FOOT NOTES

BENJAMIN ALLMON

ODYSSEY
BOOKS

Published by Odyssey Books in 2016

Copyright © Benjamin Allmon 2016

All rights reserved. No part of this book may be reproduced or transmitted by any person or entity, including internet search engines or retailers, in any form or by any means, electronic or mechanical, including photocopying (except under the statutory exceptions provisions of the *Australian Copyright Act* 1968), recording, scanning or by any information storage and retrieval system without the prior written permission of the publisher.

www.odysseybooks.com.au

National Library of Australia
Cataloguing-in-Publication entry

Author: Benjamin Allmon
Title: Foot Notes / Benjamin Allmon
ISBN: 978-1-922200-70-9 (pbk)
ISBN: 978-1-922200-71-6 (ebook)

Cover photo by Alicia Taylor
Cover design by Michelle Lovi

Permission for use of lyrics, I'll Be Gone.
Lyrics by Michael Rudd. Cellar Music Co. Pty Ltd.

For Di, for everything.

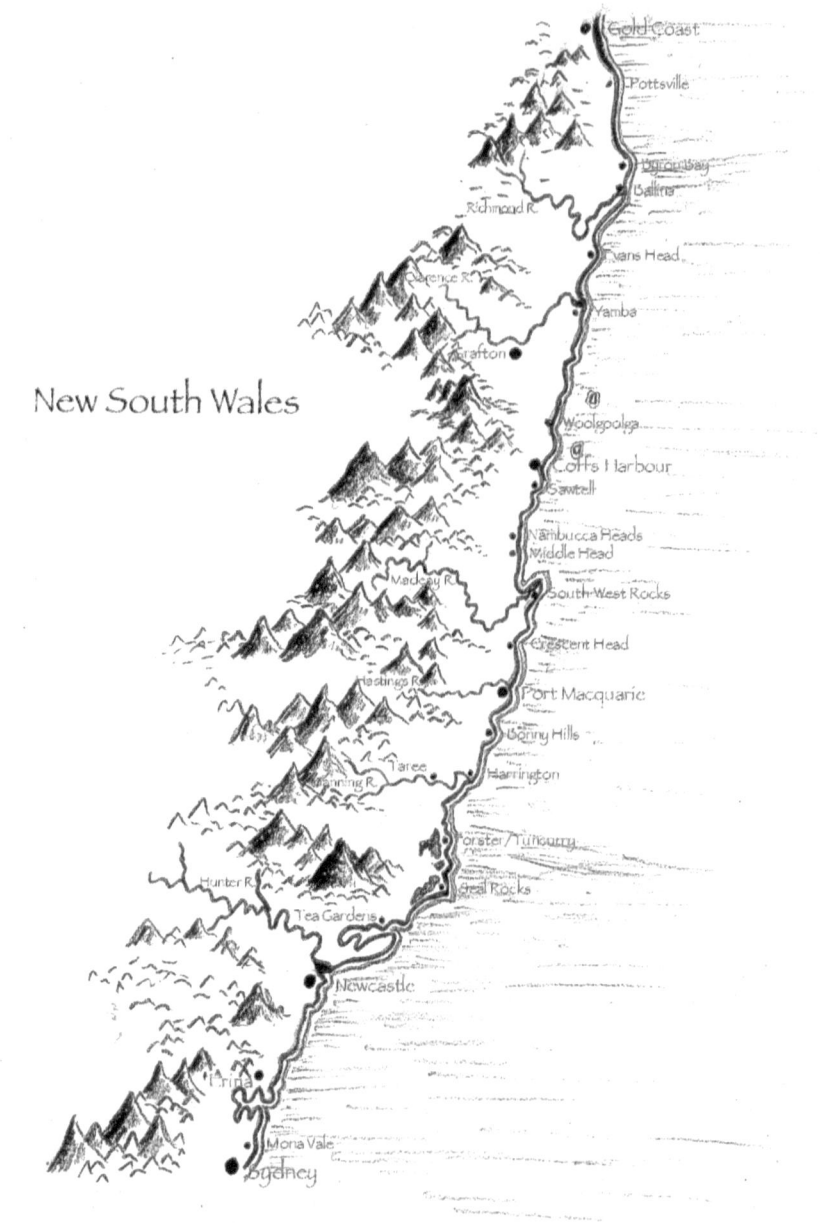

'We would walk through the country with our guitars on our shoulders, stop at people's houses, play a little music, walk on ... I didn't have no special place then. Anywhere was home. Where I do good, I stay. When it gets bad and dull, I'm gone. I knowed a lot of places ... man ... played for a lot of peoples.'

—David 'Honeyboy' Edwards (1915–2011),
last of the Delta Bluesmen

DAY 38

The people looking at me strangely as I walked off the southern end of Bluey's Beach and onto the rock shelf at the bottom of the headland should have told me something. I could feel their eyes, and whenever I turned around they were standing there, towels in hand, looking at me.

'Gawkers,' I muttered, and pressed on.

Bluey's Beach is so named for a clumsy bovine that wandered too close to the edge of the cliff-top paddock far above me. With one poorly planted hoof and a presumable lack of attention to her surroundings, Bluey slipped and went mooing into the crashing surf a hundred feet below, her cud-chewing days most certainly over but her fame ensured, posthumous though it was.

It was after four pm and the tide was rising, forcing me to rise along with it. The great shelf of rock gradually narrowed, and the surf drew closer. Soon I was forced to climb onto the next fault line of rock to get away from the incoming waves. This ledge was narrower still, perhaps only six feet wide, and covered in tiny pebbles that made footing treacherous. I was conscious of the guitar taking up the use of one of my hands.

I moved forward carefully; the fall on the last headland had made me wary. For the first time on the walk I realised how quickly things could go wrong, like it had for poor Betty and Al and their exploding caravan. If I injured my body in any way, this unconventional tour would be over. Had any album tour been called off due to the artist falling off a cliff?

I skirted and climbed, noting uneasily that I was now twenty feet up. The shelf at the bottom was now completely covered in surging water; a fall into that could result in some nasty consequences.

I think this is a mistake, the voice of my girlfriend, Di, said from her home near my cerebellum.

'Let's just get to the corner of the headland and have a look around it. The ledge might widen, or take us back onto a wide slab like the one we were just on.'

This was greeted with silence.

I pushed on, slipping slightly on the loose stones that were gradually replacing the ledge. The corner was close. I looked down and was amazed that I was now thirty feet above the crashing waves. Only they weren't crashing as much anymore, which meant the water was getting deeper. I could put my hand on the side of the cliff and feel the power of each wave rumble through the rock.

'Just a little further,' I said, to more silence. I wasn't ready to call it quits yet; I had a very good reason to find a coastal route to Seal Rocks—a bushfire was consuming the Wallingat Forest, cutting roads and threatening homes. On foot I would be slow to adapt to any change in wind direction or shift in the fire front, with potentially fatal consequences.

But when I peered around the corner of the headland, I realised the inland route might be the lesser of two evils.

The coastline as far as I could see was sheer cliffs rising from the ocean, and it was *deep* ocean. Fall in there and you might as well give it up. The current was so powerful, the waves so relentless, the distance back to Bluey's Beach so insurmountable, that death would be a pretty safe bet.

Turn back now, said Di, but to what? Walk into an inferno? I was literally caught between the Devil and the deep blue sea. I decided to take stock of my surroundings.

With the sun now behind the headland, I was shivering in cold shadow. The only sound was the wind and the water rolling over rock far below. I was utterly alone up here, and if I fell, nobody would ever know until my body washed up on the elderly nudist beach to the north, days later, bloated and nibbled by sea creatures (but still looking good when compared to the Shelly Beach Crew, God love 'em).

I looked up; far above me I could see green tufts of the paddock where Bluey had once grazed, ignorant of the fate about to befall her.

I looked down, saw stunted bushes clinging to jagged outcrops of stone and the promise of a long fall before drowning and a watery grave.

For the first time on this trip, I thought of getting out the EPIRB.[1]

I reached into the side pocket of the pack, being careful not to move around too much. The scree beneath my feet felt like it was getting ready to be evil, and I didn't want to encourage any evil.

I fumbled the device out of the pouch and raised it up in front of my face to read the instructions. Why hadn't I read them before? Why wait until now, when at any moment I could be engaged in a *real* fall, not the dress rehearsal I'd been involved in earlier today on Boomerang Head?

I slipped it around my neck and immediately felt better. If I survived the fall into the sea, then at least I could activate the thing and have some chance of rescue.

Turning to retrace my steps, I shifted my weight without thinking and the pebbles shifted underneath me. My foot slid with greasy speed out from under me, and my other leg braced for a second before buckling, unable to take all my weight. I landed on my ass but was still sliding, my free hand instinctively scrabbling for a hold. It found nothing but dirt and stone and more pebbles.

I tried rolling over onto my stomach but I was starting to build up speed now, and in another few seconds would be beyond the point of no return.

Oh God I'm really falling, my mind gibbered. *I'm really going to fall really going to fall get hurt maybe die alone out here nobody will hear me oh God*

My foot struck one of the bushy outcrops and my descent stopped

---

1   Electronic Position Indicating Radio Beacons.

for a moment, long enough for me to turn over to look, to feel for something to grab on to. As I did, however, the weight of the pack-stool swung my body out and off the cliff face, and in a heart-stopping, stomach-dropping moment I was on the knife-edge of gravity. I didn't even want to windmill my arm for fear of tipping the balance. The bush hadn't been designed to support a fully grown man wearing a pack, and it started to give way. I had a second or two in which to make a decision, and I thrust my hand blindly at the cliff face.

Oh please please please

My hand disappeared into a hole in the earth, some animal's den, just as gravity pulled me down after the bush. I dug my fingers into the soil inside the hole with every ounce of strength I possessed. I looked to my left and saw another small scraggly tree and, praying it wouldn't uproot, slung my other arm up and wedged the guitar behind it.

It held.

With both hands free now, I was able to hold myself in place while I figured out my next move. I craned my head back and looked up the cliff.

There was something coiled above me, flicking its tail only inches from my face.

Snake!

I instinctively recoiled, but in doing so almost threw myself off the cliff. I dug my fingers into the soil. I could feel fingernails peeling but I didn't care. I looked up again, terrified of the snake striking at my face. If that happened I would be going off the cliff, I would be helpless to stop myself. What kind of snake lived on the side of a cliff anyway? Was my arm in its den?

It was still there, still flicking its tail, still right next to my hand … but something about it was wrong.

Very wrong.

It was a snake's skin all right, but the owner wasn't inside it. This was just its husk, and the tail I had thought I had seen flicking was actually the wind stirring the desiccated membrane.

I hauled myself up, chuckling weakly, more in shock than amusement. I found a moderately flat section wide enough to sit on, pulled the guitar out from its position behind the bush, and breathed a deep sigh of relief. My hat was still on, amazingly, as was the pack. There had been a moment there where I had genuinely thought I was going to die.

Nobody knew where you were, Di said reprovingly.

I stood up on legs that were shaking like a newborn colt's. I hoped they were still able to carry me away, but first I figured I was owed a souvenir from this experience, if only as a reminder of how close I came to playing that great gig in the sky. I bent down and freed the snakeskin from the bush it was caught on and stuffed it into the leather band around my Akubra. Then I got off the headland as fast as I could.

Walking into a bushfire didn't seem so bad anymore.

12 MONTHS EARLIER ...

'Have you seen this?' I said, flapping *Rolling Stone's* 50th Anniversary of Rock at my flatmate, Ken, who shook his head and continued rolling a cigarette from the butts we'd piled together on the table. It was 2005, and times were tough. My guitar lay propped on the threadbare couch next to him, missing the A string I was too poor to replace. Incomplete, it looked like a grinning, gap-toothed hillbilly. 'There's a piece in here about Muddy Waters, written by Billy Gibbons.'

'The ZZ Top guy?'

'Yeah. Check this out: "Muddy told us a story once about his friends Freddie King and Little Walter walking from Dallas to Chicago. I've always had that image in my mind of two guys walking from the South to the North. Everyone else in the Great Migration took the train. I hope they weren't carrying their equipment."'

An idea occurred to me.

'Wouldn't it be funny if I picked up that guitar, walked out the front door, got to the corner, and then kept going? What if, when I got to the edge of town, I just kept walking? What if *that* was how I toured my album? Just see how far I could go with the guitar ...'

'Madness, Allmon,' Ken said, but he was smiling.

'I know, but still ...'

'It *is* a pretty interesting idea, I guess ...'

'I'd need a cooler name though.'

'Like Muddy Waters?'

'Yeah, something suitably vagabond-esque.'

'How about Smokey?' Ken said, holding up the result of his careful tobacco scrounging.

'Perfect,' I said, taking the cigarette and looking around for the matches. 'Maybe it's not as crazy as it sounds … and I've done the usual circuit, the pubs and cafés, for years. I just can't get excited by it anymore. But this … this might just work. A Walking Tour, a modern-day troubadour …'

'But you get lost on the way to the kitchen,' Ken said. I ignored this for the uncouth slur that it was, finally finding the matchbox.

I had been sitting on it.

Maybe my observation skills were a wee bit below par.

'I'll walk to Sydney, like those guys walked to Chicago,' I said, and lit our last cigarette for the week. Ken nodded and refrained from further comment, taking it from my fingers as it rapidly burned away.

I looked around the apartment. We had the couch, a beanbag and a coffee table, and two mattresses on the floor upstairs. Our ancient television silently blared snow—it was broken and we couldn't afford to get it fixed, had grown to like the static. Patterns appeared if you looked long enough.

The setting sun washed our place in scarlet light, giving it a feel of impending doom, and rightly so—it was condemned. They were tearing it down to put up a new high-rise apartment block. Story of the Gold Coast. Out with the old, in with the rendered. You can remake yourself in a day in this city, be anyone you want to be, provided nobody looks too closely.

'I'm twenty-seven,' I said to Ken as he butted the smoke. 'Robert Johnson had already changed the course of music and gone to that Great Gig in the Sky by this point. Ditto Jim Morrison, Cobain, Hendrix, Joplin …' I trailed off, inordinately depressed I'd made it past the Death Age. Still here. Still nobody. Still working for minimum wage. Still driving a car that required a golf club hitting the starter motor to get going.

Still broke.

Soon to be homeless.

It wasn't supposed to be this way.

I couldn't admit it to Ken, but it felt like the album I was recording,

The Dark Carnival, was probably my last shot at making rock a career. Over ten years trying to get noticed, get to the next level, and it looked no closer than it had in 1994, the year I began playing bass, the year Cobain was replaced on the great conveyor belt of life by Justin Bieber.

My high school friends and I had decided we'd be the '90s Metallica… even though Metallica were still conspicuously alive and active. Undeterred, we called ourselves Valhalla and commenced strumming and putting rudimentary lyrics to crude melodies.

A car accident in 1995 nearly did for me, shattering my spine; for a year, every gig I played was in a back brace, fortunate to be playing (or walking) at all. With Metallica selfishly showing no signs of stopping, coupled with head-banging restrictions due to my neck and back, I put down the battle-axe bass and picked up an acoustic guitar, determined to teach myself how to be James Taylor. By 1997 I was an accredited audio engineer, so I wouldn't have to rely on anyone else to record my masterpieces.

The acoustic band I joined, All But Well, came to the attention of an inordinately patient publisher, Marty Ryan, and his wife Kylie. We recorded some demos that were fun and mostly awful, yet which drew some interest from a new band up the road from us, Savage Garden. Pride meant that we (mainly me) declined their interest in recording one of our tunes, for our songs were, like, our children, man. We (mainly me) were idiots.[2]

In 2000, Marty—prematurely greying by this stage—arranged for me to live and work with award-winning Nashville-based songwriter Heather Field. She had worked with Tina Arena, Rick Price and Troy Cassar-Daley. When I arrived I realised I was in another league entirely. My flatmate was Keith Urban's friend and FOH[3] engineer, Steve Law.

---

2 Savage Garden set a record later that year, winning ten ARIA (Australian Recording Industry Association) awards, as the Guinness Book of Records delights in informing me. They went on to sell twenty-five million albums.

3 Front-of-House. The guy responsible for your sound at a venue, good FOH engineers are like a pair of jeans that fit well; you hang on to them until they are falling apart.

He'd just finished doing the sound at the Sydney Olympics' Closing Ceremony (where Savage Garden had also appeared, naturally).

Upstairs in Heather's studio, men with formidable command over their instruments were recording an album. When they asked if I was a muso, I mumbled something about inspecting for termites and beat a hasty retreat, unwilling to admit I had anything more than a nodding acquaintance with music (which, relatively speaking, I didn't).

Heather was good, but Heather was hard. Up until that moment I had been the best (and only) lyricist I knew. Nobody ever challenged my lyrics.

Until Heather.

'Why is the woman like a river? You can't just put that line in and not give me a reason. And this obsession with putting the word "dream" in your songs ... every song has this word in it somewhere! You are hereby forbidden to use that word as long as you are under my roof.'

'But—'

'You're lazy, Ben. You are lazy because you have some talent, and no one is lazier than the moderately talented. And those around you who say, "Oh Ben, you're so good, what a good songwriter you are" aren't songwriters, and they are doing you no favours. *Real songwriters know the difference between what sounds pretty and means nothing, and what is honest and means everything.* Do you want to be a real songwriter, Ben?'

'Yes.'

'Then listen and learn. You *can* be good, if you want to be. If you'll let me help you.'

But looking back, I don't think I took her seriously. Or, rather, I was too proud to take on board all that she had to offer. I learned valuable lessons from Heather, but they were ones that took years to flower, planted as they were in the sour soil of my pride.

Five years later and here I was, proudly recording, producing and playing most of the instruments on *The Dark Carnival* myself (not that I had the money to pay for others to do those things anyway).

When asked what style of music I played I typically answered— with some pride—'everything', and *The Dark Carnival* was the proof. Twelve songs with elements of reggae, blues, rock, metal, folk, hip-hop, funk and jazz.

Often in the same song.

Never to that song's advantage, I might add—if I may indulge in a cooking metaphor, just because you have a forty-bottle spice rack doesn't mean you should add all forty to the meal. It is simply overwhelming, too many flavours rioting and competing so that in the end none are distinct, and the meal thoroughly ruined.

Not that I was aware of this, you see.

In producing *The Dark Carnival*, I had effectively ransacked the spice rack … and raided the pantry as well. If two ounces of turmeric (or saxophone) was good, my reasoning went, imagine how spectacular twenty could be!

I was at long last recording the album I had always wanted, or, perhaps to put it more accurately, recording *all* the albums I'd always wanted, mashing them together in one overindulgent stew.

I was inordinately proud of my 'recipe'.

But how to promote this preposterous dish?

I had no band to replicate the songs out on the road. Worse, I had been a solo artist for years, used to getting my own way, not compromising on my vision—I felt ill-suited to bands now.

Still, if I wanted to replicate these multi-instrument songs I was so proud of with any fidelity, I'd need a seven or eight piece band. Four piece bands are hard enough to keep together—I shuddered at the idea of twice that many. Very few venues would book such a large band, and even if they did, wouldn't pay more than they would for a four-piece … which meant half rations for everyone, which meant amateur musicians, which meant headaches.

Pros view such gigs as a pay cheque and a chance to indulge in something different for a while, but I could never offer enough to support a cadre of them. Amateurs do it for the love, but as Toto knew, love isn't always on time; I couldn't imagine trying to organise a *rehearsal* for eight people with conflicting work, study and family commitments, let alone a tour.

There didn't seem to be any way to make this happen.

The Billy Gibbons' quote changed all that.

I knew of the bluesmen of the Great Migration, the 1900–1970 exodus of six million African-Americans from the southern states. They were musicians who lived a life utterly foreign to me, sharecroppers in the Deep South who sang in voices and rhythms that had been shaped by centuries of slavery and hardship.

Muddy Waters, Howlin Wolf and the electric bluesmen interested me, but it was their predecessors—the acoustic vagabonds—that truly fascinated me. Outsiders like Charley Patton, Son House, Tommy Johnson, Skip James, Johnny Shines … and Robert Johnson, the greatest rambler of them all. Guys who didn't have a place in regular society, but it was okay—they had made the road their home, the place where they made sense. Their concert hall was the highway, or the train station, or the back room of a store—intimate venues well suited to a solo guitarist and a pocketful of songs.

Rambling was the answer to my dilemma.

Why should I fear being broke? Or homeless? I had my hands and my head, and if I couldn't earn enough with the guitar, there was always manual work; practically all I'd ever done for employment anyway. And I was used to being poor—certainly not in the league of the bluesmen, but poor enough.

For years I'd lived from pay cheque to pay cheque, working low-paid jobs that required the least amount of cerebral input so as to focus on music. I'd subsist on nothing but a couple of peanut butter sandwiches for days, too proud to admit to friends or family that I was so drastically low on money my food budget for that week had gone on rent or fuel to get to work.

Meanwhile, my friends were buying their first homes, getting promoted in jobs that had stealthily (at least to me) become careers, weddings and kids were replacing partying and casual sex, but I was still pursuing a fantasy I'd had since hearing Cliff Burton at sixteen.

What had been cool ten years ago was now starting to seem a little sad, a little pitiable, a little desperate—I was starting to hear phrases like, 'You've given it your best shot, but it didn't pan out. Maybe it's time to think about a real career.' Or, worse somehow, 'Really, you're *still* playing? Wow? No, I mean, good on you, hang in there, I'm sure it's a matter of time.'

But time was something I no longer had limitless supplies of, or so it seemed.

The Walking Tour solved all of this; it was crazy enough and bold enough that if offered a shortcut to national attention—and its concomitant likelihood of earning folding money—while being interesting and not dependent upon a band to succeed. I would rework my songs so that they could be played on my old acoustic guitar.

'I'm going to do it,' I said to the empty room—Ken had left for work sometime during my reverie. 'It'll take a while to get everything ready, but I'm really going to do it,' I said, testing the idea aloud to see how it sounded. The guitar grinned its foolish agreement, as though delighted by the prospect, too stupid to know what it was getting itself into.

It didn't matter that I hadn't camped outdoors for longer than two consecutive nights since school. Pride dictated that I could do it, and pride furthermore assured me that the tour would be a rousing success—simply by my doing it. My career was practically assured the moment I set foot upon the sand.

Pride, the soundtrack to my life.

The cure for pride, I've found, is to go for a really long walk.

Clears it right up.

How Not To Prepare For Life On The Road, 1 March 2006
- 1 packstool, circa 1952[4]
- 1 sleeping bag (packs down to a tiny, decidedly pumpkiny entity)
- 1 battery-operated Coleman lantern
- 1 Kmart telescopic fishing rod (5-foot pole, 3-pound line, good for catching ageing guppies)
- 3 garbage bags (in lieu of raincoat/tent)
- 2 pairs of flares, 4 shirts, 3 socks and 1 pair of shorts
- 1 small tackle box comprising 1 hook, 1 sinker and 47 swivels
- 1 decrepit medical kit (a couple of bandages, a box of codeine

---

4   It was an old fabric affair that had belonged to my stepfather. He must have picked it up around the time plastic lawn flamingos were coming into vogue. It was a nylon bag, hung in a metal frame, which converted into a little fold-out stool. I couldn't decide if this was an advantage or a frivolous liability.

sporting a picture of a woman with a decidedly '70s 'fro, a few bits of gauze and an ancient bottle of mercurochrome)
- 1 $25 mobile phone (no satellite capability)
- 1 EPIRB (the only nod towards sense, a bit sketchy on how it worked though …)
- Several muesli bars, half a loaf of bread and a jar of peanut butter
- Toiletries
- Pocketknife and a larger, rusty fishing knife in belt sheath
- Hash cookies

This was supposed to see me through one thousand kilometres of coastline. There is no mention of a tent, because there wasn't one; I blithely told everyone I would just sleep in the dunes, wrapped in my sleeping bag.

There is also no mention of maps, and that is because I forgot to bring any. There *was* a cartoon representation of Australia on the cover of my notebook—complete with a singlet-wearing kangaroo that, if the scale were to be believed, I'd do well to avoid.

In addition to the packstool was the camel-pack, a marvellous water-carrying device that held one and a half litres. It had a length of plastic tube through which you can drink on the move with little effort, a far cry from the canteens of school camps that looked like a goitre and would catch on every passing branch.

There was my guitar in its soft leather case—light but terribly ungainly. I spent a few moments trying to sling it over my back, attach it to the packstool—any configuration that left my hands free—to no avail. I couldn't very well leave it behind, so I wrapped it in one of the garbage bags to protect it from the rain and carried it alongside.

Around my neck hung a silver necklace my girlfriend Di gave me as we stood saying our farewells on her doorstep.

'To keep you safe,' she said. The weight of it against my chest was heavy.

Suddenly, I didn't want to go. What had seemed like fun a few months ago when talking to Ken now seemed scary, impossible.

'I don't want you to go,' she said.

'You're going too,' I said. In a week she would be flying to the

Bahamas for a six-month contract as staff aboard *Sovereign of the Seas*. We'd committed to these plans before we'd gotten together—after years of friendship—on New Year's Day. Two months had shown how much fun dating a friend could be … what we hadn't been prepared for was falling in love. Now, these mutually exclusive adventures were intruding on our fledgling love like ghastly chaperones. I would see her next in September when her contract ended. Unless, of course, she liked it over there and renewed for another six months, in which case, who knew when we would next be able to hold each other? How could we survive being apart for so long so soon? It would be easier if one of us abandoned their dream, but neither could, and I wouldn't have been with a woman who would.

'I'm not your Penelope,' she said with a wan smile. She had been crying.

'I don't feel much like Odysseus,' I said, hoping for a smile, but it was not a morning for smiles. We looked at the rain hammering down just beyond the front porch, flooding the lawn. 'I have to do this,' I said.

'I know.'

'I'm getting too old for this hand to mouth life. Something has to change.' I said what until now had been unsayable. 'I think this is the last shot.'

'It'll work, babe, I know it will,' she said, but the sound of the rain hitting the roof was so loud I could barely hear her.

It had been raining for a fortnight. Since Valentine's Day I had been waiting for a break in the weather, but it never came. This morning, the waiting had become unbearable—I couldn't remain primed for this any longer. Doubts had begun to multiply, threatening to overwhelm the pride that held me on this course of action whether I wanted to pursue it or not—I had told too many people what I was doing to back down now. Like a politician elected on a raft of ill-thought-through policies, I now had to deliver on my outrageous promises.

It was hard to know whether to say 'so long' or make declarations of undying love—at no point over the next week would I be further away than a day's drive, yet it felt like I was bound for Mercury. So we just held each other until Ken and another friend, Ryan (who owned a car that didn't require a golf club to start it) arrived to take me to Pottsville and the start of the journey.

'Remember that I love you,' she said as I walked away, the smell of her perfume still on my shirt. I turned as I got into the car and saw her waving silhouette framed in the doorway, and then we were moving and she was gone.

Why am I doing this?

BOOK ONE
GOING DOWN THE ROAD

'Sometimes the customers threw something in the hats. Sometimes they took something out of the hats. Sometimes they took the hats.'

—George Burns

Chapter One: Spider and the Far North

DAY 1

Pottsville. The journey began in this unlikely corner of New South Wales instead of the teeming Gold Coast beaches in case it became apparent that I wasn't up to the job and could retreat into the dunes and rueful obscurity.

'You sure you don't need maps?' Ken said as he bade me farewell.

'So long as I keep the ocean on my left I should be right,' I replied, delighted at my wit. Ken shook his head sadly and patted me on the shoulder, no doubt believing it was the last time he'd see me alive.

I looked at the beach ahead. Thousands of footprints from those who had passed this way before me blurred into a senseless tangle until it seemed to be *all* footprints. I wanted to walk on fresh sand, free from the morass of others' passage, so I went down close to the water's edge. It was hard-packed and easier to walk on, but as I was revelling in my trailblazing a strong wave suddenly drenched my boots, soaking through to my socked feet. I stopped and looked around sheepishly.

There were a few fishermen and surfers about, and I wondered whether I should try to play for them. The thing was, my vision of this tour hadn't really featured that many grubby fishermen eyeing me warily. I'd anticipated playing to music *aficionados*, punters with a philosophical bent, or at the very least folks who liked their music *alfresco*. These filthy lunatics were all wrong, and the surfers were too busy catching waves to be of any use to me.

Still, this was the tour, and it had to start sometime.

Just not now.

Feeling embarrassed and awkward, I adjusted the pack (quietly appalled by its weight) and set off again, carrying the mute guitar self-consciously alongside. With the ocean roaring its welcome to the weeks ahead and the fisherfolk eyeing me still (with their good eye, at least), I began to doubt the wisdom of this touring method.

Sadly, this belated appreciation of what everyone had been telling me for months—that such an unconventional approach would never work—came as Ken and Ryan drove off, back to Queensland and sanity.

Troubled, I kept walking, making squelching noises as I went.

After about half a kilometre I spotted a rocky breakwater extending out into the surf. With foreboding I approached it, something in the pack gouging my kidneys as I did. Sure enough, the narrow Mooball Creek separated me from the other side of the beach, running too swift and deep to cross. I looked upstream, where it widened and slowed as it meandered out from Pottsville town.

Strewn along the muddy banks like flotsam were more fishermen, visions in gumboots and flannelette. I turned away from this disheartening sight and examined the river again.

Unbelievable, I thought, *not twenty minutes in and this*.

Are you sure you don't need maps? Ken had said, and it occurred to me that a map might have told me about Mooball Creek.

Walking over to the nearest tree, I sat down and took the opportunity to rearrange the packstool. I found the kidney-gouger wasn't an armour-plated pineapple after all but the Coleman lantern. As I struggled to fit it back into my pack, I noticed these fishermen were staring at me as well.

They all looked a little too alike for comfort. It wasn't just the proliferation of knitted beanies and the disquieting abundance of cauliflower ears. It was something subtler. Unnerved, I decided not to hold the first concert of the tour here, either.

I wasn't in a position to judge, however. With the wind picking up, my hat was jammed down around my ears like an aerosol cap. I had gone from the Rakish Vagabond look to something much less palatable. Slack-jawed Yokel, perhaps.

I made it across the creek by way of a small wooden bridge. The rain had ceased and my fears were lessening somewhat. It was good to be finally doing this; like performing, the worst part is always waiting. Once you are committed, many of the things you fretted over cease to overwhelm your mind ... although this was perhaps less like playing a gig and more like a skydiver jumping out of a plane to see if the parachute works.

I found the beach again, and a sense of anticipation filled me as the wind struck me full force. Grey rock formations grew out of the seething ocean, and the beach looked long and uninterrupted by people or rivers. Far out to sea there were squalls moving along the horizon, great dark clouds dragging their gauzy curtain of rain behind them like bridal trains.

Uncomplicated joy. It is rare to find such a thing as an adult; sadly, it seems, adulthood and joy unfettered are as compatible as mogwai and water.

I bent a little into the southerly and started walking in earnest, smiling.

* * *

The smile was gone by sunset when I was exposed to the raw power of an autumn squall. In the space of a minute, the wind went from steady to freight train force, sending stinging sand into my nose and mouth, and knocking me back apace. I looked around uneasily and saw the birds fleeing for cover. To the south, a solid wall of rain advanced rapidly toward me.

A quick scan of my surroundings showed there was little in the way of protection, so I sat down where I was and hurriedly prepared for the downpour. Tearing into the packstool and pulling out all three garbage bags, I wrapped the guitar in one and the pack with the other two. Pulling my hat down to new real estate on my bonce—just above my nose—I looked at my feeble preparations.

The garbage bags were involved in a frenzied breed of respiration as the wind filled them up like lungs. They looked very small against the vastness of the beach. Tilting my head right back and looking along my nose to keep the hat on, I was shocked to see the storm already upon me.

This rapid disruption in the normal order of things unsettled me on some fundamental level. It was the speed with which the storm came on that exposed just how green I was, how corroded my survival mechanisms were as a twenty-first century male.

As it hit, I sat on the sand, legs drawn up and resting my head on my knees, the hat taking the brunt of the rain. It only seemed like a minute or two and the worst of it was over—off to terrorise some other hapless adventurer farther north—but in those few minutes I had been comprehensively drenched.

I picked the plastic bags carefully off my gear and shook the water from them, stuffing them into the back pocket of the pack, readily available if the need should arise again. Shaken more than I cared to admit, I started moving again, scanning the southern horizon for signs of impending pandemonium. The sea breeze, still robust, dried me off quickly.

It didn't get truly dark until after seven pm, at which point I realised I needed to find a place to camp. It was another example of how unprepared I was for this life that I had not thought to look for a campsite before now; in the dark it was going to be extremely difficult to pick a suitable spot. Cursing my lack of camping savvy, I stopped and looked around.

The coming of night.

I stood on the empty beach and watched the shadows drape themselves over the earth with bleak totality. I felt utterly alone and terribly small.

Nightfall is a different beast in the city. Light-pollution dilutes its authority, the sounds of traffic mute its impact, but perhaps most importantly there is the knowledge that there are other humans all around you. You may not see them, but you know they are there. Being an animal that evolved as a member of a family, a band, a tribe, the constant presence of people around us is so ingrained in our genetics it goes all but unnoticed.

Until it is taken away.

Standing on a beach I had never been on before as the dark flooded the land and sea and sky, feeling my own darkness rising within as if to meet it, I was scared again. Here in the sparsely populated far north, anything could happen to me. There was nobody to watch over me, no walls around me as I slept, and no cover from the elements if it started raining.

I cast an eye over the immediate dunes, which were a shallow affair for the most part. I picked the one that looked the most generous and set up the packstool in the soft sand, working it around until it was stable, then sat down and tried to relax.

The sky was cheerless, no colours of sunset played upon the foam of the dumping waves, all the birds were in for the night, and all the fisher folk had gone home to watch the nightly freight of televised reality.

I found it hard to reconcile that this time the night before, I too had been watching television, with Di sprawled comfortably next to me on the couch reading a book on the Bahamas. We'd had a light dinner. Neither of us had felt much like eating. Now, poking listlessly through my meagre supplies, I wished for one more night of luxury, one more night of civilisation, one more night to be like everyone else.

The wind had abated a fraction, but it would be a hairy night just the same. I wondered what would happen if it rained. Maybe I should have brought a tent.

I pulled my boots off and unrolled the sleeping bag for the first time. It was a gift from Di several days earlier when she saw I wasn't going to bother with even that, the most basic of necessities. It was warm, dry, and best of all afforded protection from the plague of bloodsuckers that appeared with nightfall.

I lay down with her occupying most of the frequencies in my head. I could still smell her perfume on my shirt.

I stared up but saw no stars.

Why am I doing this?

* * *

Eventually the clouds broke up into ragged patchwork, but the stars I had longed for looked cold and distant. It was only then that I became aware of a light to the south. It winked off and on, stabbing out over the ocean towards me.

It was the Cape Byron Lighthouse, the easternmost point of the country.

I was sleeping at the edge of the world.

DAY 3

A mid-morning storm passed quickly, but as I neared the Belongil Creek I could see more of them lined up to the south-east. They made me think of elephants linked up trunk to tail, and I had a bad feeling just looking at them.

The outlook worsened when I got to the creek itself. It marked the northern boundary of Byron Bay, and in mellower conditions was probably a delightful waist-deep wade.

Today, however, surf was rushing up the river, where it collided with water coming the other way. On the out rush, only a few feet of water covered the sandbars beneath the surface; the subsequent surge of the next wave, however, would have sent me floating into town like hairy flotsam. The water boiled and spewed foam and seaweed like a terrifying engine run amok. The longer I watched the more it impressed itself upon me—these were no ordinary swells.

I had my thoughts confirmed at that moment by a passer-by.

'You'll never get across that today, mate,' said a man in his forties.

'No, I guess you're right. Can you normally cross this river?' I asked.

He nodded.

'I take it these aren't normal conditions, then?'

He gave me a grim smile. 'No, there's a big front coming. The last couple of weeks have been pretty wet, but the radio says there's worse on the way. What you're seeing down there is the result of some pretty heavy flooding all through the catchment, coupled with a king tide.'

He looked me over briefly. 'If I were you I'd go to the backpackers' hostel in town. Lie up for a few days, wait for this to blow over.'

* * *

I walked into town through light drizzle. The streets were empty; under eaves, awnings and bus shelters gathered a motley bunch ranging from ragamuffin to resplendent, sharing cover from the elements. A vicious wind hollered down Jonson Street, freezing rain in its throat and piling up rubbish in the overflowing gutters. I sat down outside the Laundromat, watching as umbrella-less folk scarpered between buildings. In this weather, Byron looked like a waterlogged shoe.

A guy sauntered over to me, about fifty. From the tattoos on his hands and the teeth missing from his smile, I judged he wasn't the mayor. I watched him come over and pick up my guitar.

'Nice fuckin axe! I got one like this down in Lennox. Yeah.'

He turned this last word into something exotic. Ye-eh. The vowel had two tones, almost as if protesting the truth of the statement.

'Thanks,' I said, trying to mask the disquiet I felt watching his battered hands strum a few exploratory chords that sounded like an old man falling down a flight of stairs.

'Yeah, got a good fuckin harmonica too. I'm a fuckin legend on the old harp. Yeah.'

'Yeah?'

'Do I fuckin know you?' he said, looking directly, alarmingly, at me. 'I know you, cunt. What's ya name?'

'Smokey,' I said, trying out the new name.

'Smokey, oh yeah, that'd be fuckin right!' he wheezed, winking at me as though we had a secret. He thrust his hand out. There were dark brown nicotine stains on his fingers. 'Name's Spider,' he said proudly, and as we shook I noticed a tattoo of a spider on the back of his hand.

'Pleased to meet you, Spider. Nice weather, huh?'

'Yeah,' he said in a voice that was suddenly thoughtful, conspiratorial. 'I know you. You did time down at Long Bay, din'cha?'

'Not me. Must have been someone else,' I said, smiling.

'Bullshit,' he said, as though I was just being coy and he knew it, he was trig, he could dig it. 'Sure you were. I knew it was you.'

'No, honestly, never been there,' I said, the smile faltering a bit.

'Really? I coulda swore it was you. You've gotta fuckin twin, mate.'

He went on like this for several more minutes. I realised that Spider was off his chops. I racked my brain for an exit line, a way to extricate myself from this circuitous conversation, bail before Spider asked for money or dope or whatever he was building to. Finally, inspiration struck. I said I was off to check on lodging for the night.

'You'll never find any here, mate. Booked up, she is. You should come down to the creek. I've got a tent down there. Yeah.'

'Nah, thanks anyway, Spider,' I said, privately thinking I'd sooner put the Admiral into a pencil sharpener.

Spider looked at me as though I was mad.

'Yer fuckin mad,' he said, then squinted at me again in that alarming way of his. 'What the fuck are you doin in town anyway, son?'

'I'm on my way to Sydney. I'm walking there to—'

'Fuckin what!!? Walk to the fuckin Big Smoke? You're madder than I thought. You'll never fuckin make it. Never in a million years. In this!!?' he yelled, gesturing wildly above his head with both arms (not doing much for his image with the tourists ... not that he'd have given a shit), indicating the wind and rain.

'Well, you see—' I started again.

'Never make it, never make it ...' he trailed off, as though the concept of someone engaged in foolishness on such a grand scale had drained him of all energy, possibly the will to live. He sat down on the bench I'd just vacated.

I continued saddling up and said goodbye to Spider, now adrift on his inner sea. My mad escapade had proven too much for him. I left to see if his prediction about accommodation was true.

After finding no room in any inn, I reluctantly returned to the streets. *Australian Idol* tryouts were on, and every room in town was booked. I guess that to the residents of Byron Bay and the potential *Idols* I looked like a particularly destitute aspirant, one of the crazy ones paraded at the start of the season as amusing spectacle/cautionary tale.

It started teeming again, so I found shelter outside a dentist's surgery. I was writing out a draft of my will when a shadow fell over the page, accompanied by, 'Well, well, well, me old mate Smokey.' He sat down next to me.

'Hi Spider, how's it going?' *Jesus, what are the odds of this?* I was out of excuses to leave without the possibility of upsetting Spider, and with this realisation I couldn't refrain from sighing.

'Fuckin walkin to Sydney, eh?' He was smiling, and seemed slightly more with it than before. His voice had taken on a fatherly tone. 'Why would you want to walk to Sydney, me old china?'

'Because I can,' I said, but my flip answer didn't seem to satisfy him.

'Why would you *do* that, mate?' He seemed honestly baffled, and I felt for him in his confusion. It was time to come clean. For Spider.

'Well, I've recorded this album, see, and I wanted to promote it in a way that gets to the essence of what music is about—'

'You sure you don't want to come back to the creek?' he interrupted. 'I got a tent with a few of the boys, they're lovely fellas, a bit down on their luck, that's all, but you'll love em, we'll grab a cask of goon, nick some scotch from the bottle-o, have ourselves a good old time.'

Clearly, my reasons for being here were of the utmost importance to this man.

'Nah, I think I'm gonna keep walking, Spider,' I said.

'Fuckin mad. Never make it!' he yelled, standing up to leave. 'Don't have any weed, do ya?' he asked, almost an afterthought. I still had a cookie, but I wasn't about to tell him.

'Sorry Spider.'

'Yeah, well, you'll never make it in this shit. Better off comin down to the creek.'

'I'll keep it in mind.'

He walked out onto the footpath and turned around, and in a ragged voice said, 'Stay away from the lighthouse, if you're really gonna head off. Nothin but fuckin junkies up there. Slit your throat for two-bob. *Don't go there after dark.*' He paused, then said reflectively, 'You never get anywhere in this shit, y'know?'

With that he walked across the road, the rain and wind buffeting him in his cheap jacket and filthy, torn jeans.

* * *

I went to one of the Internet cafés that riddled the town and asked the owner if I could recharge my phone there. He very nicely showed me to a power point, and I told him I'd return in an hour.

I walked outside for a cigarette, scanning the street for signs of Spider as the rain bucketed down, seemingly inexhaustible. From snatches of overheard conversations I learned that this storm stretched all the way up the coast to Noosa, all the way south to Coffs Harbour—six hundred kilometres in all.

Bellingen was cut off.

Ballina was going under.

They had closed all the beaches on the Gold Coast.

There was worse on the way.

This last one I heard more than once, and it worried me.

I hadn't reckoned on weather this bad. The tempest had been building all afternoon and was only intensifying if the premature twilight was any indication. It was four o'clock, but already the streetlights were on. I had nowhere to stay, and I didn't fancy a night on the streets. The creek was out, unless I wanted Spider and his merry men for drunken company until the wee hours. Apparently the lighthouse was also out; I had no reason to disbelieve Spider on this.

The alternative was going down to the beach.

No protection on the beach.

With no buildings to impede it, the wind would be terrific. I could only imagine what the surf would look like. Suffolk Park was five kilometres and a couple of creeks away, Lennox Head twelve clicks beyond that.

Should I keep moving? Or stay put?

What of Suffolk Park itself? Could it offer any more protection than Byron could? I sat next to the bike racks and signs advertising cheap tents and realised I didn't know what to do.

* * *

I collected the phone and set off in the direction of Tallow Beach, which sits at the southern base of Cape Byron. I figured I'd have a look at the conditions on the beach and make a decision based on what I saw. It beat sitting around in this sodden town.

On my way past the bottle shop, I saw a familiar figure sitting in a wicker chair outside.

Spider.

He now had a guitar he'd found God knows where. It was missing a few strings (the same could be said for the guitarist) but he was strumming it enthusiastically all the same. A few of his mates were gathered around an old table. I ambled over, smiling in spite of myself.

Sitting next to Spider was a guy with an extravagant beard; hair sprouted from just below his eyes and rioted down the rest of his face. He buried a harmonica in there and soon I could hear the strains of Spectrum's 'I'll Be Gone' emerging somewhat muffled through the growth. Spider started singing.

'Someday I'll have money

Money isn't easy to come by

By the time it's come by I'll be gone …'

Despite, or perhaps because of, the atonal delivery, Spider and his cronies achieved a kind of scruffy poignancy there in the gathering dusk that the *Idol* hopefuls could never hope to match. For these guys, the lyrics weren't just fanciful interpretation. They were a way of life.

'Money isn't easy to come by

Lovin' isn't easy to come by …'

I shook hands with a few of them and set off again for Tallow Beach. As I reached the corner I heard Spider yelling something behind me. I turned around to see him waving his arms above his head.

'*Never make it!*'

* * *

I walked down the steep hill to Tallow Beach. There I found a toilet block, a small picnic area, and a series of walking trails leading off into the Arakwal Forest. In more clement weather it was probably a popular tourist spot. With day rapidly dying in the bleak conditions it was deserted. Small rivers cut channels in the roadside mud; the car park was a lake, empty of vehicles.

I could already hear the surf.

I walked down a sandy track through the bushes, noting with

unease the way the foliage above me rippled with the blustery weather. Cresting the tertiary dune I beheld the beach.

The sea was a jagged body of mountains and deep valleys, white peaked and sending spray hundreds of feet through the air. The wind was so strong it prevented me from going further. The guitar acted like a sail, whipping out to catch the wind and yanking my wrist around the wrong way. My hat started peeling off, and I clapped my hand over it to keep it on. New places started getting wet, as the rain was flying horizontally. I did a quick survey of my inner voices; there was a general consensus to get the righteous fuck off the beach. I complied.

As I cowered amongst the pigface I considered my options.
   a. Somehow continue on down the beach and hope the storm would abate (surely it couldn't keep this pitch for very long)
   b. Stay here and sleep in the picnic area. I wasn't sure whether the cops or rangers would perform rounds and send me packing or worse, given my finances, fine me.
   c. Go back into Byron. Sleep in a park or just stay up all night and finish my will by the light of a streetlamp.

None of them seemed very appealing. For some reason (I cannot adequately describe what thought processes there were, if any) I decided to continue on along the sand.

I grabbed the guitar around the neck like a rifle, jumped over the dune and staggered into the wind. Constantly tugging my hat back down as it slid up my slick forehead, I was totally drenched in seconds. So was the pack. The garbage bags were tattered flags trailing out behind me.

After two hours and only making it a kilometre or so, I'd had enough. I spotted a faint wallaby trail leading into the Arakwal Forest behind the dunes. It promised relief from the strengthening wind and I followed it down into a small gully where it fanned out into a clearing. The ground was remarkably free of debris; I wondered if this was a man-made clearing, and if so, who had made it? In the far corner there was a hollow formed beneath a bush, clearly the den of an animal or the bedroom of the clearing's occupant.

I looked around but all I could see was wet green forest; I could have been in New Guinea. I set up the stool and sat down. I'd thought the trees and the gully would conspire to protect me from the worst of it, but it was only marginally better than the open beach. It was dark, about seven pm. I looked for any damage to my equipment, but a full analysis would have to wait until morning.

The gale continued to intensify over the next few hours. Old rotten boughs tore loose and went crashing unseen into the undergrowth. Sleep was impossible. Every time I'd start to drift off I'd hear a branch snap, and I'd try staring everywhere at once.

It was too dark to see anything, but my mind was conjuring up a couple of guys creeping through the undergrowth with knives clenched in their remaining teeth. A stupid fantasy—what kind of person goes on a killing spree in cyclonic conditions?—that was nevertheless wholly believable in this hellish darkness. The bad vibes that seemed to surround Byron had infected me; I was delirious with them.

But terror can only last for so long, and I crawled into the den at around midnight, with vague thoughts of sleeping in there. I was wrung out, and a great apathy overcame me. I dozed in the mud, hearing footsteps and low voices.

* * *

I awoke with a start, sat up and collided with the roof of the den. I rolled over and crawled out, rubbing my head. Sitting on the stool, I noted with dismay that my gear was sitting in shallow pools. The guitar seemed to regard me with mute reproach. I sat there and avoided looking at it, amazed that the storm showed no sign of flagging.

By three am, I'd had enough. I was shivering uncontrollably. Up until then I'd only read that phrase in books. Now I had first-hand experience. It was the wind-chill factor, of course—the kind of cold that enters your body like cancer, eating heat and leaving barren, frozen places inside you.

I gathered up everything and made for the beach. In my mind I was seeing the toilet block back at Tallow Beach. By now it seemed like a glorious haven of peace and security. It offered better protection from the elements and maybe I could hang up my clothes to let them dry. This little spark of hope was enough to get me going. Spider had been right; I'd been a fool to try anything in this.

* * *

Walking was easier with a tailwind. I even managed to gallop for long stretches using the guitar as a sail; a hairy man in outrageous flares, guitar held aloft like some talismanic spinnaker, hurtling through the pre-dawn maelstrom on his way to the Toilets of Tallow Beach.

I spent a spooky few minutes inspecting the dark caves of the men's and women's amenities with my lantern, half expecting a ghostly pale hand to reach out of the murk or, worse, a raddled face grinning evilly and smacking its chops. The light from the Coleman was stark, comfortless, and only seemed to intensify the shadows.

Satisfied that I was alone, I repaired to the female side, where there was more room and a long wooden bench that would serve as a bed. I stripped off, certain that no one would be coming in for the next few hours. I hung up the clothes and separated all the wet stuff in my pack. Lastly, I unrolled the sleeping bag for the first time that night and poured my cold naked body into its dry confines. Heaven.

I turned the lamp down low, made sure the pocketknife was in reach (if threatened I could offer a manicure or to open a bottle of wine) and thought about Di. I felt very far from her. The rain had washed the smell of her from my shirt. I fell into a light sleep listening to the wild night rage and fume outside, this long, strange day finally at an end.

DAY 4

Someone was shining a torch in my face. I registered this slowly, unsure of where I was. Then the events of the night came back to me, and my eyes flew open. I half-rose before I recalled I was naked underneath the sleeping bag.

I was badly scared.

Fortunately, so was the torch-bearing stranger. He stumbled back into the stall door and said, 'It's okay, mate. I'm the cleaner.'

Relief flooded through me.

'Oh. Shit. Sorry. Am I in your road?'

'Nah mate, you're right. Just checkin the stalls.'

He eyed me speculatively, perhaps making sure I was bolted together right. I did my best, but was hampered by the fact that my clothes were hanging from every conceivable structure; I was clearly nude in a duck-down sleeping bag in the women's toilets during a gale, and at five am, no less. I smiled at him, but bedraggled as I was, succeeded only in removing any remaining shreds of seemliness. I clearly wasn't a threat, however, so he relaxed and began tidying up the cubicles.

'Yep. Bit wet out there, eh?' he said with admirable understatement.

'I know. I just had to get out of it for a couple of hours.'

'Ah, don't worry about it mate. You could stay in here all weekend, won't be anyone comin down. This shit's set in. Forecast says it'll be like this till Tuesday.'

Tuesday.

It was only Saturday.

I couldn't stand the idea of being here for another three days, cooped up in the women's toilet. My cleaning buddy didn't notice my misery. He was cataloguing disaster with grim relish.

'Worst storm in thirty years, they reckon. Bellingen's cut off; they're sandbagging the town right now. Lismore's in all sorts. Ballina's going under, wouldn't be surprised if the Richmond burst her banks. Big storms off the coast, seas up around six metres, no boats going out this weekend. Gonna work on me tan.' He turned to me on his way out, and said, 'You right, mate? Need anything? There's a backpackers' in town, y'know. Better than this,' he said, waving vaguely at the roof and walls. In the weird light of my lantern and his torch he looked like a third-rate Phantom of the Opera.

'I'll be heading in come morning,' I said without much hope. I'd have loved to be snug in a bunk in the hostel, but it was fully booked and I suspected little would change with the wet weekend ahead.

'Good idea,' he said. 'Get a few more winks. Hooroo.'

He shuffled out into the early morning dark and I was alone again. I tried to think about what to do come light, but my mind was having none of it and pulled the plug.

I slept until seven am.

* * *

I hung up the phone and looked around the Tallow Beach carpark. A tawny frogmouth sat in the branch above me, still as stone. Water dripped from green leaves. For the moment, the wind had dropped.

All was calm but me.

I was feeling about as low as I can ever remember. Due to timing issues and my budget constraints, the first pressing of the album had only just been completed and delivered from the printers. But they were faulty; the gatefold cover I'd hoped for was actually just a slip of thin paper printed on both sides. The cover art, a sketch by my friend and artist Bill Higginson, relied on the foldout to be effective. Coupled with barely visible printing on the disk itself, it was a fiasco. What I had was, effectively, five hundred coasters. Coasters that had cleaned me out financially. There were a dozen being shipped to Evans Head, sixty kilometres to the south, for my inspection.

In the wake of this news I'd called Di.

Satisfied I was not in any imminent danger, she had then given voice to all the things that were rattling around in my head.

I couldn't be expected to walk or promote anything in this horrendous weather.

I wasn't adequately prepared for travelling.

There were more storms on the way.

She missed me.

She could be there in an hour, pick me up, and take me back to sanity and a warm bed with her in it.

I was close to saying yes. It would be nice to give up, let someone else take over and decide what to do, when to say enough. A strange lethargy was creeping over me, smothering the will to go on. In the end I said I'd think about it and call her back.

Only three days in and I was ready to give up. What was going on? Was I so weak that I was undone by rain and wind and Spider's doom-laden assessment of my chances? I listened and at first could hear no dissenting voice. I listened some more.

My phone beeped, indicating a text had arrived. Still listening for a murmur of fortitude, I saw the message was, coincidentally, from Bill. Having survived childhood leukaemia, he possesses an unfailingly positive outlook, which I find mostly endearing and occasionally annoying.

At least you don't have to worry about dehydration.

'Wanker,' I muttered, shoving the phone back into my pocket and trying not to smile.

But it got me thinking. All I'd had so far was rain. I didn't yet know what it was like to walk in the sunshine. There was something else, too; the suspicion that if I quit now, I'd never try again.

I could see it now; go back to the Gold Coast, go back to the blue-collar work. No one would blame me—there's no sin in making an honest living, chase the Australian Dream instead of my crazy one. After a while I'd forget what had moved me to attempt such folly in the first place. Get a mortgage, organise my superannuation, raise a family. A good life.

But lying in bed late at night, I'd wonder what might have been different if I'd pushed on for Ballina during the Big Storm of '06.

I called Di back and told her not to saddle up the rescue pony just yet. I told her I was still resolved to go on. I told her I loved her and that I was going to Ballina.

* * *

On the road leading out of town I saw Spider one last time. He was on the other side of the road, gently swaying beneath a bus shelter, bottle in hand, grinning at nothing in particular. Another storm was barrelling down, and I wondered what he did night after night, year after year. The tent by the creek, I suppose. Or nothing. The Spiders of the world get by. Or they don't. Same goes for the Smokeys. Tough old world.

He saw me and raised his arm in a half-arsed wave, yelling, 'Never make it!' and then a bus erased my view of him.

So long, Spider.

DAY 8

Four days later I was in the Evans Head post office, sporting a welcome sunburn thanks to the return of fine weather the day before. I had been holed up in Ballina for three days, watching the Richmond get higher while my spirits sank lower. Finally, the break in the weather came, and I'd had a pleasantly uneventful journey to this tiny seaside hamlet.

My phone had been beeping all morning—Di was leaving the country today. The thought of her being beyond my reach for so long made me feel gloomy and panicked at the same time, and I was restless as I stood in the queue, fielding sidelong glances.

There was something else bothering me—part of me was glad she was going. Knowing she wasn't an hour and a half away by car meant I could concentrate on the tour, not spend hours thinking of her, lying in our bed alone, presumably catatonic with woe at my absence. But if I loved her, should I feel relieved she was going? I felt guilty, shabby.

When I got to the counter the package of discs was there and, despite the manufacturing debacle, it was good seeing this album I'd spent so much of the previous year immersed in finally whole. The word made flesh, so to speak.

I sent copies to every radio station I could locate in the Yellow Pages, along with a cover letter explaining my method of touring. Although my funds were running low, I went into an Internet café and tried to organise a deal with an online distributor, Somersault.[5]

Spend any longer than, say, two days trying to promote your music and you'll realise that without distribution most radio stations won't go near you. This is based on the sensible principle that if the station's listeners like your song there has to be somewhere they can buy it. Furthermore, a distribution deal implies a level of skill and professionalism that stations like; it soothes them.

No distribution also means no album sales,[6] unless it is to softhearted relatives and friends. Publishers are good and managers are better (as long as they are ethical), but distribution is the milkshake that brings the boys to the yard.

Hence the Internet café.

Ultimately, however, I was unable to send in my application due to the wretched computer bleating anxious error messages. Out of time and ready cash, distribution would have to wait.

Having discharged my promotional duties in as responsible a manner as I could muster, I figured I would find a picnic table by the river and pull out the guitar. It was time to do the job. The tour, delayed by forces beyond my control, could finally begin in earnest. All I needed was an audience.

After a while, a couple of teenagers sat down at my table, each with a cigarette poking awkwardly out of an uncertain mouth. They smoked furtively as I played a bluesier number, which went down okay. Pretty soon a few other folks, tourists from their attire, had gathered around and I had something approaching an audience.

I embarrassed myself in an attempt at James Taylor's 'My Travelling Star', but saved the gig from disaster with a decent 'Don't Think Twice', Dylan's wry breakup song. After that, there were requests for songs I didn't know or for songs that I detested, so I jammed on a few of my

---

5   Which has since gone to that great database in the sky, sadly.
6   This of course has changed with the rise of social media—in early 2006 YouTube and MySpace were in their infancy, Facebook not even out of the university womb. Now, they are indispensable tools to the independent musician's marketing team.

own songs until everyone, including my two fellow smokers, went on their way. Nothing like a few originals to send 'em running.

But the tour had officially kicked off.

Chapter Two: The Yuraygir

DAY 10

Yamba was the last town before the vast unknown that was the Yuraygir; sixty-five kilometres of coastline with only four tiny hamlets. At over three hundred square kilometres, there wouldn't be another tract of wilderness to rival it on the tour, and it would stretch my survival abilities—such as they were—to their limit.

I'd had no further success in getting distribution, and my forays into gigging on Yamba's streets were met with sideways glances and no outward enthusiasm—unsurprising when my competition was Ladies Day at the Yamba Bowls Club. I acknowledged I had been trumped and beat a dignified retreat to the sand, vowing to return after nightfall and try again.

Sadly, Yamba wasn't overly blessed with beaches for camping. So far I had managed to avoid camping in a town, and I was worried about being discovered by the police, rangers, or wankers whose idea of fun is to beat up sleeping musicians.

With the sun already setting there was no other option, so I nestled my back against the rocky breakwater on Town Beach and self-consciously spread my sleeping bag out. It was full night by now; against the white sand shining beneath the moon I was a stark black silhouette, as conspicuous as a toupee.

I wondered how I was going to relax enough to get any sleep; from the town I could hear the sounds of drunken revelry, above me on the breakwater I could hear fishermen swearing and laughing, and before me I could see a throng of teenagers grab-arsing around on the moonlit beach. Remembering my vow to give gigging in Yamba another try, I left my stuff in the deep shadows formed by the boulders of the breakwater, and went in search of an audience.

I returned to my little camp some time later, unable to compete with the electricity-fuelled music and noise of Yamba's inhabitants; a jukebox delivering the unmistakable bawl of Jimmy Barnes, old cars with Swiss cheese mufflers grumbling and bald tyres squealing, breaking glass followed by laughter, a drunken sporting team mangling a Rod Stewart number.

The problem with being musically stripped back was that nobody else *was*—everyone was adding strips, if anything … and by going the other way I was risking being outstripped.

I eventually slipped into an uneasy doze that never truly deepened into sleep, and several times I awoke to find I had neighbours. I checked my phone—it was three am. These were probably the last of the revellers, either too hammered to remember the way home or unwilling to face a lecture from an angry spouse.

The one closest to me had fallen asleep facedown on the sand, having attempted to do some stripping back of his own; his pants were pooled around his feet and his underwear glowing softly in the dark. His snoring was muffled but insistent. I gave up on sleep and sat up, wondering again whether I'd made a mistake touring this way, and watched the east for signs of life.

DAY 11

Sunset the next day found me on a deserted beach in the northernmost reaches of the formidable Yuraygir, twenty kilometres and a thousand years from Town Beach.

The quality of the light had a spooky, purplish-golden, smoky cast to it. All around me, the world seemed to thrum with an energy that was lovely because it was so fleeting, as though the Earth was giving a mighty, silent shout before it surrendered to the dark.

On the sand, a mob of kangaroos was gathered. Kangaroos on the beach somehow don't look right. Too big. Too furry. Beyond them, the foam of a spent wave glowed delicate pink, and behind that stretched the vast, simple geometry of the sea.

Above us was the majesty of Red Cliff. It rose out of the earth to hang above the ocean like a scarlet mirage, as if someone has caught the sunset in rock like a creature trapped in amber, preserved there and glowing with its own luminescence.

It was humbling to think that this spectacle had happened every sunset for millions of years. Millions. I had happened along at the right time on a cloudless evening. It will go on doing it long after I am dead. My tour—and I—seemed supremely insignificant, dwarfed by the age and size of this vagabond continent.

All too quickly it was over, the colour draining out of the cliff face like blood from a wound, until all that remained was dull ochre swiftly overcome by shadow.

Lightning played on the horizon as the waves sacrificed themselves on the beach. It was far out to sea, and I could not hear any thunder. Above, the stars were sprayed across the darkening sky like droplets of foam from some wave that broke eons ago. I smiled and lay down, hearing the surf whisper over the sand, remembering the raucous night before. For the first time I felt the shackles of my old life—my normal life—give a little.

Until now, I'd wondered whether I'd keep walking.

Now, I wondered if I'd want to stop.

DAY 13

Somnolent is a good way of describing Brooms Head. At half past nine on a Monday morning the liveliest thing in town was an erection I was sporting for no particular reason. The two unfortunate women who ran the local store were treated to a whole lotta me, whether they wanted it or not.

The store was like so many other small town establishments along the coast; the only store. Newsagent, grocer, petrol station, fishmonger, video shop, post office, butcher, baker and toyshop all underneath one roof. Always with an old guy sitting out front rolling cigarettes and wearing an undershirt (even in summer) who looks at you as though you just crawled out of a pond. There is nothing like the gimlet gaze of some old local to really drive home your status as an outsider.

The storeowners themselves are usually tremendous folk who will do almost anything to make you feel welcome, and Brooms Head was no exception. I bought a pie, went outside and sat down at a picnic table to eat it. Fielded a few suspicious looks from townsfolk, but I was getting used to that.

Once you let your hair grow beyond a certain point you have to take such regard in your stride, especially when you throw in the guitar, the heavy stubble, the weird packstool and the flares. Not to mention the unnerving geometry inside my pants. Come to think of it, I'm amazed I wasn't run out of town.

* * *

By the time I reached the Sandon River it was just on low tide; even so, it was too deep to ford at the mouth. I wasn't overly dismayed, for I had faced several such instances already where a solution had presented itself, like the footbridge in Pottsville.

That optimism took a blow, however, when I was informed there was no bridge upriver; indeed the only road south was the Pacific Highway, about thirty kilometres inland, running from Grafton to the southernmost hamlet of the Yuraygir, Red Rock.

Sandon was the end of the line; a bucolic shantytown sprawled over a narrow peninsula. It was with some hesitancy that I approached a group of drunken fishermen to ask if one could ferry me across in his dinghy.

None were willing to take me across, although a few were only too happy to inform me of the sharks they had pulled out of this estuary. One helpful soul told me to paddle across on the guitar, another to use it as a weapon if I was attacked. I checked my sides to see if they were splitting and wandered away, disheartened.

I didn't want to backtrack. The thought of walking all day only to go back via the same route was immensely depressing. That's the problem with *walking* in the wrong direction; it takes you so long to figure out you've fucked up.

Of course, if you'd brought maps …

'Yeah yeah, I know,' I muttered, setting off.

My only chance as I saw it was that this river widened and got shallower somewhere upstream. But even though the outgoing tide had left most of the riverbed exposed, deep channels remained.

Just how deep and how fast the current I had no way of gauging, so I continued to follow the peninsula around, hoping for a break. I was heading due north by this time, and had left the fishermen far behind.

I was about to give up when I spotted a place that seemed to offer a chance at fording, but I couldn't judge the width of the deep section from where I stood since it was over near the far bank.

I started out across the exposed sand, figuring I was going to have to swim at least a little to continue this course. At first there were small pools of seawater that I had no trouble avoiding, but as I got further from the shore they became more frequent and grew in size. After I blundered into the second or third one I gave up and simply walked through them. I figured the rest of me would be wet soon enough.

I stopped on a sandbank that resembled the back of a breeching whale; the opposite shore was tantalisingly close. Just a trench of dark water twenty feet wide and God knows how deep and I would be on my way to Minnie Water. I took three, maybe four steps towards it, then stopped.

I looked down in shock at my foot disappearing into the sand. Wrenching it free before it could sink further, I took another step. This time I sank up to my ankle. Lifting my other foot, I then put it down tentatively and found the sand held.

For a moment.

As soon as I transferred my weight, however, I plunged through the thin crust and sank up to my calf. Worse still, my right foot was still sinking. The sand seemed to have the consistency of meringue. Soon I was knee-deep in the bank, and panic was struggling against the chains I had made for it over the past fortnight.

Quicksand, a treacherous voice whispered.

As I sank farther, the sand now reaching the top of my knees, I realised I could really be in trouble.

Panic.

Standing there buried up to my knees in the middle of the Sandon River

and don't forget the tide will be coming in soon

I couldn't help but instinctively yank my leg upward, and got nothing for my efforts except losing my balance and landing on my ass.

'Looking good, Allmon,' I muttered.

I unhooked the pack and lay it down on the sand, placing the guitar on top to prevent the leather case from getting damp. Then I reached down and grabbed my left leg around the thigh, took a deep breath, and heaved upwards.

Nothing.

The watery sand had perfectly moulded itself around my leg; I may as well have been dipped in cement.

I looked around for a fisherman, a boat—anyone I could summon for help. As far as I could see there was nothing but sand, water and trees. Nobody was going to come to my aid, no matter how loud I yelled.

You could be here for a while, good buddy, the traitorous voice said, its tone speculative, dispassionate.

Digging my fingers into the sand around my thigh, I gave a tremendous heave and was relieved to feel the greedy clutch of the bank give a little. Encouraged, I heaved again. A little more movement this time, and I said to the voice, 'See? It was ridiculous to think I'd never get out of this. I'm the hero of this story, and the hero never suffers as ignominious a fate as being stuck in a sandbank until he drowns or is consumed by nibbling crabs.'

Everyone is the hero of their own story, came the reply, *and they all believe it right up until they are written out in Season Three.*

I had no response to that, but it was easier to ignore him now; a few more tugs and I'd be halfway home. As it turns out, it only took one more attempt. I gave an almighty yank and my leg came free with stupid ease—unprepared for it, I once again went flailing onto my ass, arms windmilling.

The seat of my pants was soaked, I noticed. I looked at the water and was disturbed at how it had crept, stealthy-quick, around me. Water was lapping at the crest of the bank, pooling around my gear. A glance behind me revealed crabs hightailing it for the shore as the low places filled up and threatened to strand them.

I proceeded to work on the right leg with renewed determination, but found it rooted in place just as firmly as its twin had been. The minutes ticked by as I gradually worked myself free, sweating under the westering sun. Finally, with a throaty *schloooop*, it came free, and I was on my ass for a third time, wet and weary but immensely grateful.

I saddled up and looked again at the holes left by my legs in the churned sand—testament to a struggle that ten minutes ago I was not sure I'd win. I looked at the river and its unknown depths … possibly shark-infested, if one were to believe the wits back at the beach.

Then I looked back at the Sandon shore and the line of trees that bracketed the road that would take me back to Brooms Head. From there I could walk west until I picked up the Pacific Highway in Grafton, which in turn would carry me over fifty kilometres south to Red Rock.

It would be the long way around, and I would have to spend at least one night by the side of the road, but I would be on dry land and passing through towns that could satisfy my food and water needs.

Looking over the river to the far bank showed it to be pretty hairy; by the time I swam the river, negotiated my way through the dense scrub and mangroves, and got back to the beach it would be dark and I'd be exhausted.

Providing I didn't get lost.

I knew I wouldn't make Minnie Water until well after midnight if I did decide to keep walking, and even then, there was no guarantee of water, despite the town's name.

In the end it made more sense to backtrack, rather than push on into the unknown. But a sense of failure gripped me nonetheless, the fear that, regardless of whether I swam the Sandon River or not, I was in over my head.

* * *

A few hours later I was on a long, straight, unremarkable stretch of road disappearing into shimmering heat haze. The land on either side was just as flat and unremarkable. A lone brumby patrolled the periphery of my vision, white mane wild in the wind of his own making, keeping an eye on me. Trees were giving way to pastures and bottomlands, and I had long since lost sight of the river. I was sunburned and thirsty and decided to step off the road to have a rest and a drink.

Sidestepping my way down the dry and crumbly soil of the shoulder until I reached the bottom, I saw some old logs half-buried in the sandy soil and made my way over to them, relishing the shade cast by a grove of stunted eucalypts.

Sitting down on a log, I noticed a pile of bones partially hidden in the scraggly grass. I nudged them around with the toe of my boot as I drank my fill. At first I thought it to be the remains of a calf, or perhaps a sheep. The skull was wrong though. It had the long snout of a canine, but the teeth were not what you would associate with a meat eater; they were all molars and flattened incisors. I didn't know what it was.

I bent down to examine it closer.

A tremendous roar came from behind me. I jumped and whirled around, not knowing what to expect. But it was just a car, barrelling along with a muffler you could read a newspaper through, judging by the sound. From its speakers came the sound of the Allman Brothers Band, distorted by volume but still identifiable.

Cos there's a man down there
Might be your man, I don't know ...

I ducked down out of sight; why, I am not completely certain. For some reason I didn't want to be seen, didn't want to be discovered out here by whoever drove that old Holden.

As I straightened up again, I had an unexpected vision of myself: sunburnt, dusty, and with the beginnings of a full beard, crouching over the bones of an unknown beast in some forgotten corner of NSW, in this shabby golgotha by the road.

Who was I becoming?

For no reason at all, I bent over and picked up the jawbone of the dead creature. I stuffed it into my back pocket, saddled up, and started walking north again along the road, keeping one ear cocked for the sound of a V8 and the Allman Brothers coming up behind.

* * *

Exhausted, I slept in the sand a few miles north of Broom Head, close to where I'd been the night before. In the dream that followed, I was pulling myself out of the sandbank once more, only to walk a few steps before I sank again. On the far shore I could see a vast herd of brumbies running alongside the river. I wanted to join them, but I couldn't free myself from the clutching sand.

I could hear the Allman Brothers again. Across the river, revealed in glimpses through the endless torrent of wild horses, was the dusty black Holden HZ, looking like a fragment of another era, a bleak refugee of time transported from the wasteland of days long dead.

Leaning against it was a man in jeans

cos there's a man down there
his face hidden by a black Akubra. Through the blur of horseflesh, I saw him raise his head to look at me. I wanted to turn away
might be your man, I don't know
but instead I just watched, transfixed, watching the shadow cast by the hat move slowly up his face like an eclipse.

I awoke with a start, sitting up on the empty beach, looking around trying to get my bearings.

The waves crashed on the sand, the sky scored by shining stars, and in my mind the final seconds of the dream played repeatedly like a badly grooved record. The man in the black hat had been me; his face, revealed in the last frame of the dream, had been mine. But I hadn't looked good. I'd grown prematurely old, emaciated, worn.

I slept poorly for the rest of the night.

DAY 14

*W*hap!

The apple struck me from behind, exploding into a shower of green and white meteorites raining wetly down around me.

'… *ya fuckin loser* …' came the cry as the car sped past me on its way to Grafton, followed by young male laughter. I stopped walking in shock that rapidly morphed into mounting anger.

There had been no mention of idiots throwing things from cars in the honeyed tales of the ramblers I had read. Had Charlie Patton, father of the Delta Blues, been subjected to it? Of course he had, I concluded after a moment's reflection, and far worse, given the place and times in which he lived. Maybe the apple was a rite of passage, a sign I was venturing across some mystical barrier from mere vagrant to *bona fide* vagabond.

The Test of Fruit.

Despite my rationalising, it was hard to maintain my good cheer as I picked small pieces of Granny Smith from my hat and shirt, hearing again that jeering cry, the harsh laughter. I found myself glaring at every car that passed, daring someone to throw so much as a seedless grape.

It was in this mood that the old Datsun ambled past, puffing its way to Grafton like a tired pony. It was the kind of car you would expect a mutton-chopped teacher to drive on his way to downtown Eccentricity. The car's brake lights flashed.

It came to a halt, reverse lights sputtering into life, and then the driver was backing *across* the road towards me. The car made that asthmatic whinnying sound older vehicles make when called upon to reverse, and I could see the silhouette of the driver checking over his shoulder as he came.

Astonished by this behaviour, I simply went on standing there as the car stopped, the door opened, and a guy with a budding set of muttonchops leant out to greet me.

'Hello. Do you need a ride?'

'Hi. No thanks, I'm fine,' I said, as I had said in answer to the previous folks' queries that morning.

'Where are you going?'

'Grafton.'

'Long way to Grafton on foot. Why don't you just hop in and I'll give you a quick lift up the road?'

'Well, that's nice of you to offer, but—'

As I spoke I was thinking of all the miles ahead, all the potential pieces of airborne fruit. I thought of this tour, which wasn't turning out the way I'd planned at all. I'd been on the road for two weeks so far and had yet to sell an album. Being apple-worthy was the most enthusiastic response I'd so far engendered, and this revelation left me feeling low and friendless.

He smiled.

That was how I met Simon of Brooms Head; fledgling guitarist, Datsun-owner and, unsurprisingly, a teacher.

* * *

'So let me get this straight. You quit your job, sold your car, have no home, and now you're walking to Sydney to promote an album nobody has heard? Is that about it?' he said as we drove west in the late morning sunshine.

'Uh-huh.'

'Well Smokey, I take it you're not married, or have any kids.'

I smiled. 'No. I have a girlfriend though.'

'What's her name?'

'Di.'
'Serious?'
'Yeah.'
'That's good.'

We sat silently for a bit, looking out through the windscreen at the world coming at us. Simon's car smelled of books, dog, and the barest hint of his aftershave. The radio murmured in a soothing undertone.

'Are you married?' I asked.

'I was. We're divorced. We tried to make it work, but we'd just grown apart.'

'That's too bad. Kids?'

'One,' he said, smiling. 'Ralph. He's fifteen. He's learning guitar.'

'How long has he been playing?'

'Oh, I bought him an acoustic about two years ago. He's really good on it. I'm trying to get him to teach me, but I'm not very good. My desire outweighs my ability.'

'It's the same for me with carpentry ...'

Our conversation went on like this for the next ten minutes or so, exchanging slices of our lives until we'd built ourselves a pretty good conversation, and Simon's 'quick lift up the road' ended up taking me into Grafton.

* * *

We pulled into the carpark of the school where he worked. The building was unassuming in aspect and the only thing moving in the carpark was a kid trying to kill himself on his skateboard.

'I've got to run in and grab some stuff, Smokey,' Simon said, switching the car off. Then, before I could unbuckle myself, he said, 'Do you want me to leave the keys so you can listen to the radio?'

Staggered at this show of trust in a stranger that he'd met twenty minutes ago, I was at a loss for words. Simon didn't strike me as a fool, and I could tell by his eyes that he was already going to leave the keys no matter what I said. I was moved by this display of faith, especially so as I tend to be regarded with some caution due to my appearance.

'Sure Simon, if you're fine with that.'

'No problem. Change the channel if you like. Back soon.'

With that he was off, waving at a car that had just pulled in several spaces down from ours. The owner of the car was clearly a friend, cheerfully beeping the horn at him.

I sat still for a few minutes, looking at nothing in particular. I was sitting in a stranger's car, parked in a town I'd never been to. My guitar sat on the back seat, looking perfectly at home yet utterly abstract. A sense of unreality swamped me, and so I continued to sit there, doing nothing. The radio murmured of stock market activity in comfortingly boring tones. I didn't want to change the channel.

What got me out of the car and back to reality was the need to have a smoke. It had been over an hour since my last, and my nicotine centre was starting to send urgent requests to my brain.

It felt good to stand up and stretch, aware of the stiffness in my calves, the soft burn of my tendons, the huge blisters on my feet. I suspected this was just the beginning, that by the end, these aches and pains were going to be very familiar indeed.

* * *

The Jacaranda City rolled past my window and the silence between us was natural and without tension.

'Where would you like to get out, Smokey?' Simon asked, noticing me fidgeting in the seat. We were at the southern outskirts of town and the road we were on led to Coffs Harbour, where Simon had some business to attend to.

'Anywhere here's good, I suppose.'

'Feeling a bit guilty?'

'Well, yeah. I don't want to get to Sydney and have someone say to me "hang on a second pal, you didn't walk it all!"'

'Fair enough, but from what you've told me, the bluesmen you're emulating didn't necessarily walk everywhere—they rode the rails, hitch-hiked ... maybe it's about the adventure, rather than adhering strictly to something unrealistic.'

I mulled over this before nodding. 'Maybe you're right, Simon.'

We were silent for a moment as we looked for a suitable spot to pull over, and I saw with something approaching dismay a sign for the Red Rock turnoff in twenty-two kilometres. Red Rock was the southernmost village of the Yuraygir wilderness—I'd missed two thirds of its vast forests and untouched beaches ... and some of that by car, no less. I tried to view Simon's generous lift as being all part of the adventure, like he said, but deep down I knew I couldn't afford to take another trip like this and still call it a walking tour, at least with a straight face. Simon's voice broke into my reverie.

'Can I say something, Smokey?'

'Sure.'

'It seems you were surprised by my show of faith in you back in Grafton, in the carpark. I assume that looking like Jim Morrison crossed with Charles Manson means you labour under people's surface judgements of you, and you've grown used to being viewed ... parsimoniously?'

'It's such a shame most people aren't like you, Simon, able to see past appearances,' I said, unaware I had just walked into a trap.

'But from everything you've told me about your tour so far, you've been doing precisely that yourself.'

'Come again?' I said, but in the pause before his response I quickly scanned our conversation for indicators of supercilious behaviour—I couldn't see any.

'Well, right from the first day—you deemed the fishermen as too scruffy an audience, or too slow-witted, based upon their appearance. Byron was too touristy and full of *Idols* and local louts. Did you play in Brooms Head?'

'No,' I said through lips suddenly numb.

'But you got a pie and sat on the Main Street. I would have thought it a prime time to get the guitar out and test your theory. Why didn't you?'

'I guess I thought a couple of locals wasn't worth the effort,' I said, now unable to feel my lips at all now.

'Old Tom sitting there in his undershirt you mean? He looks pretty ornery but in his day he was quite the pianist—he was probably checking out the guitar and wondering if you were going to play.'

What I'd taken for a xenophobic glare had actually been honest interest, but because of Tom's appearance I'd misinterpreted the look and written him off without further thought. Most of my face was now numb, and that which wasn't felt hot, flushed; I was appalled at my hubris, my arrogance, my pride.

'I think maybe you're waiting for a perfect audience that doesn't exist, Smokey. You know, this tour would be a success if only you had the *right* audience.' He shook his head. 'But no one is going to measure up to the standards you seem to have set. And it's surprising you'd be judgemental, given your own experience,' he said, indicating my long hair, the striped flares, the two-week-old beard.

I opened my mouth to say something, but he beat me to it.

'The reason I had no compunction at leaving you in my car with keys in the ignition is because I could tell, even from our brief chat beforehand, that under the rough exterior you are a decent man. But then, I'm a teacher—and my students' appearances get worse with every year,' he said with a smile. 'You get used to seeing ... seeking ... the person inside.'

I nodded, no longer trying to say anything. I looked out the window feeling terrible and liberated at the same time.

For most of my adult life I've tended towards the Jeff Lebowski end of the fashion spectrum, simultaneously lamenting the world's tendency towards snap judgements, shallow superficialities, and emphasis on outward appearances, while in turn and with no sense of irony exhibiting and perpetrating those very same prejudices against all and sundry. Who was I to pass judgement on my audience? On *anyone*, come to that?

Bad as this made me feel, I was excited by the idea that, by viewing *everyone* as a potential audience, every moment could be utilised musically. It could accompany conversation, or replace conversation. An audience of one was just as important as fifty, and a fisherman just as good as a well-heeled ethnomusicologist. I didn't even *need* an audience—I could just walk down an empty beach and play. The world was my stage, whenever I chose to make it so.

This was as exhilarating as it was unexpected. I'd been alarmingly blinkered regarding the tour's execution up until this point—I'd been waiting for an audience that would never appear and bypassing a hundred audiences as I went.

I couldn't have replied after such a revelation even if he'd wanted me to, but he didn't, of course, because a good teacher knows when to stay silent and let the student do the rest.

* * *

'Well, here we are,' he said as we pulled over near a wooded side road, that tone of finality in his voice that creeps in when the time for parting has come.

'Listen, Simon, I haven't got any money to give you—'

'Don't worry about it—'

'—but I do have this—'

'—honestly, I couldn't take anything—'

'—that I want you to have. It's not much, but maybe your son will dig it.' After several moments of fruitless rummaging and rooting I came up with what I wanted: a copy of the album.

'Oh no, I couldn't …' he began.

'Can and will. It's the least I can do.'

Simon was having none of it.

'How much does it go for?' he asked, pulling out a wallet that looked as though it had been new around the time Mike Walsh hosted *The Midday Show*.

'No, no, no Simon. It's …'

'Ten? Twenty? How much?' I had to remind myself that I was a hitchhiker. Had any hitcher ever had money thrust upon *them*? There he was though, and now laboriously adding another ten upon the first two. I could see he wasn't going to let me go without forking over money.

I didn't want our last words to each other to be some stupid argument, so I said, 'Ten. And that's final.'

He smiled.

I smiled back.

I got out, opened the back door and retrieved my stuff.

'Keep safe, Smokey.'

He drove away, and I bent down to pick up my packstool.

It had taken two weeks, but I had finally made my first sale of the tour.

Chapter Three: Banana Country

DAY 15

A woman and her dog approached just as I was getting a nice buzz going. They joined me where I sat playing the second gig of the tour on a wooden bench halfway up the southern slope of the glorious Woolgoolga headland. Below us, surfers and dolphins caught the last glittering, golden waves of the day.

The woman was fiftyish with a stringy, muscular body that reminded me of beef jerky, and I suspect she was taking the breather not so much for herself but for her decrepit and cheerfully overweight Newfoundland who slumped, panting at our feet, clearly done in.

'Hi!'

'Hey. Your dog looks like he's been enjoying the walk.'

'That's Harvey. He hates coming out. I've got to get him in shape, whether he likes it or not. It's not right for a dog to be so fat, don't you think?'

'Oh, I dunno. I've seen fatter.'

'Hmmph. Not right. And he farts when he walks. Whoever heard of a dog that farts when it walks?'

'Gee, he looks pretty old,' I said, noting the white on his muzzle.

Harvey knew when he was the centre of attention, and pawed at my foot while giving me a loving grin, showing old, yellowed teeth.

'Yeah, he's thirteen,' she said, warmth creeping into her voice. 'Old for a Newfie.'

We sat in silence for about three seconds. I realised this was about as much as this lady could stand before she had to break it.

'I love it up here. My husband can't understand why I do, but that's because he's an idiot. He never walks anywhere. He's fat, too,' she said with resignation. It must have been hard for her, surrounded by obese creatures all the livelong day.

'It certainly is nice this time of day.'

I could have been speaking Urdu.

'Fat husband, fat dog. It isn't healthy. Do you know that half of all Australians are overweight? *Half!*'

'Yeah, that sure is a lot. Do you live in Woolgoolga?'

'Woopi. Locals call it Woopi. I love it here, wouldn't live anywhere else. Have you seen the temple?'

'Temple?'

'The Sikh Temple. Can't miss it. Lots of minarets.'

'Are there a lot of Sikhs here?'

'Yeah. They're fine. I mean, each to their own, you know? And get this—you never see a fat Indian.'

'No, I guess not—'

'Do you?'

'No.'

'No. Uh uh. It's their diet. And they walk everywhere. Not like our blokes. Beer bellies and man-boobs. What kind of country is this?'

'I don't know,' I said, ashamed of my deplorable gender and nationality.

'I mean, there's not much eye-candy for a girl in town …'

I felt I could safely throw my mind into neutral while nodding in the right places. The sun was warm on my face and Harvey's head was heavy on my foot; he was asleep. I noodled away on the guitar, refining a song that wanted to be born, strangely comforted by her ranting …

Mindful of my conversation with Simon, I had set up shop here on the long grassy slope and played for all and none, simply enjoying the act of playing. Sometimes people stopped to listen or have a chat; others walked by with a nod or a smile. I had a couple of albums out in case people were feeling generous—I wanted that rush of the sale again—but so far none were. It didn't matter—the idea I was holding my gig here in this beautiful setting, creating a soundtrack to the afternoon, was in some ways reward enough.

Those folks who did stop were often quite interesting in their own right.

'... I'm sick of getting that crap in our inbox. I mean, it's not like either of us has an erectile problem.'

'Hmmm. I'm sorry, what?'

'Never mind. Look, I'm sorry. I can't stay and talk, I really should be getting Harvey home. It's so hard to wake him up if he falls asleep.'

I looked down at the sleeping doggy face on my boot, noting the small twitches of his salt and pepper snout as he dreamed of eating and farting and doing whatever it is an elderly dog likes doing. It seemed a shame to wake him.

'I think he's already asleep.'

'Shit,' she said, getting off the bench and kneeling next to him. She very gently tickled his paws and softly called his name.

'Haaar-veeeey.'

I thought it was going to take a lot more than that to get him up, but he whuffed, blinked, and raised his head. He looked around, trying to figure out where he was and then, as the realisation sank in, the misery in his big brown eyes was clear. He heaved a sigh and got to his feet.

'Well, see you later. Nice talking to you. My name's June, by the way.'

'Smokey.'

'Pleased to meet you, Smokey. Enjoy the rest of the day.'

Harvey gave me a goodbye lick, then waddled on up the path to the summit. As for me, I sat there drinking in the sights, trying to think of a fat Indian.

* * *

Later that night, unable to sleep, I wondered what Di was doing. She seemed very far away; our text messages had dwindled as she sailed in and out of range every few days, exacerbated by the demands on her time as she tried to adjust to her new life.

As I thought of her, my phone beeped.

Hey babe ... I'm about to go out of range, but I had to tell you about what it's been like over here ...

As I read, a bleak feeling blossomed in the centre of me, a rancid flower in bloom. She was meeting new people, seeing new places and getting swept up by a river of Ben-less days. And although she said she missed me and loved me and couldn't wait until September, I wondered.

... the appreciation for a woman my age over here is incredible, it's so different to the Gold Coast where you're invisible once you pass thirty ... the first week was funny ... when I came up the stairs in my formal outfit, the cruise director saw me, all he could say was 'Wow', which was nice ...

She had been gone a week and already her life was exotic and remote and peopled with strangers who already had in-jokes with my beloved. How much worse would it be after six months? Would we meet at Brisbane airport in the spring and realise our love had died at some point during our time apart? We had only been together for two months, for God's sake. How could we hope to endure such a lengthy separation at such a critical time in our relationship?

She was getting accustomed to life aboard the *Sovereign of the Seas*, and I felt sick at the thought of her getting used to life without me.

Troubled, I didn't reply—she would've already been out of range, anyway.

DAY 16

My arms were above my head in a 'V', the guitar held firmly in my hands. The Moonee River was up to my chest, the water clear and cool, the footing reasonably stable. My eyes were on the bottom, making sure I wasn't about to step into a trough or onto a stingray.

It was noon, or just after, judging by the sun. I'd tromped over half a dozen headlands, all of which afforded fantastic 360 degree views, but thoroughly wore me out. The workout was a welcome penance for my automobile day with Simon; this was a walking tour again, all right, and my feet left me in no doubt as to the fact.

At first I had been disheartened, seeing the telltale signs of a river on the deserted Moonee Beach; the play of currents and choppy water ahead, the narrowing peninsula, the change in flora on my right—all indicated a river mouth was imminent. Memories of the fiasco at the Sandon River were ascendant.

It was only when I stood on the bank, looking at the shallow sprawl of the Moonee, that I thought I might have a chance of fording. Where the Sandon had yielded murky unknowable straits, the Moonee was clear, calm and—best of all—shallow. On the western bank it looked incredibly lush, green and inviting. I didn't waste another moment.

I tied my boots to the packstool straps and made sure the sleeping bag was secured to the frame as well. Then I took my shirt off and stuffed it into the pack, grabbed the guitar and waded into the water, wondering about bull sharks and anything else that may inhabit an isolated, sub-tropical estuary.

I needn't have worried. The deepest it got was my shoulder, and I could see the sandy bottom the entire time. The current was mild, and I kept my footing. The sunlight reflected off the water, throwing daggers of light into my eyes. Fish swam between my legs, little ones for which I had no name. Every so often a larger one would hove into view, swimming leisurely into the school like a *largo* intrusion into a *vivacissimo* movement.

It was with genuine regret that I approached the west bank. The water dropped to my chest, then my waist, then my thighs were free, and then I was back on land. I had completed my first successful fording of the walk, and I felt immeasurably courageous … capable … hell, heroic. *Allmon braves shark-infested river in the wilderness.*

It was then I noticed that, far from forbidding boondocks, I was actually standing in a picnic ground; a toilet block squatted underneath the casuarinas, tables sprouted like curious fungi from the lush grass. Looking further upstream I noticed a family picnicking, their toddlers negotiating the river with as much ease and a great deal less fanfare than I had. Wretched urchins. *Allmon braves local infants' waterhole* didn't quite have the same ring to it.

So much for the bold adventurer.

* * *

As I reached the bus shelter, I saw that it was already occupied. A kid of about eight was sitting on the bench, swinging his legs in the mid-afternoon sunshine. He wore a school uniform that bore all the signs of roughhousing associated with boys of that age.

He looked up as I made to sit down.

'Hey mister, don't sit there,' he said, pointing above my head. His eyes were large, brown and fearful.

I looked up and saw what had drawn his attention. It was a wasp's nest, the size of a grapefruit and crawling with yellow and black critters. After the past hour of walking alongside the Pacific Highway, with semi trailers passing within a whisker of my fragile bod, a wasp's nest posed little in the way of terror.

'Meh,' I said, and sat down.

The kid sat silently, no doubt convinced he was in the presence of a madman.

I tried to configure my face into something non-threatening and said, 'What's your name?'

'Tony.'

'Hey Tony, I'm Smokey. Pleased to meet you.'

'Mmm hmm.'

'Nice day,' I said, starting to panic and latching onto weather, that great detour for a conversational roadblock.

'I guess.'

'Yeah. Not too hot.'

'Uh-huh.'

This was going nowhere.

We sat together for a few minutes without saying anything. I don't know what Tony was thinking, but I was racking my brain for things to say to a kid and coming up empty. Finally the silence was too much, and I said, 'Whatcha doin at the bus stop, Tony?'

He gave me a withering look that said he wasn't surprised I sat beneath potentially lethal wasp nests.

'Waiting for the bus.'

We sat for a few more minutes without saying anything.

Tony swung his legs.

'Are you on your way home?' I asked, trying to sound as though I possessed a rudimentary intelligence. Tony looked at me for a moment and decided to cut me a break.

'Nah. I gotta pick up Sean. He's too little to walk home alone.'

'He your brother?'

'Yeah.'

'How old is Sean?'

'He's six. I'm eight,' he said with an air of importance, 'almost nine.'

'Wow,' I replied with what I hoped was suitable awe.

'Are you a cowboy?' Tony asked, apropos of nothing.

Kid must be on drugs, I thought. I didn't know what to say.

'No.'

'Oh.' He looked disappointed. I felt unaccountably bad for not being a cowboy. 'It's just that I saw the hat … and your boots …'

Understanding dawned.

'Oh, I'm with you. No, I'm not a cowboy. I'm a guitarist. See?' I held the guitar in its leather case out for his inspection.

'Wow! Can I see it?'

'Sure thing.' I unzipped the case and started strumming. I ran off a riff or two and Tony smiled. I smiled. I was warming to my audience of one when he jumped up and pointed over my shoulder.

'The bus is coming!'

I turned around, the guitar forgotten.

A big yellow bus was slowing down as it neared us, the driver guiding it into this little side lane off the highway designed for it. The sign in the window proclaimed its destination as Coffs Harbour. An idea was forming, and I listened with only half an ear to my young companion exclaiming over how he had taken the bus way back in the first grade by himself. To hear him tell it that was around the time King John was signing the Magna Carta.

'… and no one ever waited to pick *me* up.'

'Well, Sean's lucky he's got you,' I said absently. The daring plan to ask the bus driver for a lift into town wouldn't go away—I had to get off this death-trap highway. I slid the guitar back into its case and gathered up my belongings. The doors wheezed open, and a flood of four-foot terrors poured out, hollering excitedly. I saw Tony greet a smaller version of himself dressed in shorts and a jumper, placing a fraternal arm around his shoulders.

The driver was a silhouette in the darkened bus, and I had little time to let my eyes adjust. Even without seeing his face, I could sense his wariness. Suddenly it didn't seem like a very good idea to ask for a lift, and I vacillated.

'G'day,' I said.

'Hey pal. What do you need?' He was an older guy, his voice gravelly, impatient.

'Well, I was wondering if this highway was the only way to get to Coffs Harbour.'

'What? Yeah.'

'Really? There are no back roads? No alternatives?'

'Nup. Now listen, I gotta get going, pal.'

I couldn't believe there was no other way into the city aside from the nation's busiest highway. Every minute I spent walking along it was raising the odds of me becoming a footnote on the late night edition.

... and in other news, a young man who was walking from the Gold Coast to Sydney was turned into chutney by a highballing semi just north of Coffs Harbour ...

'Hey pal! You're blockin the door.'

'Oh. Sorry.' The doors started to wheeze shut on their pneumatic hinges. A sudden impulse drove me to stick my arm out to hold them back.

'Hey! What are you doing?' the driver yelled.

'Look, I'm sorry, but ... do you ever ... ah ... let adults ride the bus?' I squeezed my head between the rubber-edged doors and looked up the aisle. Kids were grab-arsing around, shrieking and gabbling and participating in that largely lawless *interregnum* that is the Bus-Ride Home. Looking back at the driver, I found I couldn't pull my head back out, so I simply stood there, wedged and trying to smile winningly.

The driver mulled over my strange request, his shadowed face impassive. 'Well, I really shouldn't ... but—'

'Look, I don't want to get you into trouble—'

'—but I'm sure we can work something out,' he said, releasing the door, and with it my arm and head.

'Sure. How much?' I said, rubbing my neck.

'Seven bucks.'

'*Seven bucks?*'

'Yeah. Hey, this *is* a school bus you know. I mean, it's not like you're supposed to use it in the first place. It's not a taxi, pal.'

'Okay, okay, it's cool.' I pulled out a fistful of shrapnel and handed it over. 'Here you go. That should do it.'

He took the money and put it straight into his pocket without checking it. A little extra on the side, beer money for when he knocked off, perhaps. I didn't blame him. Last time I checked, bus drivers weren't on a king's ransom.

I climbed aboard and the bus fell silent immediately. I stood at the head of the aisle feeling preposterously tall; twenty little faces looked up at me solemnly, all eyes. I could hear my heart beating, could feel the sweat trickling down my back and collecting in my armpits.

I looked around for a seat, noting how small they seemed. The one behind the driver was free, and I sat down hurriedly, wanting nothing more than for the bus to get moving and break the moment. I could hear the kids whispering behind me.

'... why's his hair so long? ...'
'... he looks like my Uncle Hank ...'
'... not allowed to ...'
'... smells funny ...'

I tuned them out. Other than sniffing my shirt to confirm the fact that, yes, I was indeed pretty rank, I tried to ignore everything and stared over the driver's shoulder through the front window.

'We'll be in town in about ten minutes,' the driver said. The gruff tone was gone now; in fact, he sounded grateful to have someone closer to his own age to talk to.

'Oh, okay. I haven't been here since I was a kid. What's it like?'

'Shithole. Aha ha ha, yeah, nah, you know.'

Coffs Harbour, known to some as the Banana Capital, would be the largest town of the walk thus far. Its success with bananas is so great it has driven the townsfolk to erect at the edge of town a concrete banana the size of the bus I was currently in.

With a population of around seventy thousand, Coffs dwarfed Woolgoolga and was almost twice the size of Ballina. If I'd struggled with navigating those two towns—and I had—I was in a whole other league here. I could feel little flutters in my stomach at the thought of all those people crammed into one area, and wondered what was happening to me. Was I developing into some kind of agoraphobe?

What concerned me more, however, was where I was going to sleep. The sun was on the wester; in another few hours it would be dark. After the experience of the night on Yamba's Town Beach I wasn't too thrilled with the idea of sleeping near a city, but I was too tired to do much more walking today. Since sitting down my muscles were cooling, tightening, and all the aches of the walk were starting to tune up for a night of lusty playing. My lower back and the arches of my feet were the worst, and I wondered for the first time whether I was going to last the course in a physical sense. As people kept pointing out, it was a long way to Sydney.

The third matter weighing on me was the musical aspect of the walk. So far I'd done next to no promotion, played in front of a few dozen people and achieved a grand total of one sale. Sure, I'd sent off a bunch of copies to radio stations a week ago in Evans Head, but I'd heard nothing back. I was going to have to get off my ass and start knocking on doors, calling up stations, and getting in touch with newspapers.

Coffs Harbour, with its population and infrastructure, seemed like my best bet to achieve those aims. I wanted to do those things without carting all my gear around, however, and before I did anything I needed to clean myself up. I couldn't do any of those things staying on the beach, I realised, and my mind turned reluctantly to the idea of staying in a hotel.

Reluctantly, because I was getting desperately low on funds. I figured I had about fifty dollars to my name, and a night in a hotel would leave me penniless. I felt panic stirring and tried to focus on something more positive.

The bus stopped, and I disembarked, thanking the driver and waving to the kids who chorused their goodbye in deliriously loud voices, drawing the downtown shoppers' attention to the filthy hippie stumbling off the little kids' school bus. Overcome by the weirdness of my arrival, I set off in no particular direction in search of the cheapest lodgings I could find.

* * *

I walked into the backpacker's foyer and found it empty. I could hear voices coming from somewhere nearby, and the tinny sound of canned laughter that could only come from a television sitcom. Judging from the hour I figured it must have been *M*A*S*H*. I walked through another doorway and found a recreation room full of people watching the tube.

'... *I'll Hari-kari if you show me how, but I will not carry a gun!*' Alan

Alda was saying as all heads turned to regard me. I was reminded of the kids on the bus; the room seemed full of eyes.

One guy who was a few years older than the others stood up and ambled over. I took him to be the proprietor. 'Help you with summat, mate?'

I shook hands with him, 'I don't suppose there's any rooms left for tonight?' My experience in Byron Bay had conditioned me to expect rejection at this late hour when it came to backpacker hostels, but I was in luck.

'Yep, we've got room, so long as you don't mind sharing with Canadians. How long you plan on staying?'

'Just tonight.'

'Magic. Come in the front and I'll get you sorted out.' His accent pegged him as a Yorkshire man. He seemed friendly. Friendly or not, I wanted to know how much it would cost before we went any further.

'Seventeen dollar,' he said, adding, 'You get back a tenner in the morning. That okay?'

'Yeah, that'll be fine,' I said, handing over the cash and trying to ignore the funny things my stomach was doing, my quickening heart. 'What about Internet?' I wanted to get my promotion sorted, wanted to get that all-important distribution deal. Once I had that I could legitimately go to radio.

'Computer's in the rec room. Two dollar for thirty minute. You'll be lucky to get on though. There's a couple of Swedes got a monopoly on it. Ruddy Swedes, eh?'

We reached the door to my room. When he opened it I was positive somebody had ransacked the place. There was such utter devastation everywhere the mind shrank from it. The last time I'd seen such ruin it had been in my dorm room at college, where I'd bunked with two other guys in what was known simply as The Dungeon.

The proprietor saw my face. 'Yeah, I know. Fuckin swine. But that's Canadians for you. You don't mind, do you?'

'Well it's not the Beverly Wilshire, but then, I'm not Richard Gere,' I said, dumping my packstool on the only bare ground visible.

He laughed and shook my hand and left me to the room. I closed the door, relieved to be in for the night.

* * *

I lay in bed, unable to sleep. I was too comfortable, for one thing. The mattress felt strange, soft yet unyielding, unlike the mouldable sand beds I'd grown used to. The room, still bereft of Canadians (unless they were buried somewhere under the mounds of refuse), was unnaturally silent—I had grown accustomed to the susurrus of the surf, the constant respiration of the Pacific at night, the wind through the thin fingered casuarinas and spinifex grass. And when I stared upward, all I could see was the bottom of the bunk above me, instead of galaxies wheeling in their circular dance above.

I threw the covers back and swung my legs out of bed. I got up and padded across to the packstool, where my sleeping bag was. Clearing a place in the detritus, I unrolled it on the floor, then grabbed my shirt off the dresser and bundled it up into a makeshift pillow. I got down onto the floor and slid into the sleeping bag, resting my head on the shirt. I reached out and was comforted to feel the knife in its leather sheath lying near my head.

I fell asleep in minutes, but not before I wondered how long it would take me to readjust to normal life after this was over.

DAY 17

The next morning I was standing in the post office, mailing off letters to Triple J, the only nationwide avenue for unsigned acts to get some proper exposure.

Much like the court minstrels of the Middle Ages, a signed artist has a patron. The patron—in this instance the record company—pays for the artist to record an album, and any other incidental costs like a makeover, new equipment etc. The unsigned artist—me, for example—is essentially wandering the dodgy wilderness roads of the music scene, itinerant and homeless.

The price of the patronage for the court minstrel was that his material had to include a lot of odious odes to his benefactor. The price for the signed artist of today is that they owe the record company all the costs of producing the album, hence touring is the only way they are likely to see any money. It could be argued that being unsigned is a savvy method of retaining pure control over one's songs and career.

Of course, without a patron or record deal, the likelihood of *having* a career or anyone hearing your songs is slim; mainstream radio still plays ninety per cent signed acts—the historical connection between labels and radio stations is a long and deeply entrenched one. A signed artist implies they are marketable and will bring listeners—and hence consumers—to the station, who can then ask top dollar from advertisers. Unsigned means unproven in the market as it is understood by the radio station, and can therefore never trump the signed artist and the guarantee of revenue they bring ... as is often the case, there is little room for altruistic solos in the capitalist ensemble.

Triple J, being an arm of the many-tentacled, government/taxpayer-owned ABC and thus insulated against market forces and not having to chase the advertising dollar, can afford to run the arty, the leftfield, the critically acclaimed but unlistenable.

The unsigned.

Folks like me.

A *lot* of folks like me. Triple J receives one hundred CDs a week, every week, all year. Then there were the uploaded mp3s ... I was one voice in a very, very large choir.

I included a copy of the album with each handwritten letter. Lacking the funds even to run off more professional printed copies, I hoped the handwritten aspect could be construed as rough and raw missives from the road, in keeping with the whole ethos of the tour.

I further hoped that they would reach their intended targets at the station, knowing that in the daily flood of music they probably wouldn't. More than anyone else, however, I wanted to reach Richard Kingsmill.

The head of Triple J programming, he held one of the keys to the door that opened onto a future in music in this country. It was rumoured that even recording giant Sony only got fifteen minutes a week with Kingsmill to push their latest artists. An audience with Kingsmill was the musician's equivalent of an audience with Colonel Walter E Kurtz—a long and perilous journey with no guarantee of ever getting there. And if even you did, he may not give you the answers you sought.

If I could slip past the competition with some crazy stunt like walking to Sydney, then so much the better.

Earlier that morning I'd used the hostel's computer to once again fill out Somersault's online application form. When the time came to submit, however, an error message kept hollering for a password, just as it had in Evans Head.

As it had been six am there was nobody around to ask what the password might have been. In an effort to beat the Swedes to a computer I'd undone myself. I watched as my time ran out and the screen went dark, the computer still waiting for the password. Leery of trying again with my funds so low, I was still without distribution. Panic, and the sense that this tour was an extravagant failure in the making, wouldn't go away so easily this time.

Exacerbating my gloom was another text message from Di that had arrived while I'd slept, telling me of the cocktail-fuelled antics of her workmates at their first staff party. I needed to talk to her, needed to hear her voice. But she'd be out of range by now, cruising around the Bahamas, working hard.

On a ship full of eligible men; better looking, smarter, funnier than you, a voice whispered.

'Shut up.'

Better lovers.

'Shut up.'

I knew my fears were stupid and groundless, and so I paid them my undivided attention.

She's in the Caribbean, *for God's sake. The accent alone is enough to make you a distant memory.*

The voice was right, dammit. Reading a list of unwanted pharmaceutical side-effects sounded sexy when said with a Bahamian drawl. *May cause desquamation, mon.*

'Stop it.'

What was I so worried about? Di loved me; I knew that. I was funny, smart and didn't stop clocks when I entered rooms.

No one was a better lover than I was.

I struggled to convince myself of the last one, but I pinned my hopes on Di believing it so.

So if I knew I had nothing to worry about, then why wouldn't the fear that she was slipping away be banished by such logic?

* * *

I played for most of the morning to little notice or acclaim. A few people stopped by for a song or two, and I smiled encouragingly at them and struck up a few conversations, but on the whole Coffs was a bust. The confidence I'd felt in the wake of my sale to Simon and the *alfresco* gig on the Woolgoolga headland was beginning to wane. My idea to conduct a tour on the beaches and in the parks of the country—so elegant and simple in conception—was in reality too strange and unexpected, at least so it seemed.

People expected to see touring musicians in pubs, or in arenas, or at the very least with something more professional than a beaten acoustic, a bunch of shabby albums and a packstool that looked like a refugee from a 1950's lawn sale. Rather than coming across as a down-to-earth, no-frills production, I simply looked homeless and possibly crazy. Maybe the world wasn't ready for this. After a passing bum told me to get a job, I gave up and went in search of a wider audience at the Coffs Harbour ABC radio station.

ABC Local Radio was going to be my only chance to get on the radio in the early going, as the syndicated FM stations generally don't allow for unsigned artists and certainly not those without distribution. At least the ABC might interview me, if not play my undistributable songs.

After fruitlessly knocking on the door at the station, however, I decided it was maybe time to leave Coffs, flee from the miasma of failure that seemed to be growing thicker with each passing moment. That nobody answered the door—possibly due to my appearance—was especially disheartening, since my chance of reaching an audience as large as this would not come again until ABC's Port Macquarie station, two-hundred kilometres away.

Faced with not enough money for another night at the backpackers' and the unappealing prospect of sleeping on a well-lit beach populated by dudes even scruffier than me, I saddled up and hit the sand, Sawtell-bound. The sense of failure came with me and was getting heavier.

* * *

Picture if you will a man who stands five feet high, grey hair pulled into a ponytail and boasting a truly heroic rod. So tanned he resembles nothing so much as a walnut with legs. 'Happy Jim', it says on his rod, written in elaborate gold script.

He greeted me as though we were old friends reunited.

Jim had no sage advice, no connections to the music industry, and no money to buy an album.

What Jim had was ganja.

'Beautiful day, huh?' he said, as I dumped my stuff on the sand beside him.

'Sure is. Catch anything?'

'Yeah. Threw 'em all back though. Used to be you could pull in the big uns all day long. These days I could spend all week out here and not catch anything bigger than me old persuader.'

'Out here' was a handy little spot by the river, just before it ran its course into the frothing ocean north of Sawtell. The water was a deep, mysterious green.

'Nice here,' I said.

'Why would you live anywhere else, eh?' he said.

I looked at a nearby family. There was a boy and a girl splashing around in the shallows of the river, while the parents took the opportunity to indulge in some gentle canoodling on a picnic blanket. It was a good scene.

'What's your handle, mate?' he asked as he cast out.

'Smokey.'

'Happy Jim.' He stuck his hand out. It was as small as the rest of him, brown and weathered. He looked me up and down and said, 'You have a smoke, don'cha?'

'I'd never say no, Jim,' I said, thinking I needed a pick-me-up after Coffs Harbour.

'Well fire up the briar, Scrimpy! She's right there in the tackle box, in a little tin. Go for your life.' He turned back to the river, concentrating on reeling in his line, leaving me to have at it.

'You sure, Jim? I mean … just get stuck in?'

'Huh? Oh, sure. Shit, that's what it's for. Got plenty. I grow my own, you know. Never run dry that way.'

'No, I guess not. Do you want me to roll you one?'

''kin oath. I was just thinkin before you rocked up that I was due.'

And so we partook, first me, then Jim. I've smoked my share of weed over the years, but Jim's stash was in a league the like of which I have never encountered. I mean, there's popcorn chicken and there's *pollo scallopini al funghi*. If all you've eaten in your life is Cluck-in-a-Bucket, then that second dish is gonna blow your doors completely off, and Jim's gear was definitely the *pollo* in a world of cluck.

God knows what Faustian pact he'd made to concoct such a killer plant, but in short order I could feel my head floating away like a helium balloon. Jim was pretty spaced out himself, if the truth be known. He launched into a circuitous, difficult-to- follow tale that had something to do with Western Australia.

'Go west, Sooty, that's the ticket,' he informed me, with a conspiratorial air.

'All we need is Sweep,' I said as Jim nodded serenely.

'Yep. The west is the best, as someone once said. I was over there last year … no, wait a minute. *Two* years ago. Hang on. Maybe it was …'

I left him to it, simply enjoying the sound of his voice and the warmth of the sun on my skin. Every so often I'd tune back in, listen to stories of abalone the size your head, whale sharks twice the length of your boat. But mostly I looked at the green river and wondered whether this was a sensible response to the failure of the tour thus far. I felt as though perhaps the time for hash cookies and joints had passed, at least until I got this tour moving in the right direction.

Jim noticed my rod sticking out the packstool.

'What the hell is that?'

'Hmmmm? Oh. That. My fishing apparatus.'

I paused.

'Appariti.'

No, that wasn't quite right either.

'My rod.'

Sweet.

'Looks like crap,' Jim remarked.

'Yeah, it is. But then, I'm not much chop when it comes to the noble art of angling.'

'Well you'll never get any better with this contraption, Smucky. Mind if I take a closer look?'

'Go for it,' I replied at length; all I seemed to be capable of now was smiling beatifically at this small brown friendly gnome.

He pulled it out and had a thorough inspection of its construct. As he did he derided, cursed and mocked until he could mock no more, which was fair enough—it was a wretched Kmart gadget that had cost me twenty bucks. By any fisherman's standards it was worthy of nothing but the contempt Jim heaped upon it.

Here's the thing about stoners; they are prone to acts of alarming generosity, rarely thought through and almost never wise. Spend any time with a pothead and you will discover the truth in the adage 'possessions are fleeting', and Happy Jim was no exception.

'What you need is a decent rod. Come back to my place up the river,' he waved in the general direction of the ocean, 'and we'll get you sorted out. I've got one just like mine that you can have. More weed back there, too.'

Now, what you have to understand is that his offer was entirely genuine. It wasn't some ruse to get me to part with money, or a fanciful tale coughed up by his weed-addled brain to pass the time. I was certain there was a rod leaning up against the wall of his shack, waiting for us to go get it.

The problem was that Jim would soon forget he had given it to me, and at some stage next week he would be turning his shack upside down in a vain attempt to locate his spare rod. I couldn't do that to this lovely, generous, obliterated man.

'I couldn't do it, Jim. This one will see me through. I'm used to it.'

'No no no. I can't let you go off without a decent rod. Teach a man to fish, and all that. How can I teach you to fish with this fucking thing?'

'It's cool. Besides, I'm used to it.'

'It's no trouble, Shaggy, honest. This thing couldn't catch a cold. We'll go now, while we think on it.'

I could see it was going to take more than mere demurrals to stop him, so I played the card that would stop any stoner in their tracks.

'Jim, you'd have to pack everything up. Lug it all back to your place. Long trip …'

I could see his mind working this over, and knew long before he spoke what decision he would make. I know the Happy Jims of the world, you see, and if there's one thing they all have in common, it's apathy in the face of activity.

'Yeah. I see what you mean.'

'Be a shame to let this glorious afternoon go to waste.'

'Mmmm. I *was* kinda settled.'

'Besides, there's always next time. What do you say we have another toke and forget about it for today?'

'Yeah, good idea. You're all right, you know that, Swifty.'

'So are you, Jim. Salt of the earth.'

'Ha! Salt of the Christing earth! That's us!'

So we packed a bowl and Jim forgot all about his spare rod, which was leaning against a shack somewhere upriver, biding its time.

Chapter Four: The Gathering Storm

DAY 19

No one was offering rides across the Nambucca River. In fact, there was barely anyone around at all.

The deserted town of Nambucca Heads really drove home the shortcomings of my tour. With nobody aware of my existence, my appearance rapidly disintegrating with the tribulations of the road, and with no local knowledge of good spots to play or when the pubs had original music night (a phenomenon in these modern times as rare as a politician's *mea culpa*), the tour was in danger of simply becoming a homeless ramble with the occasional foray into starvation and dehydration.

My funds were almost gone, and I was caught on the horns of a dilemma: stay put and try to build an audience that could sustain me and hopefully provide enough to continue in due course, or push on at top speed for Sydney and hope I'd make enough busking to survive the course.

Did I want, in other words, musical success or simply an adventure with a guitar strapped to my back?

By throwing everything I had at Sydney I was perhaps missing the whole point of a walking tour: to test the concept that such an unorthodox method of touring could work. By rushing through the thing before I starved and went bankrupt, I was effectively admitting defeat, wasn't I? And if that was indeed the case, why bother pushing for Sydney at all? Why not just call it a day here in Nambucca Heads?

On the other hand, the trouble with setting up shop in a town for a few weeks to rebuild the bank balance was that winter was coming on apace, and the longer I tarried the less appealing nights spent sleeping on the sand would become.

Nambucca Heads clearly wasn't the place to earn folding money, however, so I decided to push on. When I got to a town of some size, I would reassess my dilemma.

There was an information kiosk at the edge of town. If anybody knew of a way south other than swimming the Nambucca River (where several years before a guy had been badly bitten by a shark), I figured it would be the owner.

* * *

'Nope, only way south is the highway.'

'You're kidding.'

The attendant shook her head and smiled. We were the only ones in the centre, a stark one-roomed structure with racks of maps around its periphery. Outside a hot wind whipped up dust devils and peppered the windows with fine grit.

'Sorry, dear. My advice is to go to Macksville, then once you're through the town, look for Warrell Creek. Turn left when you see it. There's a road that runs alongside it to the coast. At the end of it you'll find Scotts Head.'

'How far is Macksville?'

'On foot? Take you a few hours, I'm thinking. Also, they're upgrading the highway. A friend of mine just called and said the traffic's jammed all the way there. It's Sunday, you know, and everyone wants to get to the beach.'

I thanked her and left the kiosk, and walked the short distance to the highway. Standing by the orange crash barriers, trying not to breathe in the cloud of dust raised by the roadwork, I closed my eyes and pictured myself bedding down on the beach at Scotts Head. I could almost hear the waves sweeping over the sand, feel the cool sea breeze ruffling my hair, the welcoming cloak of night enveloping me.

I opened my eyes and looked at motionless traffic stretching as far as I could see, listened to the sound of grinding and hammering and crunching, felt the sun roasting the skin of my neck, tasted the exhaust and dirt. I started walking.

The traffic jam stretched on. Some people took the opportunity to get out and stretch their legs; others appeared to be asleep at the wheel. One guy was sunbathing on his roof, determined to get a tan whether he reached the beach or not.

I passed a car with a freight of shrieking children in the back, some crying, some whingeing, and one making a sound like an aeroplane plummeting to earth.

'Mum! Dylan broke it. Mum! Dylan broke it …

… Nyyyaaaaaarrrrrrr! Rat-a-tat-a-tat! Keeeeooowww! …

… Heeeyyyy! Give it back! Muu-uuummmm!! …'

I looked at Mum and Dad, sitting in the front. Neither moved. They looked normal enough: middle-class Australians who just happened to be cataleptic. Both stared with unseeing eyes at the dashboard, probably thinking they must have fucked up righteously in a past life to deserve this karmic Armageddon.

I passed a dog lying in the tray of a ute, panting in the heat. A pretty teenager with pimples smiled and waved at me from a Ford. I waved back. A couple of guys on motorbikes sat revving their engines in frustration or friendly competitiveness.

The road followed the river west, and gradually I tuned out the metal caterpillar of human misery to my right.

I had problems of my own.

Foremost among these was avoiding the workmen. They were everywhere, and clearly in no mood for dealing with an anomaly like me. Coming in a close second and gaining fast was a lack of water. So hot and dusty were the surroundings I was gulping the stuff down. At the rate I was going I'd be dry long before I reached Macksville.

Finally, there was the problem of my feet. They had served me well so far; apart from several whopping blisters and the occasional twinge in the arch they'd made few complaints. Now, however, I was getting a stabbing pain just behind the ball of my right foot with every second or third step. I tried flexing the foot as I walked in case it was some kind of muscle cramp, but to no avail. I pressed and kneaded to see if I could find the cause of the problem, but felt nothing. I checked the boot itself, in case there was a rock or maybe a nail come loose from the sole. Apart from some dirt and sand, the boot was innocent of debris. I put it back on, drank some more water, cursing myself for doing so

small sips Allmon, small sips

and started out again.

For the first few steps all was well. I cautiously allowed myself to hope whatever it was had sorted itself out. The next step, however, a bolt of pain lanced up from my foot and lodged in my hamstring. My leg buckled momentarily, and I thought I was going to flop onto the bitumen like a dehydrated marathon runner. I managed to keep my balance and started walking more on my left foot to compensate.

How long can you keep going with it like this? a voice murmured.

'I don't know. What choice do I have?' I said, belatedly realising I was talking to myself aloud.

You could stop, came the reply.

Part of me thought that suggestion had merit, but I wasn't ready to throw in the towel just yet. When I got to Macksville I would reassess my situation, depending on how the foot held up.

* * *

Two hours later I was struggling. My foot felt like it had a meat hook in it, pulling and gouging. Sunburn had settled deep into my arms, face and neck. The straps cut into my shoulders, abrading the skin through the shirt fabric. Salty sweat seeped into the wounds like low fire. I was out of water, my lips were cracked and my eyes were dry, red and full of grit.

It was a brown day. Brown earth, brown sky. Brown river that wandered away from the road, as if it had grown bored and sought solitude in the barrens. A cattle truck rattled by, as depressing a sight as one can imagine—all crowded flesh, fur and plaintive mooing. The smell that followed was apocalyptic.

Out of the swirling clouds of dust came an improbable sight; a contraption that looked a bit like a bicycle and car had been intimate and this was the progeny. In it (or on it) lay a man on his back, arms pumping forward and back, obviously the method of propulsion. His legs lay in useless torpor, and I realised he was a paraplegic. Behind him, stretching around the corner into Macksville, were semi-trailers, cars, buses, you name it, all trying to get to the coast and join the traffic jam. From the signs on his vehicle, he was doing some sort of ride for charity, and it looked like hard work.

We locked eyes as he passed, and it was only then that I became aware I'd stopped walking, my foot forgotten. His face was red, the cords on his neck standing out, white teeth bared in what I at first assumed was a grimace of effort but quickly realised was him smiling at me. Surprised, I smiled back, my hand going to the twelve-inch scar stretching from my back to my navel, my souvenir from the car accident of '95. We smiled at each other, separated by traffic and millimetres—the distance it takes for a bone to sever a spinal cord. Then he was gone, vanished into the dust.

I walked into Macksville with no further complaints.

* * *

After you're through Macksville, turn left at Warrell Creek. The road runs to the coast.

So the woman at the kiosk had said, but I was having doubts. It was nearing sunset, and I was worried I had taken a wrong turn somewhere. I was taking a break by the side of a narrow country road, having a smoke and wondering where I was. The map I'd purchased in the Nambucca Heads kiosk[7] was of little help; there were at least two roads I could be on, as far as I could tell, and possibly three or four.

It had been hours since I'd left Macksville, a town that seemed to consist of pubs, football fields and trucks. I thought that by now I

---

7 It is disheartening—yet unsurprising—to note that it took three weeks for me to have the wherewithal to acquire a map.

should smell the salty air of Scotts Head, but instead I was breathing in the manure of itinerant ruminants and market gardens that bracketed the road.

As the sun dove behind the wooded hills in a bloody spectacle, I observed a beat-to-shit car weaving slowly towards me, headed in the same direction as me. I butted my smoke and cautiously took a step backwards, further off the road.

There had been a couple of near misses on the highway since Macksville; one of them, a big B-Double, had blasted by so close to me it had blown the guitar out of my hand and the hat from my head. I'd passed a sign that informed me (with morbid relish, it seemed) that there had been thirteen deaths on this highway in the last three years, making it the most dangerous section of a dangerous highway.

The drunks on their way home from the day's football games had filled me with unease, but this was the worst of the lot. As I watched, it looped from one side of the road to the other, wheels crunching over the gravel of the shoulder, only to swerve belatedly back to the centre of the road. It slowed as it drew up, and I realised the driver had seen me.

The car stopped in the middle of the road, the window rolled down, and I was greeted with a bleary, red-eyed face in the gathering gloom.

'Where the fuck're you headin?'

'Ah, well, I was hoping you could tell me. Scotts Head, but I don't know if I'm on the right road.'

A wheezing laugh issued from the weathered face; it spoke of a life of devoted service to whisky and cigarettes.

'Fuckin knew you weren't from aroun ere. Driven past you three fuckin timesh today, an I said to meself just now, I said, "I wonder where this bloke thinks he's goin?" An sure enough, you're on your way to the Head.'

'I see,' I said, taking a few seconds to decipher what he'd said.

'Three timesh! An every time I'm thinkin "I gotta stop an give that bloke a lift."'

'Well. Yes. So this is the right road to Scotts Head?'

'Fuckin A. Hop in, that's what I'm tryin to tell ya, forfuckssake.'

I could smell the beery fumes coming off him from where I stood, curling the hairs in my nose and doing little to inspire me to jump on in.

'No no, I don't want to hold you up. It isn't that far to the town, I'm sure, but listen, thanks for the offer, I'll be fine, really. Besides, I've got all this stuff, and your car looks pretty full as it is, so thanks again but, you know, I'm cool …'

'Come on, son, get the fuck in. Shcotts Head is two fuckin clicks up thish fucker. Be there in no time.' He belched.

I thought of Simon; that had been a great hitching experience. Maybe this would be the same. After all, Simon had also reminded me not to judge people on appearances. Ignoring my misgivings and telling myself there couldn't be much that could go wrong in two kilometres, I shoved my stuff onto the back seat and, after being informed the passenger door didn't open, followed suit.

The driver seemed far more amicable once I was in. He turned in his seat and stuck his hand out.

'Col's the name. Pleestameetcha.'

'Likewise. Smokey.'

'Good name, Shmokey. Just like that cunt and the bandit.'

I noted with some apprehension the beer bottle wedged in his crotch as he fumbled around with the keys in the ignition.

SCREEEEECCCCHHHHHHH!

'Car's already on, Col.'

'Eh? Oh. Yeah, right.' We took off slowly and Col leant back in his seat, cocking his head towards the rear-view mirror. 'So, where you headed after the Head?' he asked, steering the car more or less up the middle of the road. We were approaching a blind crest, and I thought I could see the glow of headlights approaching. I tried my best to ignore it, fought the urge to lean forward and grab the wheel.

'Well, I'm walking to Sydney.'

'I'm from Shydney. Used to work at the track out Randwick way. Musht have been thirty yearsh ago, now. Ran bloody horshes for Aub Grey, the cunt. Never knew his ass from his elbow, did Aub. Up at three every morning, muck out the stablesh, fit, strap, shoe—the bloody works. Hey boy, which side of the fuckin road am I on?'

I was only listening with half an ear to Col, but something about that last comment rang alarm bells. I leant forward and looked at him. The scarred topography of his face was illuminated by the ghastly green glow of the dashboard lights, and he was holding his right hand over his right eye, trying to bring the road into focus.

'Bit to your left, Col,' I said in a constricted voice. I watched as he alternated hands, always keeping one eye covered, and endeavoured to follow my instruction. We made it over to the left just as a pair of headlights bore down upon us, accompanied by a horn blast and someone yelling something. The word 'maniac' was all I heard clearly.

'Hey Col, you can drop me anywhere up here, mate. Anywhere's fine.' He didn't respond, just kept switching hands, slowly waltzing the car up the road. I wished I had gotten around to finishing my will.

'You play guitar?' he rasped.

'Yeah—'

'I play fuckin guitar. No, wait, the harmonica. That the one with the bells on it?'

I was unsure how to respond. 'Tambourine?'

'Yeah, that's the one. Fuckin Mr Tambourine Man, thass me.' And with that he launched into a deplorable rendition of Dylan's 1964 masterpiece, waving his arms about for emphasis. The effect this had on his driving was negligible.

'*Eeeeeyyy, Misser Tanborime Nam, sings a thing to me. He's not sleepy. And we've got a lot of work to do now ...*'

He broke off in a fit of wheezing and coughing, which was perhaps just as well. His voice sounded like gravel rattling over corrugated iron, and that last line sounded less like Bob and suspiciously like the words to the Scooby Doo song.

'*Eeeeeeyyy, miss that tambourine, man, save a thong for me— RAAAARRRP!*' Col belched, took a swig from the bottle, scratched himself and said, 'Beautiful song, that.'

'Oh yeah, Dylan wrote a lot of good stuff,' I said, not trusting myself to say more.

'Dylan? Who the fuck's that?'

Silence descended, and I took the opportunity to look out the window. It was almost dark outside, and I could see the lights of Scotts Head approaching on our left. I thought of the Platters, and the heavenly shades of night falling.

'Dunno why you wanna go t'the Head anyway. Fuckin place is a retirement village, when it's not full of punks,' Col said, soiling the moment. He turned around in the seat to look back at me as we straddled the double whites at thirty kilometres an hour. 'I mean fuck, you shouldn't be spending the night in thish dump. You here till Sat'dy? Should come up to the cabin with me and the boys.' He picked his nose, examined the booty, and wiped it on the headrest. I did my best to take my mind away to a happier time.

'Every fuckin weekend we go up to the cabin, have a few beers, play some of the old songs. Me mate, Georgie Whittaker, plays a fuckin good guitar. You two'd get along great. Whaddaya say?'

'Oh, well. Col. Mate. *Mate*. It sounds like I'd love that, y'know, but I've gotta keep moving on …'

'Well,' he said, turning back towards the front and pawing at the wheel, 'if you change your mind, you know where to find me.'

The truth is, I had no idea where to find Col during the hours of daylight, but prudence dictated I keep my mouth shut on that dilemma. We reached the town, and Col steered the car with reasonable success to the curb outside the corner store. I thanked him for the ride.

'Ah, don't fuckin mention it. Like I said, I said, "I seen thish cunt three timesh …"'

I got out into the stillness of the twilight, relishing the cool fresh air after the dank aroma of Col and his rust bucket. He was still droning on about the Head and the cabin and poor old Aub Grey, who didn't know his ass from his elbow. I slung the pack over one shoulder and grabbed the guitar, looking at Col as I did.

He was well in the bag, and his rant gave way to a fit of hiccupping and belching. Every time he hiccupped, he'd belch or fart. It was as though his body was being startled by its own involuntary noises, a gaseous one-man band.

I was unsure whether to let him drive home, fearing he'd kill himself, or, worse, someone else. The trouble was, he would probably react badly to the suggestion he park it for the night and catch a cab. Worse still, he may insist I drive him home, and further enmeshing myself in his life was low down on my Top 40, yes sir.

'See ya Sm-*RAAAARP*-ey,' he yelled abruptly, pulling away from the curb and weaving off up the road, taking the dilemma out of my hands.

I stood and watched the one working taillight disappear into the night, telling myself I'd been in no position to stop him and not really believing myself. It had been a judgement call, and I think I botched it.

Judgement.

Perhaps Simon had been wrong about appearances—there had been less to Col than met the eye.

Troubled, I set off for the beach I had so longed for in Nambucca Heads.

*　*　*

Later as I slept, clouds swept up from the south, obliterating the stars.

DAY 20

From my vantage on Middle Head I could make out the town of South West Rocks, fifteen kilometres to the south. Turning to my left was the vast expanse of the Pacific; I could almost see the curvature of the planet in its horizon. Turning left again, and I saw where I had come from the day before, Nambucca Heads. Turning again and I beheld the west; green giving onto gold giving onto red, the bulk of Australia, this vast island drifting in the South Pacific, this ancient vessel upon whose rocky prow I stood, a young man on a great adventure.

I had found this incredible place when all I'd been looking for was a way onto the next thing, worrying I had made a mistake and would have to engage in my least favourite activity: backtracking.

Looking south I could see no signs of human habitation between me and South West Rocks, just white sands fringed by green forest. No roads, no towns, no smoke, no people. It was grand. I felt like the only person on Earth, and it felt good. I was reluctant to leave, to come down from this high place where I could see so much, so I sat down on a large flat rock and decided to eat lunch.

I guess being stricken with awe works up an appetite, because I made short work of the peanut butter and crackers. I polished off the last of the muesli bars and drank most of my water. With a full belly and a slaked thirst, I sat looking at the white caps on the ocean, the colourful little birds that flitted amongst the rocks on the ground, the shadows of clouds racing across the green-carpeted hills below. All was quiet, and I cannot recall ever being happier or more at peace.

Except … one thing was missing: someone to share it with.

* * *

What got me moving again were the gathering clouds to the south. They held rain, judging from their hue. According to the map there was no trail that led from here to the next beach. Looking around, I couldn't make out any path in the rocky terrain. Backtracking seemed imminent.

The wind was picking up again, seeming to come from all directions, and my hat blew off and went cartwheeling down the slope ahead of me. I ran after it and snagged it before it could go too far. It was only then that I noticed where it had been going—down a tiny trail.

Something in the trees caught my attention, and I walked a little closer. Tied to the trunk of a struggling banksia was a pink ribbon, indicating that someone, at some stage, had come this way. Had my hat not been blown in precisely this direction I would never have seen it. Sure I had found the way to the beach, I ran back up the hill to my gear, saddled up, and looked around one last time.

I don't know why I did what I did next. If pressed, I may say it was because the place had had such a profound effect on me, that my thoughts had been of her, that in some way she had been here with me. Maybe by leaving part of myself here I could take the memory of the day with me.

It doesn't really matter, I suppose, but somewhere on Middle Head, under a large red rock, lies the silver necklace Di gave me on the day I left.

* * *

The storm was almost upon me by the time I gained the beach, dark grey and coming in fast from the south. The sand looked very white in contrast, as did the foaming waves whipped up by the increasing wind.

I was reminded of my first storm, outside Pottsville. Then I had been terrified, scarcely able to think. Now, with three weeks under my belt, I was better prepared. The important thing was to keep my equipment dry, especially the guitar. *I* would dry out in a matter of an hour, two at the very most, but the sleeping bag, clothes and guitar would not.

I stripped off, wrapped up everything in the garbage bags until I had a watertight ball, dug a small hole in the lee of the dune, dumped my stuff into it and covered it with a few broad leaves of *Heliconia* that grew in the surrounding rainforest.

By the time I was done the storm was on me. I sat on the dune in a pair of ragged shorts and my hat, letting the rain hit my bare skin and silently marvelling at what a difference twenty days can make to one's coping mechanisms.

As it turned out, the burial of the necklace on Middle Head marked the last of the fine weather; it would rain solidly for the next six days. The rain would prove to be but one of my problems, however; for starvation and madness lay in the sodden body of the week ahead, like cancers stirring, awakening, their time come round at last like Yeats' rough beast. The halcyon days were over, and the true nature of the tour was about to reveal itself.

BOOK TWO
THE CROSSROADS

'He met the Father where he was carving.
If Father took time, he accepted it;
And he helped him and he stayed with him for sixteen years.
When the others (deities) came they stayed about eight days and then left,
And some stayed four days and left.
Esu[8] did not leave; Esu learned how the Father made hands;
He learned how to make feet,
How he made mouths, how he made eyes.
Esu learned it all.
Afterward Father said, 'All right,' he said, 'Go and sit at the crossroads;
He said, 'Everyone who is coming to see me,
He said, 'If he does not give you something,
He said, 'Do not let him pass.
He said, 'Do not let him come.'
Esu went and sat down at the crossroads.
Everyone who was coming to Father would give Esu something.'

—*Sixteen Cowries: Yoruba Divination from Africa to the New World*,
by William Russell Bascom, as told to him by Salako,
one of the last Ò̩yó̩ diviners, in 1951.

---

8 Esu's post at the intersection between the world of man and the gods is thought to be the origin of 'Devil at the Crossroads', a soul-selling myth attributed to various musicians from Robert Johnson to Led Zeppelin. A somewhat chaotic deity to the Yoruba and the unpredictable interpreter of human desires, he was often confused in Christian interpretation as Satan. He was said to walk with a limp because he had a foot in the world of man, and one in that of the gods.

Chapter Five: The Ragged Edge

DAY 21

Standing outside the Stuarts Point Everything Shop, I checked my phone.

No reception.

There was no way I could get in touch with Bill, who was engaged in album sales up north that would provide me with some desperately needed funds. I had agreed to his kind offer several days ago on the condition that he took a twenty-five per cent commission for his effort. All well and good, but now Bill didn't know where I was, and here in the technological black hole of Stuarts Point I couldn't call to tell him where to send the money.

It was Tuesday, and I had $5.60 left. Assuming that at some point today I could call him and he sent the money immediately, it would still take until next Monday before any money arrived.

There was no way my food would hold out until then.

Starvation reared its emaciated head for the first time, grinning and nodding back and forth on its stalk-like neck. I pushed the image away, but it lingered at the periphery, an idea whose time had come, as it were.

The rain started up again, this time with purpose. I stowed everything back into the pack, used a garbage bag to cover the guitar, and set off towards South West Rocks.

It quickly became apparent that there was no way to the Rocks from Stuarts Point without a boat. Yet again a river would thwart me, this time the formidable Macleay River Delta. As with Sandon and Nambucca Heads, I would have to walk inland, pick up the highway and go the long way around.

This time it was to be the royal screwing, however; forty kilometres to make about five in real terms. Not so bad in clement weather, perhaps, but it was bucketing down and by the time I reached Clybucca, it started to hail. The tiny balls of ice sounded like applause as they rattled along the semi-trailers passing within inches of my drenched and bruised bod. It was hard to disagree with the voice that was saying the tour was going from bad to worse when this was the only decent applause I'd received thus far.

Fortunately, the rain and hail eventually drowned the voice out altogether.

* * *

Standing at the junction of the Pacific Highway and the road I needed to take to the Rocks was a hitchhiker, and even from a distance I could see he fell into a category of his own.

He wasn't wearing shoes for one thing, and his bare muddy feet must have been particularly appealing to potential rides. His clothes were just as muddy, and I briefly wondered what he had been up to. He was clean-shaven, but in this respect it wasn't enough to mitigate the lack of cleanliness everywhere else. He had no possessions with him apart from a cardboard sign he'd fashioned from a beer carton, upon which he'd written SOUTH in savage capitals.

'South' left a lot of scope for a driver to deal with, not to mention the fact that the sign was also muddy.

'Hi,' I said.

'No rides today. All the people here are stuck-up wankers.' He smiled bitterly at me; most of his teeth had gone, possibly south ahead of him.

'Really?' I said, my tone indicating bafflement as to why nobody would want to be confined with a muddy, toothless, barefoot man in a cramped space for an indefinite amount of time. Selfish gits.

'Fuckin oath. If we was in the Territory, every man and his dog would be pickin us up.'

'I hope it gets better for you,' I said, just as the rain started to intensify yet again. We both looked up, then back at each other.

The hitcher managed a look of remarkably sublime cynicism, and said, 'I don't think that's on the cards, mate.'

'Best of luck, anyway,' I said as I moved on, but he didn't respond, just kept looking south, which seemed strange since his potential chauffeurs would be coming from the north, one would have thought. I thought he'd have a long wait, whichever way he was facing. Still, on the bright side, maybe the rain would rinse him off a bit.

* * *

It wasn't long before the Macleay River farmlands revealed themselves to be a wholly unsuitable place to walk. Apart from the rain, which had eased somewhat, there was the redolence that comes with a large amount of cattle confined to one area. The smell of manure was almost overwhelming, and it didn't surprise me to see that every car that passed me had its windows rolled up. The smell didn't just offend the olfactory, it kicked it in the groin and left it writhing on the ground.

Since I was the only thing other than a cow foolish enough to be out here, I was soon deemed to be the main attraction by hundreds of flies, causing me to flail about much like King Kong at the planes. Flailing proved to be no great disincentive to the flies and only succeeded in me looking completely out of my gourd to the people driving past. After me, the muddy toothless delight would look pretty good.

These flies were veterans of tail-swishing bovines; I realised I was not going to win, and so, defeated—cowed, if you will—I gave up and tried not to think of the hundreds of little legs rubbing busily together on my body.

The other thing the region had going for it was the narrow road flanked by mud. It soon became clear why my erstwhile buddy had been so thoroughly coated in the stuff—there was simply no avoiding it. I walked down the middle of the road whenever I could.

A few hours later, I passed a sign that said I was entering Jerseyville. Phone reception was still non-existent. I consulted the map and saw that I was indeed close to the Rocks. I started walking a little faster.

A campervan pulled over ahead of me and I knew in that intuitive way you acquire after long periods on the road that I was going to get a ride. It seemed faintly ironic that I should be picked up so close to my destination, but this was no match for the irony of the scene that greeted me when I opened the door and saw who had stopped to pick me up. If only the hitcher could have been there when I was picked up by a man and his dog.

* * *

'You heading to the Rocks?' the man asked.

The dog asked no questions, just grinned happily down at me from his place on the shotgun seat, tail wagging.

'Yeah.'

'Well, hop in. Put your stuff in the back.'

'Thanks,' I replied, trying to pick his accent. It sounded Irish, but I couldn't be sure due to his admirable economy with words. He was an older gent that still looked tough. I opened the sliding door on the van, revealing a tidy array of cupboards, drawers and little benches. There's something comforting about that level of order and organisation, the promise of what all those tools may create in the right hands. Being to carpentry what Lucrezia Borgia was to mixing drinks, handymen always impress me.

I climbed into the cab with the dog turning excited circles on the seat and giving me the occasional lick. The man looked ashamed of his companion's behaviour.

'That's Jake. C'mon dog, move your ass.'

Jake obliged with a rueful grin at his owner, and I sat down and shut the door. Jake promptly crawled into my lap and flopped down, looking completely at home. The driver rolled his eyes.

'Name's Pat,' he said, sticking out his hand.

'Smokey. Pleased to meet you.'

Pat checked his mirrors and pulled out. I settled back and scratched

Jake behind the ears, an act that caused him to look up at me lovingly, eyes slitted in supreme joy.

'Looks like you've made a friend.'

'Yeah, he's a beauty. What breed is he?'

'Jake? Nothing but purebred mutt, from a long line of mutts. Eh, Jakey boy?'

Knowing he was the topic of conversation, the mutt in question rolled onto his back and presented a warm furry belly for attention. His tongue lolled out the side of his mouth; the effect this had on his apparent IQ was the canine version of turning your cap sideways. His indefatigable tail wagged perilously close to the gearstick.

'So,' I said, rubbing Jake's belly, 'how long have you lived in the Rocks?'

'Oh well, me and the missus moved here back in the 1950s,' he replied, trying to use Jake's tail to get us into fourth. 'What the Christ? Ruddy dog!' Jake tried for remorse, made it briefly to contrition, then returned to blissful with unseemly haste. 'Where was I?'

'You were saying you moved here in the '50s. You must have seen a lot of changes in that time.'

'Oh aye, plenty of changes, most for the worse, but that's the way of it, I suppose. It's still a good place.'

We were silent for a moment, looking at the rain-washed countryside and the gunmetal river flowing along beside. Jake had now found something on my hand that needed licking with quiet desperation.

'What brings you out in this, lad?'

'I'm walking to Sydney, promoting an album.'

'You staying in a hotel?' said Pat, eyeing my muddy clothes and general air of destitution. I realised it was entirely possible that I reeked of manure as well, given my prolonged exposure to it this afternoon. Good thing I wasn't running for mayor.

'Ah, no, probably not. So far I've been camping on the beach.'

'I see.' Then Pat adopted the approach most people of his generation do when confronted by mystifying follies of youth—acceptance and no further inquiries, lest even more peculiarities reveal themselves.

We rolled into town, and Pat had to concentrate on navigating his mobile workshop through the afternoon traffic, leaving me free to look out the window at South West Rocks.

My first impression was of a tidy seaside town with a nice park and fantastic views of the ocean. Even in the gloomy weather it looked pleasant.

'You want to watch out for the coppers, lad,' Pat said, interrupting my sightseeing. 'They're pretty strict about folks sleeping rough in town. Just be careful, is all I'm saying.' His concern was quite touching.

'Thank you. I'll keep it in mind.'

Pat steered the van over to the side of the road that bordered the seaside park I had been admiring and said, 'Well, here you go.'

I tried shifting Jake off my lap, but he seemed reluctant to go.

'C'mon Jake, I've gotta get going,' I said in my most cajoling tone. Jake looked up at me, grinned and refused to budge. 'Maybe he wants to come,' I said to Pat.

'Aye, and he'd love that I'm sure. You'd have a hell of a time keeping him away from the ladies though.' Jake grinned at him, indicating that yes, he was a scoundrel and made no apologies for it.

I picked him up and handed him to Pat, who took him with familiarity into his arms. I collected my stuff and then stood at the passenger door to say goodbye. Jake had already reclaimed his seat, and I found myself missing his doggy warmth.

'Thanks, Pat.'

"Twas nothing, lad. I'd invite you back for a sandwich at home, but I'm not sure how the missus would fare having company without warning.'

Especially when they smelled like they'd been rolling around in manure, I thought. It was no wonder the dog had liked me; he must have assumed I was a kindred spirit.

'No worries. Thanks for the offer though.' I reached through the window and patted Jake. He gave me a parting lick and tried hooking his paw around my hand.

'Stay safe, lad, and mind what I said about the coppers.'

'I will. Take it easy, Pat.'

'I take her any way I can get her.'

And with that he drove off, leaving me to explore.

* * *

About an hour later I was still in the park, sitting at a table and playing guitar. Nobody came over to listen. It could have been due to my overall dereliction, but the weather also played a part, frequently bucketing down on unsuspecting passers-by.

Those people who were in the vicinity—screaming toddlers, fatigued parents, older folk in matching pantsuits with net bags full of grapefruit who seemed to have stepped whole and breathing from a Metamucil commercial—weren't exactly a demographic tailored to my boisterous strumming.

Just as one of the guitar strings snapped, I remembered that I had yet to contact Bill. I put the guitar down on the table and pulled out my phone. There was reception, but I discovered to my horror that I had only enough credit on my phone to send one text message—a Hail Mary pass I fervently hoped Bill would catch.

I pulled out the map and traced the coast with my finger. I needed to pick a town I'd likely be in by next Monday to have him send the money to. After some deliberation I selected Port Macquarie, eighty kilometres to the south. It was my best and possibly last chance to get on the radio and breathe life into this faltering tour. I figured it would take me three, maybe four days to walk there depending on conditions, and I could hole up over the weekend and wait for the money to roll in. I outlined the plan to Bill and impressed upon him the need for haste in this endeavour. He replied that he'd sold four albums at twenty dollars apiece. He's a good friend.

Having sorted one problem, I examined the guitar. The D-string was the one that had shuffled off the mortal coil—a critical blow. Without it I was going to have serious difficulties playing anything, and as I rummaged through my pack, I found replacements for the other five but not the one I wanted.

While I was in the pack, I made another disheartening discovery—a hole had developed along one of the seams, about the size of a fifty-cent piece.

Fifty-cent piece.

I scrabbled around, hoping to hear the jingle of the loose change that amounted to ten per cent of my remaining funds. I was greeted with silence. They must have fallen out at some point.

I was annoyed, but not disconsolate, as I still had a crumpled five-dollar note in my pocket. I reached into said pocket for reassurance it was still there, my bulwark against total bankruptcy.

It wasn't.

I checked the other pocket, ready to smile and perhaps even chuckle at my own foolishness—I mean, who *doesn't* move things around their person and then forget they've done so?

The other pocket was empty.

Now stay calm, I'm sure it's—

'I know, I tucked it into my shirt pocket for safe keeping …'

The shirt pocket was empty.

What followed was an increasingly frantic search for the elusive note, and it was a search that bore no fruit. I sat in the middle of a galaxy of possessions—unfurled sleeping bag, upended packstool, every item of clothing and knick-knack I had brought. If passers-by had thought me a hobo before, I had successfully removed whatever doubts remained by scattering my life all over the place like a bizarre picnic.

To top it all off, it started teeming. Although I moved quickly to stow everything back into the pack, I wasn't quick enough; the result being a pack full of wet belongings. I started cursing under my breath and surreptitiously gave the sky the finger.

Not surreptitious enough, it would seem. People started to actively avoid me. If I sat here much longer the cops would bust me for certain, for vagrancy and flipping the bird at clouds.

I made it to a covered picnic table and sat there letting the fact that I was now officially broke sink in. I didn't need to check my food stocks to know what I had. Half a jar of peanut butter. This was bad. How many days can a person go on peanut butter alone? And still walk ten or twenty kilometres a day over difficult terrain?

Making things worse was the fact that I was out of cigarettes as well. The supply of tobacco I kept in a small black pouch had dwindled without me noticing. With no money for tobacco I was looking at going from a pack a day habit to nothing. Withdrawals here we come.

Even my means of catching food was gone—south of Sawtell one of the packstool straps had torn along the seam, sending the contraption crashing to the ground, squarely onto the fishing rod, snapping it. The effect this had on the amount of fish caught was negligible, but still ...

I'd managed to fix the pack, but numerous repair jobs had left it looking like something Dr Frankenstein might have assembled on one of his off days. About the only thing in perfect condition was the Coleman lantern, which could not be eaten, played or smoked. Trying not to freak out, I saddled up and went looking for a place to bed down for the night, preferably somewhere sheltered like a public toilet or an out-of-the-way picnic table.

Having covered the bulk of the town in the two hours that followed, I can safely say no such place exists. There were a few public toilets, but not the kind that promote a feeling of wellbeing and security. The one near the country club was the worst of the lot, with both cubicle doors ripped off their hinges and then left lying in the urinal trough. There was an ominous piece of graffiti scrawled on the cracked mirror over the basin—*I'll be BACK!*—and that was it for me. I'd sooner spend the night in a puddle.

By six-thirty I was east of the town, struggling through a swampy twilit jungle that bordered the beach. I crossed a little wooden bridge over the swollen Saltwater Creek and went back to struggling.

I eventually made it out onto the aptly named Trial Beach, one of the few north-facing beaches on the east coast of the country. This fact only served to drive home how little distance I had actually covered for all my walking, for there, barely six kilometres away and plainly visible, was Stuarts Point. It sat there, mocking me and my hail-bruised body. It said that no matter how hard I tried, I would only ever gain ground in tiny, meaningless increments, with nothing to show for it but pain and an empty belly.

I shoved these unhelpful thoughts as far to the back of my mind as I could and went about setting up camp. I could feel them lurking, however, just out of sight, waiting for the cover of true night so they could creep back in the darkness and claim me as their own.

I sat until I was certain the dog-walkers and die-hard joggers had gone home for the night before unrolling the sleeping bag. As if on cue, the rain started up again in earnest, and I stowed the bag back into the packstool. It was going to be a long night; it had been two days since I'd slept because of the weather, and I was now entering a new phase of deterioration.

* * *

Two hours later it was still raining. It was nine o'clock, and I was starting to shiver. There was nothing to eat besides peanut butter, and nothing to smoke to quell hunger. I longed for a flask of scotch to warm me and send me to sleep at the same time. I was exhausted, but sleep would not come.

* * *

Three hours later and it was still raining. It was midnight, and my desire for sleep had become an obsession. The Ruined Toilets of the Rocks with their ominous graffiti were looking pretty good, if only I could have found my way back to them. The swampy morass behind me served as a sufficient deterrent to this course of action. Further east was the unknown quantity of the Trial Bay Gaol and its rocky peninsula jutting out into the sea. It seemed a foolish option on a night like this, a last resort, and maybe not even then.

I looked back at the town, with its comforting streetlights and well-lit park where I had sat this afternoon. Even from this distance it looked horribly illuminated though, no doubt to deter people like me. Bedding down there would be tantamount to knocking on the station door and asking to be locked up.

As I thought it, a jeep with a mounted spotlight stabbing into the night drove slowly through the town. With a jolt of unease I saw the blue and white chequered paint job. I wondered if this was routine or if something was wrong. My tired mind became convinced they had heard I was around and were looking for me in all the old, familiar places. Several times the spotlight would wash over me and I would cringe down into the wet sand, sure I would hear a bullhorn voice saying,

'YOU THERE! YOU, COWERING IN THE SAND! STAND UP AND MOVE AWAY FROM THE PACKSTOOL! WE HAVE YOU COVERED!'

They never did, and eventually they vanished back into the night, leaving that lush green Venus Flytrap park and its promise of shelter to tempt me once more. I wasn't tempted, however. Out of options, I sighed and wished fervently for the rain to stop.

* * *

Two hours later it was raining harder than ever. The town was gone, hidden behind a vast caul of rain that shifted and swayed but never thinned. My hope was gone, replaced by rage. How was this storm able to keep going? Forget abating, the fucking thing was intensifying. How was this possible?

'*Fuck off and do this somewhere else!*' I yelled. The sky took no notice, just kept dumping gallons of water on my thoroughly drenched belongings and me. The rage blocked out everything. There was the storm, there was me, and there was my rage.

'*Aaaaaarrrrgh! Just leave me the fuck alone!*' I screamed, on my feet now. There was no fear of being seen—visibility was down to twenty metres—but I wouldn't have cared anyway. I was losing it. The sky ignored me, and this only made me angrier. I was completely at its mercy, and this enraged me further. To be so helpless, so impotent, drove me to madness. A red film descended over my vision as I tore my shirt off and threw it on the ground, bared my chest at the falling rain and screamed,

'*Come on then! Come on! Come on if you think you can. Let's see what you've got!*'

* * *

Two hours later and it was still raining. It was four o'clock, and the rage was gone, replaced by deep depression. Entropy in the dark trench of morning. I was curled up in the sleeping bag, having unrolled it at some point and crawled in. It was soaked. I was soaked. The rain fell on my exposed cheek, cold and constant. I hadn't the energy to roll over or wipe away the water trickling down my neck. I no longer cared about the rain. The rain was old news. Been there, done that, got the T-shirt and tore it off and threw it on the sand.

The water had washed away the hope, doused the rage, dissolved the veneer of a civilised, thinking man. All rubbish, that concept of being civilised. Push a person far enough and they'll reach their breaking point—after that it's just survival. It had taken me three weeks, but here I was, talking to myself softly, cold comfort but better than the sound of dripping. I was close to that ragged edge.

'The certainty, the hope you felt when you set off in Pottsville, was bullshit. There *is* no hope, and to believe otherwise is dangerous.'

I was shivering.

'Your idea of walking and playing music to promote an album was ridiculous. Nobody knows you're here, and even if they did, they wouldn't care. The world just rolls on and fifty years from now you'll be dead and forgotten.'

My teeth were chattering.

'You're alone; you always were and always will be. It is only now, isolated and removed from your life, that you can see the truth. This is reality. Everything else is a lie.'

The rain was warm upon my cheek.

'It's better to know this now, rather than keep deluding yourself. I'm only telling you this for your own good. You are alone. Always remember that.'

Remember ...

'Love is a lie, the worst lie of all, because it keeps you hoping that there is something better, when there isn't. There *isn't*. She's gone. Always remember that—'

... that I love you.

I stirred. I knew that voice.

Always remember

'—you are alone.'

that I love you.

I felt something inside stirring at the memory of Di's voice, even as the rain returned with greater force than it had all night.

'I love you too,' I said, and saying the words gave me strength, picturing her gave me faith. Before this night I wouldn't have believed another person could save you, prevent you from going under, especially when they only existed in your head.

The rain intensified, but I no longer cared.
I finally fell asleep.

DAY 22

A couple of hours later I cleaned myself up as best I could and went back into town to see if I could sell some albums. I was sure I would; all I needed was to find the right spot to sit, play some guitar and smile a lot. Think positively. If I did that, people were sure to help me out.

I chose the same picnic table I'd sat at the day before, pulled out my remaining albums and arranged them on the table before me. There were six in all, and even if I sold them for only five dollars apiece I would have enough money to last me for the rest of the week.

* * *

Three hours later I had yet to sell an album, and the cheerful optimism and surety of the morning was evaporating. I had moved several times, thinking it might be like fishing and you just had to be in the right spot, but to no avail. The people who passed either ignored me or glanced up briefly then went back to inspecting their shoes.

I was clearly not the hit I had assumed I would be. Without the D string my repertoire was severely compromised, anyway. The rain had returned, making playing nearly impossible and uncomfortable to boot. Reluctantly I acknowledged that I would sell no albums here.

There was a hot dog stand maybe thirty yards away, and the smell was driving me crazy. The woman running the place kept looking at me suspiciously, and rightfully so. The smell of frying onions and reconstituted hog guts had me drooling, and I knew it was only a matter of time before I charged over and ransacked her little stall. She must have sensed my desperation, for she moved the buns to the back shelf.

To appease myself, I dug the peanut butter out of the pack and spooned a couple of fingers-full into my mouth. Seeing this must have done nothing to ease her mind.

As I savoured the peanut butter, I thought of what to do next. It was ten-thirty, and the weather looked set in. Should I stay in town or make a move south?

Charge the phone, a sensible voice said, highlighting perhaps the greatest recurring obstacle of this trip—publicly available power outlets.

'That's a good point,' I said. I was about to go into unknown territory with no food, there were no major towns after this until Port Macquarie, I had no money, and immediately south of here was a heavily forested mountain, Big Smoky, which the map told me had limited trails.

I stood up and shouldered the packstool. The woman in the hot dog stand watched as I approached, apprehension writ plainly in her stiff posture and tightly drawn mouth.

'Hi. How are you today?' I said, smiling in what I hoped was a non-threatening way.

'Not bad,' she replied, her mouth tightening even more. I realised in all probability she had seen me talking to myself moments earlier. This was going to take a hell of a lot of charm.

'That's good. Bit quiet with the weather?'

'Bit.'

'Right, right. Still, smells fantastic, doesn't it?' I said, indicating her wares.

'Uh-huh.'

Okay, enough small talk, time to hit her with the charm.

'You know, I don't suppose you could do me a favour, could you?' I said, increasing my smile until it felt like I was going to be stuck that way for the rest of my life.

'What kind of favour?' she said in a tone that indicated she'd been expecting this all along; bums always want favours—that's what makes them bums.

'It's not much really, I just need to …' I trailed off and thrust my hand into my pants to get the phone out. Her eyes widened in alarm as I rummaged in my groin; God knows what she thought I 'just needed' to do … all the while grinning like a dog that's just torn up the azaleas.

'Ah, here it is,' I said, holding up the phone. The look of relief on her face was unmistakable. 'I was hoping I could plug this in to recharge it.'

'Ah well, I really don't know—'

'I'd really appreciate it. I'm, uh, backpacking, you see, and I need to stay in touch with my family.' A small lie, but the truth of why I was here would do nothing to aid my cause.

'Um, I'm not sure. How long would it take?'

'An hour, tops. Just so it has some battery for the next couple of days until I get to Port Macquarie.'

She was a picture of indecision. She seemed a kind enough person who was naturally cautious of entering into any long-term relationship with a bum.

'Okay, but just for an hour. Have you got the cord?' I rummaged some more in the packstool, not wanting to give her any time to change her mind. I found it and held it out to her. She looked around almost furtively, as if we were engaged in a drug deal, and then took both items from me.

'Thank you so much, this is great,' I babbled, to which she nodded curtly and told me to be back in an hour.

* * *

By the time I returned to collect my phone I had reached a decision—to push on rather than remain. The longer I stayed the more likely I'd overstay my welcome and the police would pay me a visit; twenty-four hours is a long time to be in a small town looking the way I did.

The real reason for leaving was that this had been the scene of my lowest ebb so far, and everywhere I went I was reminded of that fact. I wanted new surroundings, things to take my mind off my troubles. It was perhaps the only ace in my paltry bunch of cards, that advantage of nomadic life whereby there is very little holding you to any one place.

* * *

I stumbled across the duck pond in Big Smoky's foothills some time later. Why there was a duck pond out here in the middle of nowhere was beyond my powers of understanding; the birds in question seemed just as surprised to see me.

I had the place to myself, probably because a fetid duck pond is a crappy draw for tourists, but the rain undoubtedly played a part as well. To the south the hulking body of Big Smoky loomed, his head lost in the low hanging clouds, a constant reminder of what was to come.

I ventured too close to the pond and was accosted by several of its filthy inhabitants. The quacking took on a frantic note, accompanied by much flapping of wings.

I have no time for ducks. Chickens are fine, swans are okay, turkeys are hilarious, but the duck is a devious bird with few if any redeeming qualities. People don't seem to understand my prejudice, citing geese as far worse offenders. I deny this. Geese are upfront with their hostility—there is no hidden agenda. You know where you stand with a goose.

Ducks, on the other hand, are highly suspect. Ducks are sly. Ducks are secretive. You cannot look into the eye of a duck and tell me there isn't some clandestine plan afoot in its tiny brain, some plot for mayhem. You cannot trust a duck.

I flapped my arms at them and sent them packing before continuing along the trail that led south, occasionally looking over my shoulder to see if I was being followed.

I wasn't, at least as far as I could tell, but then you never know, for you cannot trust a duck.

* * *

Walkers should exercise caution in the extreme as the Big Smoky track is steeply graded and for experienced hikers only. Those with a heart condition, asthma, children or the elderly should not undertake this walk under any circumstances. It is advised to take plenty of water and food. In case of emergency dial 000 or contact the National Parks and Wildlife Service.

All the sign needed was a *'Turn ye back, all who would enter here'*, and it would have been complete. As someone who gets turned around on his way to the bathroom, I was ill equipped to deal with the trail disappearing underneath a very recent landslide. Forced to engage the heroic undergrowth of Big Smoky, I was promptly lost and remained that way well into the afternoon.

Smokey on Big Smoky would have seemed the ideal place to hold a gig; as it turned out I spent most of my time on all fours, scrambling up Big Smoky's steep and densely vegetated body, my heart hammering away like Keith Moon at the end of 'My Generation'. I did come across some bush ginger—the momentousness of me recognising something botanical cannot be overstated—that, while deliciously citric, offers little in the way of long-term sustenance. Still, it was a welcome change from peanut butter.

For the first time I contemplated leaving the guitar behind. In the dense undergrowth it became a source of immense frustration, slowing me from tortoise-like progress to glacial. Of course I couldn't—such is the nature of friendship, you stick with your buddy through the hard times because of the joy they give you the rest of the time. And anyway, it had grinned just as naively at the prospect of this journey as I had—neither of us had known what we were getting into.

I resisted the urge to call out, partly out of fear I'd look silly if it turned out some intrepid hikers were close by, partly out of fear that they weren't. That no one was. That this dripping silent forest would just swallow my voice. This is a big country, and people go missing in it all the time. This mountainous national park covered seventy-five square kilometres, ample room for a man who struggled with carparks and shopping centres to get himself lost.

Which, it seemed, I now was.

* * *

For those who have never seen lantana, or tried to get through a forest of it, imagine a plant that actively hates you. Its branches grab at you, stabbing you with tiny needles. When it isn't drawing blood, it simply denies you progress because of its sheer impregnability. Furthermore, the damn thing is poisonous, so you can't eat your way through it.

My clothes were torn, the packstool fabric ripped, and my arms and face were scratched and stinging. The netting of the camel pack insisted on snagging every branch. I was conscious of my eyes more than anything else—in a lantana thicket there is ample opportunity for that soft jelly to be skewered on a prickly limb.

Eventually, mercifully, I could hear the surf pounding the beach on the southern side of Smoky Cape. By now I was on my belly, following an animal track and pushing the packstool ahead of me, dragging the guitar behind me, and had stuffed the camel pack down my shirt.

By the time I staggered out onto the beach, covered in farmer's friends and muttering darkly about ducks, I was on the brink of exhaustion. I was also out of water—amazing, given the inclement conditions, but there you go—and more than a little delirious. It was on nightfall. Parched and tired, I decided to keep going and hope something appeared.

I looked around and saw a break in the dunes about three hundred metres to the south. As it turns out, it was a sandy track into a campground, which went by the name of—you guessed it—the Smoky Cape Campground. The paucity of ideas in naming things around here was rubbing off, and I was looking forward to taking a Smoky Nap right after taking a Smoky Leak.

I looked up to see what the weather was doing and saw no stars; it seemed another wet night was in store, and I had no desire to go through a repeat performance of the previous night.

Looking at one of the picnic tables, an idea occurred to me. I rummaged around and found the Coleman lantern. Switching it on, I had a look under the table and saw sandy soil littered with cigarette butts and a few ice cream wrappers. With those gone and a bit of work it would make a handy shelter against the night.

Ten minutes later I was in the sleeping bag, my head propped up on the packstool, which was acting as a pillow. I'd draped the three garbage bags over the table, so that in case it rained the water couldn't drip through the gaps in the beams. To hold them down in case the wind picked up I had placed my tin cup on the place where all three converged. It would act not just as a paperweight, but also as a miniature water tank if it rained.

The rest of my gear was tucked away with me beneath the table. It was cramped quarters to be sure; with the cross beams and the two seats attached to the table base I had about twenty centimetres of clearance. I didn't care though, because for the first time since the return of the rain three days ago I was sheltered for the night. I actually hoped it *would* rain, thereby filling my cup and giving me water for the next day. As a bonus, I'd found two twenty-cent pieces during my housekeeping—I was no longer broke.

Looking forward to sleep and escaping the cravings for all that I lacked, I dozed off to the achingly beautiful sound of the wind soughing through the casuarinas, my last thought to be careful not to bang my head on the crossbeam when I woke up.

DAY 23

I opened my eyes, sat up, and cracked my head on the crossbeam. '*Aaaah, fuck!*' I said in a breathy voice, lying down again and rubbing my head. Judging by the light it was about seven o'clock and overcast. I felt my sleeping bag and found it dry. My shelter had worked.

The next thing I became aware of was my thirst. I remembered my tin cup and slithered out of the sleeping bag to check on it.

It too was dry.

I looked up at the sky, cloud-laden and ominous. I thought back to the previous night at Trial Bay, with the vast curtain of rain obscuring the Rocks. Thought about the recent days of rain where I could have wrung my fill from the very air around me and still never run out. This was the first night where I had hoped it *would* rain, where I *needed* it to rain.

I looked back into the cup.

Nothing.

As I stowed it away and began the day's walking, it started raining. I was reminded of the Yiddish proverb; *Mann traoch, Gott lauch.*

Man plans, God laughs.

* * *

Arriving in Hat Head was a disappointment.

My opinion of the town was perhaps jaundiced as I had been

counting on it to do more than it could. Over the course of the morning I had been building it up in my mind as a haven of crystal clear water, generous folk with a spare steak cooking on the barbecue, soft green hills to lie down in and watch the clouds drift by. Perhaps a cheerful cigarette vendor, handing out free samples.

Instead, the only thing drifting by was a plastic bag across Straight Street. Hat Head was a tourist town in the offest part of its off-season. There was a working tap—and thank God for small mercies—but the water was not so much crystalline as it was brown. The barbecue facilities were ample, but I was the only one present, and with nothing to cook the empty hotplates mocked me. If there was a cigarette vendor, I didn't see him. I had been a fool—towns like the one in my imagination only exist in books.

I sat down and scraped two fingers-full of peanut butter into my mouth. The last hour had been exquisite torture; badly dehydrated yet walking at a punishing clip to get to the town and its brown water. My mind was starting to wander, and increasingly over the course of the morning I had been afflicted with attacks of the giggles. Other times I would become irrationally angry at the tiniest thing—soft sand, stinging wind, cold rain. I was tired, all the time.

Hat Head gets its rather unique name from the headland that sits at the easternmost point of the town; it looks as though some giant Mexican sank and left his sombrero as a floating marker.

South of the town the land becomes a series of high headlands covered in scraggly heath and bush. As I negotiated these, the sun finally put in an appearance, and with the day heating up at an alarming rate I was glad I had filled the camel pack, even though the water was warm and tasted of the pipe it had issued from. The sunlight felt good on my face, and I was once again reminded of just how much impact the weather has on my mood.

The effect the sun had on my malnourished mind, however, soon became apparent.

The wind began to pick up as I progressed over the hills and down onto little postage stamp beaches in between them. It was on one of those little beaches where I finally ran out of peanut butter.

The faithful little jar, which had been my only source of sustenance for the last two days, was empty. It was as though I had lost a friend. I sat there on the beach and felt absurdly like crying.

I picked it up, not wanting to look at it anymore, but not wanting to leave it here. It had been a redoubtable companion, always giving of itself and never asking anything in return. What better friend could you ask for? I couldn't throw it away, not after what we'd been through. I stuffed it back into the pack and then went on sitting there, feeling hopeless.

What was happening to me? One moment I was fine, the next I was disconsolate and nearly weeping.

It's starvation, Ben, a voice said. *You're exhibiting the signs of one who has taken the first step on the path of deterioration.*

The voice was soft, the tone sombre, Attenborough-ish.

'I'm sorry,' I said, not knowing why, only that it was true.

It is a sorry state in which you find yourself. With no more food you will last only a few days. Your body needs vitamins. You've got to be less than sixty kilograms and with no food at all your weight will plummet. There will be precious little walking left in you after today. With no energy from carbohydrates or protein, you will not make it past Crescent Head.

'What else will happen to me?' I asked, not really wanting to know but wanting desperately to know.

Any number of things. Headaches. Delirium. Your vision may begin to blur. Muscle loss, fatigue and ultimately loss of coordination will plague you. Since you've had very little in the way of vitamins over the last three weeks, your tender gums will worsen, as will the red patches appearing on your skin even now. These are the hallmarks of Vitamin C and niacin deficiency, better known as scurvy and pellagra.

'Whoopee,' I said listlessly.

As I said, unless you eat—and eat the right things—you will never get past Crescent Head.

'Right. Crescent Head better be good, then.'

I watched as my finger made little whorls in the sand, feeling the wind seek me out and ruffle my hair. A little flock of black dots swarmed across my vision, as though proving the voice's grim prognosis was already at work. My heart was racing and wouldn't slow down. I looked around, blinking, trying to clear my eyes. I happened to glance up the steep trail that crested the next headland and looked away.

'I'm pretty tired. Maybe we should call it a day and stay here the night. Whaddaya say?'

Just get over this last headland and then you can rest.

I got to my feet. My head spun from the change in altitude, and I felt like I do when I've had two beers more than my limit. When my head cleared I bent over and picked up the packstool.

It looked like shit; my spare shirt poked out of the rip in the seam in an effort to prevent anything else from falling out. Not that I had much to lose. I shrugged into it, feeling the iron frame dig into its now accustomed place in the small of my back. It was lighter than when I had begun this back in Pottsville, but in that moment it felt like I had loaded it with rocks.

I picked up the guitar and brushed the sand from it, feeling sorry for the leather case it was in, the damage that had been done to it through exposure to the elements. Everything I owned seemed to be taking on a sentience, a personality, a life of its own. I felt empathy for my battered accoutrements, felt bad that I was putting them through this suffering.

The path up the headland consisted of a crumbly mixture of clay and gravel, and I was mindful of my condition as I ascended. I stopped for a moment as a wave of dizziness swamped me and made the mistake of looking down. The ocean was a long way down, and I had a moment of vertigo where the ground seemed to rush towards me at the same time as it rushed away. I looked back up at the bright blue sky in a hurry, feeling a bit queasy.

Eventually I gained the top of the head. The wind up here was terrific, knocking me back apace. I had to stop and regain my breath, bent over and with my hand on my knee.

As I stood there, I noticed something was wrong—wrong with the way the light was hitting my battered Blundstones and the ground they were on. I looked up and saw two things that hit me hard. First, the wind appeared to be pushing more rain this way, from the east this time, in over the sea. It seemed the sunshine of the afternoon had been nothing more than a brief reprieve.

The second thing—the more disturbing thing—was the position of the sun. If the story it told were to be believed, it was *late* afternoon, when by my reckoning it should have been one o'clock, two at the latest.

'Are you where you're supposed to be?' I whispered at the sun, but it didn't reply, just went on staring at the advancing clouds like a ruined king about to be engulfed in revolution. I pulled out the phone and looked at the time.

Four pm.

I couldn't believe it. I looked again, thinking it might have been a trick of my addled brain, but sure enough, it was now four-o-one.

'How long was I sitting on the beach?' I asked. There was no answer, but the silence that followed was a knowing silence. 'How long?' I demanded.

At least two hours, possibly three, the voice said. *I warned you this might happen. You—we—must eat. Never mind the fact that you've eaten nothing but peanut butter for two days, you haven't eaten decent food in two weeks.*

'But how could I sit there for two hours and not remember?'

You greyed-out, possibly, or dozed off. Who knows? The important thing is to get food, get to Crescent Head. And get down off this headland, because—

'—that doesn't look like any ordinary storm coming,' I finished, and got moving.

* * *

The long beach between Hat Head and Crescent Head is really more of a miniature desert. The dunes have progressed far inland. I'd read somewhere that those dunes are expanding. Walking is the correct term.

Walking dunes, walking man. As the afternoon light turned a bruised purplish-yellow it was the eeriest environment I had encountered. Coming in from the east was the vanguard of the storm; an ominous spectacle. I had a feeling this wasn't going to be like the steady rain of the past week—this was the Big Boy, and he was heading right at me.

The wind had cranked up until walking was impossible (unless you are a dune, presumably). Flying sand stung my eyes, arms and legs, and there was not a soul to be seen in the water or on the beach. My hat flew off with a particularly strong gust and running after it proved to be the end of my endurance. It was time to find shelter and a place to recuperate for the final push tomorrow.

There was nothing in the way of shelter but beach, the vast plain of dunes behind it, and the swampy morass of the Hat Head National Park behind them. Nowhere to hide, and almost out of time.

The uncontrollable giggling and the scary vagueness that had plagued me all day evaporated, revealing a cold survivalist that knew we were down to it now, that ragged edge. I carried my gear inland, over the high tertiary dunes with their antimacassar of greenery. To the west was a great expanse of sand, dotted with mounds reminiscent of those that termites build. They stretched as far as I could see, and again the strangeness of this region struck me. I hid the packstool under a large bush.

Standing on the crest of the dune, I was quietly appalled by what I saw. The sky was purplish-black, the ocean dead flat beneath the thunderheads where the rain fell in a torrent, but closer to shore the wind had whipped up the water into towering swells that crashed against each other in white frothing mayhem. The heat was still terrific, and I was sweating, although from the humidity or fear, I couldn't be sure.

Given what was coming, I started burrowing into the dune, pulling armfuls of sand away in an effort to make a hole. It was soft dry sand; the dune shifted and replaced whatever I excavated. Eventually I got to the wetter sand, and after a few minutes had a respectable burrow in which to put my gear. Just as I did, the sun gave one final stab of defiant light before it was completely overrun by clouds. I tried not to think about what was coming, but of course found myself unable to think of anything else.

What is it about aberrations in the normal order of things that hold us spellbound? I have heard of people just standing, watching a tornado bear down upon them. Or watch in mute fascination as a bushfire rages towards their home. Earthquakes, tsunamis, avalanches—they are so big, render us so utterly helpless, that they can override the survival instinct and hold us rooted to the spot.

I clambered up the dune and stood on the crest again, watching it come.

The wind was too strong, so I sat, watching it come.

I took my hat off and held it in my hands, watching it come.

Lightning danced around the edges of the green-black clouds, occasionally snaking down in jagged lines, seeking the surface. The grim rumble of thunder rolled across the water towards me.

I had been right when I'd said this was no ordinary storm. This made Byron look like a light drizzle and the past week a spray from the garden hose. This dwarfed reason and denied all prayers. I was fucked, plain and simple.

Yet still I sat, watching it come.

The wind, which had been whipping my hair out behind me like a flag, stopped. It didn't fade away, didn't abate—it ceased to exist. The surf was suddenly becalmed, and all was silent. Although it was only five o'clock, everything was dark. The temperature plummeted. No birds chirped, no crickets hummed, nothing. There was just me, and the storm suspended above like the executioner's axe, poised to fall.

Then, as the storm crossed onto land, there was a brilliant flash of lightning followed immediately by a tremendous, deafening roar of thunder, and the heavens opened.

Time started again, the freezing rain jolting me out of my stupor. I scrambled back down the lee side of my dune, struggling to find my little cubby. Another burst of light, and this time the thunder pealed directly above me, so close it was shocking. A little scream escaped me—I was reduced to the cowering animal, the primitive creature we all are beneath our language, clothes and superannuation. My lips were pulled back into the rictus of fear, certain that at any moment the lightning would strike and I'd be nothing more than a small pile of ash and a couple of pieces of melted jewellery.

I found my stash and started to dig a hole for myself as well, burrowed furiously as the storm raged around me, deeper and deeper until I crawled into what I had made and listened to the tempest unleashing its fury upon the earth. I didn't think it could maintain that level of intensity for long, but then, I was no longer sure of anything. If I could lose two hours and not know then my judgement could no longer be relied upon.

BANG!

The storm was right on top of me, and I pressed myself as hard as I could into the shallow hole.

'Oh please let me get through this in one piece,' I said, closing my eyes against another flash of lightning. I cringed, waiting for the boom, and then cried out when it hit.

The storm raged on, and I lost all sense of time. A minute could have been a second or an hour. Water started pooling in the base of my hole, turning it into a wholly uncomfortable place to be. It was preferable to being out in the open, however. No way was I going to risk it out there, not on top of the highest dune in a lightning storm.

I clutched the jawbone and prayed I'd live through the night. At some point, miraculously, I dozed off, the sound of cannon-fire in my ears.

DAY 23, LATER ...

I woke up with a small scream. I still had the jawbone in my hand. I was breathing hard and trying to look everywhere at once. It was still dark, felt like three am. The rain had stopped, but fear still clung to me like a rancid blanket.

A gripping pain in my stomach effectively broke the spell, and I dropped the bone and put a hand on my belly, rubbing it and wondering what it was. Withdrawals? Hunger? A muscle I pulled and didn't remember doing so?

The cramp came again, stronger this time, and I suppressed a groan. I had an idea what this was. The cramp came again, moving lower, and I was forced to unbuckle my jeans and pull them off.

I started crawling down the dune, away from my camp. The cramps came faster and with greater intensity, and I was forced to stop until they passed. When they did, I crawled the rest of the way down the dune, onto the flat sandy ground and over to the base of one of the mounds. Using it to pull myself upright, I let the festivities ensue.

* * *

Twenty minutes later I was crawling back to my cubby, hot and sweating and feeling like throwing up. Before I made it to the dune, I did just that. I had nothing in me to lose, however, and all that came up was acidic water and bile. I wiped my face with the back of my hand

and kept crawling, spitting to clear the foul taste.

I made it back to my camp, dug through the packstool and found the flattened roll of toilet paper I'd had the wisdom to bring. I wondered what had brought this biological carnival on.

'Can't have been anything I ate,' I said, chuckling. It felt good to chuckle. Chuckling pushed the intestinal nightmare a little further away, took my mind off my rebellious stomach.

Something in the water seemed most likely. I had thought the reason the water was discoloured and tasted funny was due to the pipe from which it had come, but perhaps there had been an extra bonus prize in there as well. Or it could have simply been the lack of nutrition, the loss of vitamins and salts, my body deconstructing itself.

I hoped it wasn't the water, because having just lost most of my fluids I needed water more than ever. I wanted to rinse the taste out of my mouth, wanted to drink my fill—but what if it was a vicious cycle? Throw up, drink, and throw up again. I'd never make it to Crescent Head on that sort of program. I eyed the camel pack suspiciously and decided to give the water a miss for now.

I'd do anything not to feel like this, I thought, staring up into the darkness and wondering if there was any sleep left in the night. *Actually, if we're wishing for things, I'd do anything to save this faltering tour.*

Had the ramblers at the crossroads had similar thoughts? Been willing to cut any sort of deal for success? Esu didn't work for free though; you had to give him something. I felt into my pocket. Was forty cents enough?

Before I could ponder this further, I dozed off.

Chapter Six: All or Nothing

DAY 24

I opened my eyes and saw a bird circling in a white sky. I sat up, hot and disoriented. It was nine am; I'd slept in.

I became aware of how thirsty I was, and that brought back to mind the ordeals of the night. My mouth felt all furry, and I longed to take a drink, but stopped myself as I hoisted the camel pack. Should I risk it? I knew the answer; there was no way I could walk the fifteen or so kilometres to Crescent Head without water, so I took a few swigs to see how my body handled it.

While I waited for the results I stripped off and bathed in the shallows, unwilling to venture out beyond where I could stand. I knew that if I got stuck in a rip, I'd have precious little energy to do anything about it.

By the time I waded ashore I felt somewhat better. The future of the tour hinged upon what happened today. If Crescent Head turned out to be another Hat Head I was done for. I would have to call Bill or Ken and have them come get me. The tour would be over and I would have to resign myself to more traditional methods of promoting the album. I doubted that I would ever have the gumption to try this again, and I had a feeling that my failure would gnaw at me for years to come.

* * *

The walk along the beach was a blur. Several hours passed where all I did was put one foot in front of the other, mindlessly picking them and putting them down. Three squalls blew in from the east, and each time they threatened I turned the pace on and got ahead of where they crossed onto land. It was exhilarating, pitting myself against the elements and winning the race, but the toll they took on me was great.

By the time I reached Crescent Head I was exhausted and relieved to get under the cover of a rotunda just as the fourth squall hit. Beach-goers all around me were fleeing for the shelter of their cars or similar rotundas that dotted the seaside park as the rain fell. I sat on the table and regained my breath, wishing for something to eat. At least the Hat Head water hadn't come back up for an encore.

I looked around and saw a healthy little tourist town that managed to avoid all the trashy pitfalls of similar towns to the north. Even the caravan park had an air of respectability that was as startling as it was welcome. I think it's fair to say I fell in love with Crescent Head at first sight.

Still, I was desperately hungry. I spied an ATM and hoped that by some miraculous fiduciary oversight the bank had accidentally transferred thousands of dollars into my account.

-$164.20

'Great. Awesome. Overdrawn. Fucking bank fees!' I hollered, before reminding myself that I was back amongst people now, and to keep my interior discussions … well, interior.

Walking past a small fruit shop on the corner of the block with two tables and chairs set up outside, the sight of all those healthy snacks so conveniently packaged in their own skin had my mouth watering. Apples, so green and red and shiny. Hands of bananas reclining on display, offering themselves up to all and sundry with nary a murmur of complaint. A platoon of oranges fairly bristling with Vitamin C—the cure for this scurvy dog. A solitary pineapple, a beautiful relic of summer. It was a wholesome scene, and one I entered into almost without thinking. It wasn't until the proprietor came out from a back room that I realised I was in her store with no money to buy anything.

'Hello,' she said brightly, the first person to seem genuinely pleased to see me since Happy Jim. It cheered me more than it normally would, after the last few days. 'Are you right?'

'Yeah, fine thanks. Just looking for the moment,' I said, as though I was actually planning a purchase. That was a joke. I subtly felt in my pocket where the two twenty-cent pieces rubbed together. I'd planned on using them in case Crescent Head turned out to be a bust and I needed to call Bill from a payphone to come and get me.

'Well, if you need me just yell out,' she said, and proceeded to arrange a display of drinks.

I walked around the little store, making a show of inspecting various fruits, all the while feeling the weight of those two coins in my pocket.

It could all end here, today, I thought.

Maybe that's for the best, said a voice that sounded like Di. *You're getting worse, not eating, getting sick, losing your-*

She didn't finish the thought, but I knew what she had been about to say.

Losing your mind.

Was that what was happening? I thought about the nightmares, the hours I lost on the beach south of Hat Head, the long wet night in Trial Bay. The way my thoughts were like fish: slippery, hard to hold onto for long. The way my mood would suddenly shift without warning, the increasing frequency with which I talked to myself and, worse, the times I did so *unaware* that I was doing so.

Maybe she was only half-right.

Maybe I'd already lost my mind.

'Of course, there may not have been that much to lose,' I muttered, then realised in horror that I'd spoken aloud.

'Excuse me?' the woman said, smiling.

I just stood there dumbly, with no idea of what to say to her.

Her smile was starting to wane, replaced by a look of polite puzzlement that would soon give way to wariness if I didn't say something.

'I ... ah ...'

She leant forward, her eyebrows raised and nodding slightly in that encouraging way when you're wanting to help the person finish their sentence and end the uncomfortable moment that is spinning out between you.

Go on, Ben. Ask. What is it that you want? Di asked softly.

I responded without thinking, feeling the coins in my pocket as I did. *To walk.*

Then go on, take the risk. All or nothing.

'... well, how much fruit can I buy for forty cents?' I finished, and couldn't meet her eyes as I did. I felt embarrassed, certain she was going to laugh and tell me to take a hike, and that would be it.

I kept staring at my boots.

'Well, the apples are twenty cents each, and the bananas are the same. Which do you like?'

I looked up in surprise, saw her looking at me in that frank, inquiring way, still smiling, and replied, 'Both, I guess.'

'One of each then?'

'Uh, yeah. That sounds great,' I said dazedly, trying to comprehend the fact I was still here, and about to enter into a transaction to boot. Twenty cents for an apple couldn't be right, surely.

She walked behind the counter to fetch a bag, and said over her shoulder, 'You look like you've come a long way.'

'Um, yeah. I've come down from the border.'

'Hitch-hiking?'

'No. Well, occasionally.' My concentration was focused on which banana I would select, which one looked the ripest. 'I'm walking to Sydney to promote this album I recorded. I thought I'd, you know, do the tour a bit differently.' I reached down and picked up an enormous specimen, hefting it and marvelling at its weight.

I became aware of the silence. I looked over and saw the woman standing behind the counter, holding a plastic bag, looking at me. I had a sudden moment of panic, fearing I had said something crazy, something that had rooted her to the spot. I had, but it was a concept I no longer thought of as crazy.

'You're walking to Sydney?' she said, her face seemingly all eyes.

'Well, yes. You know, promote the album in a different way, and get to see a bit of the country while I'm at it. I think I'll take this one,' I said, holding up the gargantuan banana like a smooth yellow trophy.

She ignored this last and said, 'How long have you been walking?'

'A little over three weeks.' My eyes were now drawn to the apples, and the four or five different varieties she had on display. God, I was so hungry, it was a wonder I wasn't drooling. 'What's the difference between the pink lady and the Fuji?'

'Where have you been sleeping? What have you been eating?' she asked, clearly not interested in the apples.

'On the beach for the most part. I've got this sleeping bag my girlfriend gave me. As for eating, well, not much over the last week. As you can probably guess, I'm pretty broke.' And that was putting it mildly, given the deficit in my bank account.

She kept looking at me for a moment, lips pursed and brow furrowed slightly, then her face cleared and she came up to me. Holding out the bag, she said, 'Here. Fill it up. Whatever you want. I'm just sorry I've only got fruit and veg.'

I reached out and took the bag, still holding the banana. I thought I understood what she was saying, but my brain was pretty fuzzy these days.

'Did you say "fill it up"?'

She smiled, a beautiful warm smile, so open and guileless it did more to banish the horrors of the last few days than anything else had, and nodded.

'Really, thank you, but I can't—'

'I insist. Go on. Just bring it over to the counter when you're done.'

'Thank you. I don't know what to say …'

'Sue.'

'Ben,' I said, wanting to tell her my real name for some reason. I stuck my hand out to shake, then realised I was still holding the banana. We both laughed.

'Go on, Ben, fill it up. I'll be out the back for a sec.'

I wandered around the shop, feeling terribly excited. *Fill it up*, Sue had told me, a blank cheque that made me giddy.

Don't be greedy though, I told myself. *Don't abuse this generosity*.

In the end I only took two bananas and two apples. I chose the Granny Smiths, in honour of getting hit with one on the road to Grafton. I couldn't wait to bite into that crisp green skin and the juicy flesh beneath.

I took my little bag up to the counter. I could hear the rustling of a plastic bag from some unseen room out the back.

'Ah, Sue?' I called.

'Just a minute,' she said.

I had time to think of some way I could repay her, and realised forlornly that I had very little to offer besides a jawbone and an empty peanut butter jar. I slung the packstool to the floor and rooted around for something that wasn't torn, sandy, muddy or scampering. Nothing. When I straightened up Sue was standing there behind the counter, looking at me curiously. She was holding another plastic bag.

'Is that all you got?' she asked, pointing at my bag of fruit.

'Yeah, it's heaps, really. More than enough.'

'Come on, Ben, you can do better than that. Grab some more bananas, they're full of potassium.'

I picked up two more bananas and put them into the bag, feeling guilty and good at the same time.

'That's better,' she said, and held out her own bag to me. I looked inside and saw she had wrapped up some cheese and crackers for me. I looked back up at her. She shrugged and said, 'It's not much, but the cheese has calcium. Good for your bones.'

'Sue, I don't know what to say. Thank you so much.'

'Don't mention it.'

I handed her the forty cents, insisting when I could see she wasn't going to accept it. Thanking her again, I walked back outside in a daze and sat at one of her tables. Without thinking I peeled a banana and ate it in two bites. Then I did the same with another.

FOOD! my body cried, and I smiled, truly happy for the first time in days. I stopped myself from tearing into a third banana and contemplated the apples. I also had cheese and crackers. God, so much variety. I felt like running around shouting for joy. The rain was falling again, but underneath Sue's awning I was sheltered.

Sue. How I wanted to repay her … but with what? I was totally, unequivocally broke, and all I had to show for this crappy tour was bleeding gums and a bunch of unsold albums …

I reached down and opened the little compartment where I kept the discs. I found the least damaged one and put it on the table, happy I had something to give after all.

As I did Sue ran past me, out into the rain and over to a small car parked on the opposite side of the road. I wondered what she was doing as she leant into the driver's side and picked something up. I tried to see what it was, but couldn't make it out. As she walked past me back into the store she said, 'Stay there.'

I stayed where I was, craning my neck back to look through the door to see what she was up to. I could see little in the dimness, however, and could hear nothing over the rain and occasional passing car. I wanted to go in and give her the copy of the album, but since she seemed to want me to stay where I was, I didn't.

A few minutes later she emerged again, holding a small white plate with a white bowl in the centre of it. She put it down in front of me and I saw she had filled the bowl with steaming pumpkin soup. Surrounding the bowl were four quarters of a buttered sandwich. It had been a thermos she had gone to the car for, I realised; she had run out into the rain to fetch me her thermos of homemade soup, probably her lunch. I felt my throat close up and my mouth tremble.

'I hope you like pumpkin soup,' she said, patting me on the shoulder.

I looked up at her and couldn't say anything. My mouth opened and nothing came out but air. I nodded. It was all I could manage. She returned my nod, smiling not so much with her mouth but her eyes, and went back inside.

I looked back at my soup and saw she'd stirred in a little cream. That did it. A choked sob escaped me, and I furiously wiped at my eyes, determined not to break down. I picked up the spoon and tried the soup to distract myself. The first swallow was hard because my throat was still closed up. After that my body took over, demanding more of that hot goodness so thick it was almost a solid. I made short work of the sandwiches, which she'd cut into quarters like you do for kids. Then I sat there, watching the rain fall onto the road, feeling warm and full and wonderful.

A few minutes later I stood up and carried the plate back inside. Sue was standing behind the counter and smiled as I approached.

'Good?' she asked.

'The best,' I said, putting the plate and bowl down and the album next to it.

'What's this?'

'This is the reason I'm here, the reason I'm walking to Sydney. I want you to have it. It's my way of thanking you. I've got nothing else to offer.'

She picked it up and turned it over, saying as she did, 'I can't just take this, Ben. How much is it?'

'Uh uh, no way Sue. I won't accept anything.'

I could see she wanted to argue, but saw from my face it wouldn't do any good. So instead she did something touching: she took the disc out and went into the back room where the radio played softly.

In a moment the drum signature that opens the first track, 'Riff Raff', replaced the news. It was so strange to hear my music coming out of speakers that belonged to a woman I'd only just met, in this town I'd never been to before. I had a moment of unreality, as I'm sure anyone does when their work is on show in a strange new environment.

Sue re-emerged from the back room, and we talked for a few more minutes as my song filled her shop. No customers came in while we did, but if they had they would have seen two people talking as naturally and easily as old friends.

Six people saved me that day in Crescent Head, but it is Sue that I remember best. She was the first, and it was she who restored not only my faith in people, but in myself. She gave me more than food, more than kindness. She gave me the best gift of all.

Hope.

* * *

I was sitting at a picnic table in Crescent Head's glorious park. The blue sky had returned, and the sun had replaced the rain. I'd given up on writing the will; instead I was writing a letter to Di, wanting to tell her about the shift in fortunes I'd experienced here. As I wrote I munched on a slice of cheese, trying to make it last and not doing a very good job. I'd already eaten one of the apples. The juice had stung my tender gums, but it was good pain, a welcome pain. It meant that at long last my body was getting the vitamins it needed.

A shadow fell over the page as I sat there writing, and I looked up.

A man stood there smiling at me through a rhododendron of a beard, thumbs hooked into his pockets and a large belly hanging over his belt. His eyes were friendly, caught in a net of wrinkles that spoke of many years spent outdoors. He looked like a farmer, but wearing sandals instead of gumboots.

'Travelled a long way, I reckon,' he said in a broad dialect. He was country, all right, even without the gumboots.

'Reckon,' I replied, smiling.

'Saw ya sittin here and I thought, "Now there's a bloke with a story to tell."'

'Yeah, it's a pretty strange one too.'

'Reckon it would be at that,' he said, still smiling. It seemed to me that everybody in this town was happy. 'Name's Woody,' he said, sitting down next to me and shaking my hand.

'Smokey,' I replied.

'So what are you doin sittin here, Smokey?'

'Well,' I said, putting the pen down, 'I'm resting for the moment. I'm on my way to Sydney. I guess you could say I'm on tour.'

'On tour? What for?'

I hesitated. Men like Woody understand manly pursuits, traditional values, and hard work. They don't have much time for crazy, seemingly pointless endeavours like mine.

'Well, an album. I recorded an album, and I wanted to tour it differently, so I thought I'd walk to Sydney. You know, like a troubadour, or a wandering minstrel.' He was looking at me, his expression unreadable beneath the beard. 'Or something,' I finished lamely.

He continued looking at me impassively, then said, 'That's the most brilliant bloody idea I've ever heard of.'

I did a double take. He laughed when he saw that.

'No, I mean it. You've gotta do something different. And you're givin it a go. Bloody brilliant, son.'

I laughed and said, 'Well, Woody, not many people are in your boat. Most people look at me as though I'm nuts.'

'Well, and you'll pardon my French, but,' he leant in and lowered his voice to a conspiratorial level, 'fuck 'em.' We both laughed.

'What about you, Woody?' I asked.

'Not much to tell, mate. Been a farmer for forty years out past Gunnedah in the wheat belt. When the missus and I retired we moved here.' He looked around and breathed in deeply. 'We used to come here every year for our holiday. The kids loved it; the beach, the surf. I always wanted to move here when I gave up the farm.'

He paused and looked around. I did the same.

'Why would you live anywhere else, eh?' he said, echoing the mantra I'd heard time and again during my travels. If there's one thing Australians like to do, it's invite you to reflect upon the horror of living somewhere else. I actually think it's one of our best qualities: the sense to realise we are lucky to be here, a country free from war, religious persecution, and unexpected badger attacks.

'Yeah, I see what you mean.'

We sat in silence for a while, just watching the day happen around us, Smokey and Woody in the autumn afternoon.

'Well, I better get going,' he said eventually, getting to his feet. 'The missus is at the doctor's, and I reckon she's about done by now. Nice to meet you, son.'

'Likewise Woody, and I hope she's all right.'

I watched him amble off before returning to my letter. I was just finishing it when I heard someone call my name.

'Hey! Smokey!'

I turned around and saw Woody approaching. Behind him I could see what must have been his car, idling in the parking lot. There was a silhouette in the passenger seat that must have been Mrs Woody. I walked over to meet him halfway. He was reaching into his pocket, pulling out a battered old leather wallet.

'You're givin it a go, son, and I reckon that's gotta be worth something,' he said, holding out a ten-dollar bill. I couldn't believe what I was seeing. He must have misinterpreted my look of shock, because he added, 'Look, don't think of it as charity. I'm not saying you need it, just that I figure it's a long way to Sydney and any help's gotta be a good thing.'

'No, it's not that, I mean … shit Woody, I don't know what to say.'

'No need to say anything, mate. Just take it. And good luck.'

I reached out to take the bill, then stopped myself and ran over to my pack. I found what I wanted and ran back to Woody, who wore a puzzled expression.

I held out the album to him and said, 'It probably isn't your cup of tea, but I want you to have it anyway.' He looked absurdly touched by the gesture and started shaking his head. 'Please,' I said, 'I insist.'

Still shaking his head, he took it from me. 'I dunno son, if it'll make you feel better then I will, but that's not why I—'

'I know. But it's a fair swap. And if you don't like the music on it, then at least it'll make a good coaster.'

He laughed at that, and we shook hands and parted. He walked back to his car and his wife, my album looking too small and fragile in his large farmer's fist, still shaking his head. I think he was pleased all the same.

I looked down at my own hand, and the blue note in it.

Ten dollars. In that moment it looked like a hundred. This was more money than I'd had in ages. But what to buy?

Cigarettes, a craven voice whispered.

Would Woody want you spending this on cigarettes? asked Di in a deceptively offhand way.

'No, I suppose not,' I replied, ashamed of myself. 'It'll have to be food.'

Better.

As I blissfully mulled over all the things ten dollars can buy, two guys of a similar age to me passed by on their way to the barbecues. They smiled as they went, one of them mumbling something about breakfast. I nodded and returned the smile, thinking again that everybody in this town was pretty damn friendly.

I walked over to them as they unloaded a bag of food to cook on the hotplates.

'Hey, I don't suppose you could watch my stuff for a few minutes?' I asked.

'No probs,' said the first guy, a blond with a surfer's look about him. The other guy, who looked like there was a Mediterranean somewhere in his immediate ancestry, gave me the thumbs up.

'Cheers,' I said, and went off in search of a place to spend my money.

* * *

It must be said, ten dollars goes a long way if you're really trying. After a longing look at the cigarette display behind the Everything Store counter, I made a beeline for the bread section. I then wandered over to the spreads. I took my time, not wanting to make a decision I might come to regret later on. The options were seemingly endless, yet each one posed a problem.

Vegemite—needed butter.

Anchovy paste—hideously expensive for so small an amount.

Jam—too messy.

Honey—potential to attract a plague of insects.

As I stood there drooling and debating the various merits of sandwich accoutrements, my eye happened upon a jar of home-brand peanut butter. It was the same brand that had served me so faithfully up until now, and I knew it could be counted upon. What I needed in the days and weeks to come was dependability, and it had proven itself in that department many times over. I grabbed a jar and knew I'd made the right decision.

I scratched my chin, thinking of what else to buy. Feeling the beard made me think of my appearance, and of the possibility of promotion and media coverage in the larger towns to the south. I picked up a disposable razor to this end, one of those plastic ones that cost fifty cents.

Having acted responsibly with the cash so far, I thought I owed it to myself to live a little, and made for the confectionary aisle. I had few qualms grabbing a bag of party mix and a box of crackers, then hurried over to the cashier with my booty.

The woman who rang up my purchases was engaged in a good-natured argument with the woman serving alongside her.

'... as if you had a chance with him. He's *married*, for God's sake!'

'More of a chance than you, you old cow,' said her friend, which set them both cackling. I smiled in that polite way you do when there's a joke going but you're not in on it.

'Don't pay any attention to her, darl,' my cashier said to me. 'She's just jealous cos I got all this and she didn't.' She gestured to her stout body provocatively, which set them both into fresh gales of raucous laughter.

'That'll be eight dollars exactly,' she said, and I handed over the bill, sorry to see it go but glad I had exchanged it for enough food to see me through another few days. I thought briefly about spending the last two dollars, then thought better of it. I'd be wise to have an emergency fund in the uncertain weeks ahead.

The realisation that I was again thinking in the longer term came as a pleasant surprise.

* * *

'Hey guys, thanks for watching my stuff,' I said upon returning.

'Sweet as, dude. Hey, do you want an egg and bacon sanga?' said Blondie.

'Are you serious?' I said, barely able to control myself. This day just kept getting better and better.

'Sure. Pull up a chair, dude. You want sauce?'

'No, I'm good. Wow, thanks.'

'Happy to share. This is breakfast. We drove up from Sydney last night for the long weekend. Didn't get here until two. Had a couple of beers and dropped right off. Hey, speaking of which, you want a beer?'

I laughed. 'Sure! Are you married, man? Cos I think I'm in love.'

Blondie filled up a paper cup with Coopers, one of my favourite beers and easily the best thing to come out of South Australia. It was my first beer of the tour, and it tasted good. I was reborn; a man who, just three hours ago, had been contemplating the end of his dream.

'My name's Smokey,' I said, shaking hands with Blondie.

'Cam,' he replied, then introduced his swarthy companion. 'This is Maurice.'

'Please, call me Morrie,' he said, holding out his hand.

'Are you French, Morrie?' I asked.

'Oui.'

'What brings you here?'

'Ah, well. It is the long story. I'm here for another few weeks, then it is New Zealand.'

'Morrie's a real ladies' man, wants to cash in on both sides of the Tasman,' Cam said.

'So, what brings you up from Sydney?' I asked, smiling.

'Surf. We live in a flat in Bondi, but we wanted to get away from the rat race for a bit,' Cam said. 'We're gonna do here, then work our way back south—Point Plomer, Seal Rocks, you know, the usual.'

'So, how come you are here?' Morrie asked.

I went into my spiel, pointing over to the table where my guitar was leaning.

'Sorry … you walked here from the border?' Cam said, a bit dazedly.

'Um, yeah, pretty much.'

'And how long did you say you've been without food?' Morrie inquired.

'Well, I ran out of peanut butter about this time yesterday, but I haven't really eaten properly this week.'

'I dunno how you keep going, dude. If it was me I'd be calling someone to come and pick me the fuck up,' said Cam.

'Yeah, well, you know,' I replied, growing uncomfortable with their impressed looks. 'That's why this burger is so awesome. I can't thank you enough. And the beer.'

Cam waved this away. 'Oh fuck, that's nothing dude. This is like something out of a movie; like bumping into Forrest Gump and shit. How long do you think it'll take till you get to Sydney?'

I thought about this for a second. This morning I had pretty much given up on making it to Sydney. It was too far away, too many things could go wrong before I got there. But after today's events, maybe it wasn't completely outside the realm of possibility.

'I'm not really sure,' I said, 'but probably another three weeks.'

'Three weeks!' Cam cried, and Morrie just shook his head, smiling. 'Dude, that's one long motherfucker of a walk. Hey listen, when you get to Sydney, you're welcome to crash at ours. We've got this cool place near the beach.'

'Well, I might just take you up on that,' I said, thinking he was just being polite. I was quite surprised, therefore, when he asked me for a pen to write his number down.

'I'm serious, dude, call anytime,' he said as he wrote. I wanted to pinch myself to check this was real, not some mad fantasy wrought by my addled mind as I lay prostrate under the sun somewhere in the Hat Head desert. Cam and Morrie's generosity could not go unrewarded, and so I gave them a copy of *The Dark Carnival*.

'It's a bit different,' I said as he took it with far more reverence than it deserved. I hate qualifying my stuff, but I don't think there is an artist alive who hasn't felt the need to point out the flaws in his work before someone else might. It's a terrible habit—one should let the art speak for itself and make no apologies for it—but one that's damn hard to break. We talked for a while longer before shaking hands and promising to catch up once I arrived in Sydney.[9]

* * *

I pulled out my phone and checked the time. Two-thirty pm. I noticed the battery getting a bit low and figured I wouldn't have too much trouble finding a shopkeeper in this magical town who could recharge it for me.

The first place I tried was a beach-side café and bar, and the chef was an Indian guy who only too happily took the phone from me and told me to come back whenever I wanted to pick it up.

An hour or so later I went back to the café to get it. I saw that there was a message from Bill.

Benny boy. Just sent the money, woman at the post office said it would be there Tuesday. Eighty bucks, hope it helps.

The chef, still cheerful—which seemed at odds with most of the chefs I've worked with over the years—finished plating up and smiled at me.

'You seem pretty happy today,' I said.

'Who wouldn't be?' he said. He gestured out the huge glass wall that overlooked the surf and the beach. 'Look at that. Hard to be sad with such a view.'

'Very true. Well, thank you—'

'I see you are a guitarist,' he interrupted, pointing at the guitar in my hand.

'Yeah. How'd you guess?'

---

9   We never did, but the following day I bumped into them on the exquisitely titled Delicate Nobby Head, where we shared a joint and watched a guy surfing the break with his pants on his head—giving us good view of his delicate nobby, regrettably.

He laughed and said, 'Are you staying for long? Rick will want to meet you.'

Before I could answer, a man in board shorts and a Hawaiian shirt walked in through the front door, and the chef hailed him.

'Rick! Come here!'

Rick looked like he'd been a surfer for most of his life. The sun had bleached his hair, and his tanned face broke into a smile when he saw me. We shook hands as the chef introduced us.

'Are you a guitarist too?' I asked him.

'No mate, I'm the owner. What brings you to our neck of the woods?'

I told him of my journey, and of the album I was promoting. He got very excited at that.

'Have you got a copy of the album with you?'

I realised I might have given my last copy to the boys at the barbecue. I rooted around in the pack and found one survivor, missing the front cover.

'How much?' he asked, inspecting the dodgy print job on the disc.

'Well, I've been selling them for ten dollars, but please take it as payment for charging the phone.'

'Nah, fuck that. I tell you what—because it's damaged I'll give you five.' He paused, then said, 'Screw it, I like you. Have ten.' He punched a button on the cash register and handed me a note. I couldn't believe the turn of events. I was rich!

'Thanks Rick,' I said. He waved it away, then reached into his pocket and pulled out a card.

'Here's my card, Smokey. I want to stock your album, so when you get your next shipment, make sure you send us some. We do the same with a few of the locals. I'm dead serious about promoting independent musicians, even if you are a Queenslander.'

'I'll remember that.' I tucked the card into my pocket.

'Good on you, Smokey. Will we see you around town?'

I was faced with a dilemma. I had planned to push on to Port Macquarie, two days walk to the south. I figured I could busk there for a few days until the $80 arrived. Port Macquarie housed a radio station and a population of seventy thousand that could feasibly sustain me for a decent amount of time.

Crescent Head, although overflowing with kindly folk practically falling over themselves to offer me food or money, had no radio station and a population of a thousand. This town had been the apogee of the coastal communities I'd seen in twenty-four days of walking, but it seemed too small to sustain me.

'Well, the thing is, I'm pretty broke, and was planning on busking in Port Mac. But if the action around here is enough ...'

Rick shook his head. 'It used to be, back in the '60s and '70s,' he said, 'but it's pretty quiet these days. I think you'd struggle.' That decided me. I thanked him for his honesty, his help and his money.

'Good luck, Smokey,' he said, and the chef smiled and waved as I left. 'Don't forget to send us those discs.'

'I won't,' I said, feeling inordinately pleased that someone wanted my work. It is, after the act of creation itself, the best feeling an artist can have.

For the next hour or so I drifted around Crescent Head in a happy daze. I did spend some of the ten dollars on cigarettes this time, feeling guilty but not guilty enough to stop myself. At $4.85 they were cheapest, nastiest smokes I could find, but sweet Jesus that first drag tasted good.

As the evening started drawing down, I stood for a moment by the side of the road leading south, looking back at the little town dozing in the late afternoon sunshine. I silently blessed Rick and the Chef, Cam and Morrie, Woody ... and Sue. Without her intervention and generosity I am sure that instead of pushing on south this afternoon, I'd be sitting in Bill's van, heading back home. The wish I had made the previous night that the tour be saved had come true, and I hadn't had to sell my soul for it to happen.

Had I thought such towns only existed in books? How wrong I had been.

'Thank you,' I murmured, then turned and left.

DAY 25

My first campsite the following night seemed fine at first. Beneath the Point Plomer casuarinas had been an inspired choice, I'd thought, providing shelter from the brisk southerly and the frequent showers it brought. With the departure of the sun, however, it turned into an insect funhouse, swarming with jack jumper ants, huntsman spiders, bush cockroaches and a terrifying creature I later discovered was a *belostomatid* (picture a scorpion-like creature the length of your palm that can fly). I decided to go off in search of less plague-ridden quarters, venturing further up a fire trail into the darkened forest behind the dunes.

My second choice for a campsite was worse. I found a clearing and was fumbling with the lantern to inspect it when a sudden gust of wind set the trees dancing. I caught movement off to my left and quickly held the Coleman aloft like a talisman against the increasingly wild night. On the ground I could see the usual galaxy of beer bottles and empty cigarette packets that adorn so many Australian campsites. What caught my attention wasn't on the ground, however.

It was in the trees.

There was a dismembered animal strung up from the branches, swinging back and forth in the strengthening night breeze. In the stark light of the lantern the limbs cast shadows that capered like imps on the trees behind. Once it had been a kangaroo—now it was an atrocity.

I staggered a bit, the lantern sending up strobing images of a foot, the long nails shining blackly in the fractured light; a tail, the fur still on it; a grinning skull, the fur—and eyes—long gone. Someone had threaded the rope through the eye sockets. I fought a momentary urge to pull the jawbone free and stuff it into my pocket.

I started backing out of the clearing and felt something bump my shoulder. I turned around and saw a net bag full of feathers swinging toward me, turning as it did and revealing a protruding beak, a talon, a tiny quiver of bones that had once been a wing. The wind drove it into my face, smelling of corruption, decay.

I batted it away, not knowing what sort of bird it had been, not particularly wanting to know. I bumped something that rattled like a head full of loose teeth; turning, I saw a spine, long and white and dangling from a branch … it *must* have belonged to the kangaroo, but it looked almost like—

No! Don't even think about it!

I made for the clearing's entrance, eyes never leaving the ghastly mobiles until I was on the trail once again, where I let out a relieved breath. Unless there was a local taxidermist who was into impressionistic art then the people around here had *way* too much time on their hands. I especially didn't want to be around if the 'artists' came back. It was too easy to imagine some surfer stumbling across parts of me strung up from a she-oak in two months' time.

I remembered the brand new toilet I'd had the pleasure of using that afternoon at the Point Plomer beach-side park. With another storm building and every other option looking infested, inundated or decorated by maniacs, I figured the toilet to be the best bet.

My third choice—sleeping in the public toilet—was one of my better decisions (you try not to reflect too much on where your life has led you when such a sentence passes your lips). Ten feet by six, there was ample room to stretch out. I locked the door and lay down in the sleeping bag, listening to the rain beat a tattoo on the Perspex roof. It cannot be said enough—hearing rain and not getting wet is the best soundtrack to fall asleep to, it really is.

The walls didn't quite reach the ground, and I could feel a cold breeze coming through the gap. The rain only wet the edges of the concrete, however; I was dry and safe. I sniffed the air and caught the faintest trace of pine and nothing else. Best of all, no wildlife.

Perfect, or as near as you can come out here on the road.

And it was … in theory.

At some unknown hour I awoke, stiff beyond all comprehension and needing to use the toilet. This wasn't what had woken me, however. It was the sound of voices. The rain had stopped at some point while I'd slept, so the voices carried clearly through the night air.

Who could be out here at this hour? The decorators of the clearing? Adrenalin flooded my system, waking me up fast.

'Come on mate, what're you doin, waiting for a fuckin invitation? Just throw it in.'

I could hear a bang, which sounded like the tailgate on a ute being shut. I rolled over and looked out through the gap between the walls and the floor. I could see nothing in the dark—the moon had either set or clouds were still covering it.

'Yeah yeah, keep your shirt on,' a second voice said. 'Christ! Just lemme go to the dunny, then we'll go.' As Number Two spoke his words became clearer, and I realised he was coming my way.

Oh no.

'Fucking hell, any longer and I'm gonna send down roots. Just go in the bushes before it starts raining again,' Number One complained.

Yes, go in the bushes, for the love of God. Listen to your mate, he talks sense. No need to come over here. Unless—

'Mate, I'm not taking a crap in the wet bushes,' Number Two said, 'I'll be five minutes tops.'

'Damn you, Number Two,' I cursed under my breath, and stifled a giggle. A giggling toilet would surely arouse suspicion.

I could hear footsteps getting nearer, could hear him whistling something tunelessly. Any second he was going to burst in here and find me curled up in my sleeping bag like a strange caterpillar undergoing metamorphosis in the most unlikely of places. And what was I going to say to him?

It's not what it looks like, Number Two; I'm actually filming a documentary on Australia's most commodious toilets …

This is going to sound mad, but I'm actually travelling through time, putting right what once went wrong …

Ah yes, I'm glad you're here, Number Two, for I'm about to reveal the murderer ...

I'd be lucky if he ran off screaming into the night. What seemed more likely was he'd figure I was some deranged pervert who lurked in toilets, waiting to spring on unsuspecting victims before serenading them on the guitar, and call the authorities.

The footsteps stopped. From my position, nose pressed to the concrete and looking out through the gap, I could see his sneakers. One of the laces was untied. He stood on the other side of the door, and I knew my time of reckoning had come.

There was a thump against the door. Then another one, harder this time.

'What the fuck ...' he said to himself, then he banged on the door a third time. I looked up and remembered I'd locked the door before I'd gone to sleep.

What happens now? I wondered.

What happened was Number Two put his shoulder to the door and *rammed* it. The whole structure shook under the impact, and I turned just in time to see the guitar lean outwards and fall towards the floor.

I threw a hand out and caught it inches above the floor, preventing it from giving me away with a musical thump, but it had been close. I was sweating, could feel my shirt sticking to my back.

'What the fuck's going on, mate? I thought you had to go,' Number One yelled from the ute.

'Some idiot's locked the bloody door,' he yelled back. His voice was shockingly loud and close, and a moment of unreality washed over me.

I wonder what would happen if I suddenly opened the door and said, 'Gentlemen, I give you your idiot.'

'What?' Number One yelled back.

'Bloody kids or something. I can't get in.' Number Two sounded righteously pissed off, and I realised if he *did* discover me in here I was more likely to get a beating rather than a quizzical look. '*FUCK!*' he screamed, and thumped the door again. I looked at the lock, but it was solid. After all, this was a brand new toilet. The Impregnable Toilet of Point Plomer.

'Well, come on then. Let's go home. You'll just have to hang on.' Number One sounded slightly amused by the whole thing.

'But I really need to go,' Two said, and I felt sorry for him. Not sorry enough to let him in though. I heard his footsteps fading away, then the sound of the ute starting up. I cautiously opened the door and saw I had the park to myself once more.

Relief.

A cool night wind blew in off the ocean as I stood in the doorway, looking south. I could see Port Macquarie glowing in the dark distance; a careless scatter of lights—red, green, blue, white—like beautiful gems on the black cloth of the ocean.

The rain started up again, and I closed the door and lay back down. Just as I was dozing off, I remembered something I'd forgotten in all the excitement.

I needed to use the toilet.

Ah, Number Two, I thought as I sat there in the darkness, *if only you knew.*

Chapter Seven: Nano-Fame

DAY 29

It was a fine moment opening Bill's envelope in the post office and seeing the four crisp twenties inside. Holding them was like holding my ticket for re-admittance to the world. Feeling giddy, I went in search of the radio station, where the disc I had mailed from Evans Head should have arrived weeks ago. On the way I stopped in at a guitar shop and bought a D string to replace the one that had broken in South West Rocks.

At Coffs Harbour's ABC, the first broadcast station on my route, there had been no answer on the phone or when I knocked repeatedly on the door. I worried the same result awaited me here, but I needn't have.

'You're doing what?' asked a chirpy lady who introduced herself as Fiona as we shook hands at the station doorstep.

'Walking to Sydney. I sent you a copy of the album and a letter about a fortnight ago? Maybe it didn't arrive.'

'Well I don't know, pilgrim. I've been on holiday. Do you mind if I just go and check with our producer? I'll be back in a sec.'

'Sure, no worries,' I said as she disappeared back into the building, letting the door latch shut behind her. I stood there for a few minutes, wondering whether this was how disc jockeys dealt with undesirables.

Sure, Mr Allmon, sure we got your letter, now just let me go inside and lock the door and oh, don't bother waiting, we have a file for albums like yours and it begins with 'R'. 'R' is for recycling, Mr Allmon; we're very conscientious here at the ABC about recycling unwanted junk ...

The door swung open several minutes later, and Fiona stuck her head out.

'I'm sorry I took so long.' She looked at me for a second, perhaps noting my pained expression. 'Thought I wasn't coming back, didn't you?' she said, grinning.

'Not at all,' I said stiffly.

'Well, I had a chance to skim over what you wrote. It sounds interesting, very unusual. I can't find the album you sent though. Have you got a copy with you?'

I handed her one of the fresh shipment that had arrived along with the money Bill sent.

'What I'll do is have a listen, and if there's something there that's suitable I'll give you a call. I'm not promising anything, you understand, but I'll let you know either way. Are there any tracks in particular I should play?'

Mental jam.

'Radio-friendly?'

One of the songs, 'Killing Time', had been played on Gold Coast ABC a year or so earlier; all the others were unknown quantities. I realised then that although I had written to a lot of stations expressing my desire to get airplay, I had very few songs that were playable.

The short ones were too strange, lacking choruses or friendly themes. The more user-friendly tracks ran far too long for any station other than the ones run by cranks out of their own garage. At seven minutes you'd better have a damn good tune, a 'Stairway to Heaven' or 'Bohemian Rhapsody' ... the sad truth was that my songs just weren't in that league. Moreover, the last track on the album was a piano instrumental, for God's sake. Apart from 'Song for Guy', I couldn't think of a piano instrumental that gets any airplay, and again, I'm no Reggie Dwight.

In my desire to create something unique—an album with absolutely no theme and adhering to no genre whatsoever—I had created myself right out of the market. Still, I had to say something.

'I'd listen to "Killing Time", maybe "Vagabond Odyssey", or "Dark Carnival". Although the latter might be a bit long.'

'Okay, great,' said Fiona. 'I'll give you a bell in a few hours.' She turned to go back inside, then stopped and turned around. 'How long are you in town for?'

'Well, that depends on what you think of the songs.'

'I see.' With that she went back in, and as the door swung closed I let out a little breath I'd been holding the whole time we talked.

I was one step closer to getting on the air.

* * *

I walked out of the internet café with a list of every local newspaper and radio station between Port Mac and Sydney.

The task now was to write an article on myself that could be submitted to the papers, announcing my itinerary and accompanied by a copy of the album. Before I wrote a word, I pulled out a map of the state. I pored over it like a general planning an upcoming campaign, plotting my course and developing a strategy.

There were five major urban centres still to come, and I estimated I was perhaps three or four weeks from Sydney; enough time for this to still work, or so I believed.

First there was the Manning River region. At the heart of it sat Taree, a large inland town sadly known more for its problems with crime and unemployment than its music scene. With twenty thousand people, however, it provided a large listener base.

The next major population centre was the twin towns of Forster-Tuncurry in the Great Lakes Shire; a beautiful region that, with the oldest median age in the state at fifty-one, could be a blessing (the community radio listener base is predominantly over fifty-five[10]) or a curse (people in their fifties being less likely to go for the style of music I was peddling).

---

10 Community Radio National Listener Survey 2010.

After that was a long stretch of smaller coastal communities until I hit the sprawling metropolis of Newcastle. In Newcastle I had the potential to reach half a million. I planned to stay in the region as long as it took to get on the radio, although I felt a flutter of nervousness even this far out at the thought of being surrounded by so many people.

After Newcastle was the Central Coast, home to three hundred thousand people. I believed that Erina would be the key, a large satellite of Gosford, the heart of the region. Erina was where the Central Coast ABC station was. Make it onto the radio there, and I stood a good chance of word reaching the goal, the prize, the fabled piñata.

Sydney.

If I could crack Sydney, the largest city in the country with four million people, then it wasn't too far-fetched to imagine the tour becoming national news. The album, weird assortment of genres and noises that it was, could get national airplay. As the largest city in Oceania and the only Australian city most foreigners knew, Sydney was the only place in the country where I stood a chance of attracting international attention. The idea that such an insane concept as a walking tour could theoretically get me onto the international stage was as staggering as it was unlikely.

It was also putting a lot of carts before the horse. First I had to crack Port Macquarie, and to do that I was totally at the mercy of one Fiona Wyllie. If she knocked me back, it would mean a total reappraisal of what I could hope for. Without radio support, the chances of anyone knowing I was doing this thing were slim. I could maybe get an article or two into the local papers but they couldn't reach as many people or convey my music the way radio could. Television was beyond the range of my ambition, and word of mouth was just too damn slow.

Without radio coverage, I figured I'd still complete the tour, but it would be a blow to have nobody hear my stuff. After all, that was the reason I was doing this, so that I could make a living from music. Wasn't it?

Why are you doing this? a voice asked as it had on the day I left, but I shut it out.

* * *

The phone rang—I lunged for it, hoping it was Fiona. It was a woman's voice, but not Fiona's.

It was Di.

My woman.

At least, I hoped she still was.

'*What's going on!* I haven't heard from you in days! Is everything all right?'

I'd spent the last of my phone credit on my mailing instructions to Bill in South West Rocks, and realised with shock that had been over a week ago. I apologised and told her the situation, hastily adding I was once again solvent.

'Thank God,' she said, and I could hear in her voice she was close to tears. 'I've been *so* worried, I thought something had happened.' I felt terrible, not just because I'd caused her to worry, but because I'd been worrying about her for a very different reason, one which, if her holding back tears was any indication, I'd had no need, or right, to. '*Has* something happened?' she demanded.

I thought of Big Smoky, of Hat Head, and how close I'd come to the ragged edge, but decided to say nothing of it. 'No, just experiencing a lack of fiduciary buoyancy,' I said, forcing a smile into my voice.

'How am I supposed to know you're okay if you can't text me?' Di said in a tone best described as amused exasperation that was nevertheless better than the frantic, close-to-crying one of a few moments ago.

'Uh, I don't know,' I said, displaying the quick-witted repartee that had wooed her in the first place.

'Listen, save your money; *I'll* put credit on your phone. I'll do the thirty dollar recharge, but if you need more just tell me. I'm not going to go through the next however many weeks without any way of keeping in touch. It's hard enough as it is,' she finished, and now she *was* crying a little.

I closed my eyes. It was hard all right. I felt my throat constrict and fought it—if she suspected all had not been well there would be questions. My vision blurred, and I swiped a hand across my eyes, forcing myself to smile.

'That's great, babe, but how are you going to do that from the Bahamas?'

She then went into a lengthy and wholly incomprehensible explanation of the prestidigitation required to put credit on another's phone from the other side of the world.

'Riiiiight,' I said.

'You didn't understand any of that, did you?'

'I—'

'*Did* you?'

'Not as such, no.'

'It's a good thing you're cute.'

'I am cute.'

'But stupid.'

'No argument there. Can you afford it though?'

'Of course I can. I love you. I want you to be able to text me as much as possible. I miss you.'

I let the words wash over me, a soothing balm for a wound that had been festering more than I had suspected, somewhere deep inside, growing worse with every day we spent apart. I clutched the phone and took a deep breath.

'I miss you too.'

'I'll do it now, so send me a text tonight and let me know you're okay, okay? Listen, I've gotta go, we're sailing out of range, but remember that I—'

There was smooth silence, the sound of ten thousand kilometres between us. It didn't matter—I knew how that sentence ended. The trick was remembering it as the tide of days sought to wash it away.

'I love you too,' I said to the silence.

* * *

At about three pm the phone rang again.

'Hello?'

'Smokey?'

'Fiona?'

'Yes. I've had a listen to … ah … "Killing Time" …'

'Yes,' I said, suddenly tense.

'I *love* it. And I've had the chance to read your story properly. My

God, what a brilliant idea! Like a troubadour of old. We'd love to have you on for an interview, if you're happy to do it tomorrow?'

I tried to control the grin that wanted to spread across my face.

'Yeah, that'd be great. What time would you want me?'

'How does eleven am sound?'

'Great!'

'How do you feel about playing a song live on air?'

About three years earlier I'd been invited to play live on the radio for Gold Coast ABC, and it had not gone well. The condition of the invitation was that after they played your song, you had to play a cover. I had attempted a rendition of James Taylor's 'Carolina in my Mind', an ill-advised prospect when neither your guitar chops nor your vocals are up to his incredible calibre. Taking on the Big T is just too much to expect from a poor schlep like me, and as much as I hate to think about it, it showed.

The unfortunate disc jockey had sat there with what she must have assumed was a look of encouragement but in reality was a grimace of pain. I battled gamely on through the bridge, but even I could not ignore the irony of Taylor's lyrics when he wrote,

... and it seems like it goes on like this forever

you must forgive me ...

and sweet Jesus, when your playing sounds as bad as mine did that morning, forever is exactly what it feels like, and no amount of forgiveness from the listener can possibly make up for it.

By the time it was over, I had a mental picture of the Gold Coast breathing a sigh of relief and going about their day. Certainly the deejay, Briony Petch, moved with unseemly haste to the traffic report. So you can understand the icy panic freezing all productive thought at Fiona's innocent remark.

'Smokey?' she asked, in a tone that indicated she thought she had lost me.

I unlocked my jaw, defrosted my brain, and said, 'Sure thing. I'd love to play something.'

Nooooo! cried the voice of three years ago.

'Fantastic. You just need to get here a few minutes early so we can get you set up.'

'No problem.'

I hung up and stood there for a moment. After all the mayhem and madness and untimely erections, I had finally gotten something right.

I was going to be on the radio.

DAY 30

'I'm sitting here with Smokey, a young man who is on tour for his debut album *The Dark Carnival*, but he's doing it a little bit … differently? Is that how you'd put it, Smokey?'

'Ah, yeah.'

'Just sit forward a little so we can hear you, thanks.'

'Oh sorry, is that better?'

'Perfect. We need to hear what you've got to say, because you're on a real adventure, aren't you?'

'Yes.'

'For all our listeners in the Mid-North Coast, I want you to picture a man who looks a cross between Jim Morrison and well … maybe Malcolm Douglas?'[11]

'Or Charles Manson's younger, more deranged sibling.'

Fiona snorted into her microphone, briefly dispelling the aura of professionalism that surrounded her, before recovering her composure and continuing. The snort helped put me at ease, however, and I felt less intimidated by the thought there were actual people listening to my answers, judging the merit of what suddenly seemed a foolish concept.

---

11 Wonderful old bearded Australian nature-documentary-maker from an era before presenters were the slick, gym-sculpted, sickeningly effervescent tossers they now are.

'He wandered in here the other day with a guitar across his back, an album in his hand and a unique story of how he came to be in Port Macquarie: he's walking to Sydney. Tell us about your idea of touring, Smokey, and how it's going so far. You've come from Queensland, haven't you?'

'Just about. Pottsville.'

'How long has it taken you?'

'Four weeks so far.'

'*Four weeks*! Where have you been sleeping?'

'On the beach, mostly. I have a sleeping bag and it does me just fine …'

'No tent?'

'Ah, no.'

'So what happens when it rains?'

The memory of me standing on Trial Bay beach, ripping my shirt off and screaming into the maelstrom flared briefly in my mind.

'Well, I get wet, I guess.'

'He gets wet, folks. Well Smokey, to ask the obvious, why?'

'I guess I wanted to show there's no single right way to do something. I mean, everybody has grown accustomed to musicians touring a certain way, a way that just didn't inspire me. Night after night in pubs, playing for three regulars who are busy working on their cirrhosis. Then I read about the Delta Bluesmen of the Great Migration, roaming the countryside and playing their guitars … I figured that by walking and immersing myself in the places I was playing, I'd have a better time than if I was just rocking up at a pub and then hurrying off for the next thing.'

'I imagine it's a more satisfying way of interacting with the listener, too.'

'Exactly. Music seems to work best when there is a connection between the two parties, but the modern methods of playing those songs live do everything to break that connection. Gargantuan stadiums, towering stages, security guards, advertising placards, barricades. Even on the smaller side of things, you're still separated from your audience by the fact you're standing facing each other. I guess what I wanted was to sit in the midst of my audience, face the same way.'

'Have you gotten a lot of coverage?'

'No, you're my first.'

'You always remember your first, Smokey.'

'So I'm told. I'm hoping it's the start of something big. So to speak.'

'You should be so lucky,' she quipped, to which I laughed. 'Well, you can be pretty sure nobody else is doing something of this nature.'

'I'm hoping it could start a chain reaction. Others might start to downsize, get back to more traditional modes of exposure, like the Deltamen, or the minstrels of the Middle Ages. Instead of everybody piling into a massive stadium, or crowding into a pub, they could be hearing their favourite bands in the local park, or on the beach, or sitting in their back yard.'

She nodded encouragingly, and I started to warm to the topic.

'No admission fee, no ticket booth, no overpriced vendors, no advertisers, no security busting you for smoking something or taking pictures … it could be a renaissance for the music scene. There's an immediacy, and intimacy, that I'm positive the musos and the punters would prefer. No barriers. Other people can join in if they've got a guitar or a bongo, and there's a place where you can light a bonfire and cook up a heap of food.'

I looked meaningfully at the clock, but Fiona kept nodding.

'The costly tours, the pollution caused by aeroplanes and truck convoys and the amount of electricity needed to light a stadium, the separation of fan from musician—all this could be cured at a stroke.'

'I think the music business executives would be the ones having a stroke,' she said dryly. 'But go on.'

'Okay, so a band like Coldplay announce a tour of the beaches Down Under, and instead of charging you a fortnight's rent money, people can pay whatever they want, whatever they think the gig is worth, or however much they can afford. Chuck it in a hat, like buskers have.'

'Nobody would pay though, not if they didn't have to.'

'I'm not so sure. There are restaurants with no prices on their menus, and the patrons just pay whatever they think is fair.'

'Yes, I think I read about that somewhere,' she said.

'You'd think they go broke in the first week, but they don't. It's because they have faith in human nature. It a case of playing off everybody's innate sense of fairness, of value. The owners report that some people pay less than what the meal used to be worth, and others pay more. It balances out. Or that they get less for every meal, but the volume of custom goes up, which balances out too.

'I don't think we put enough faith in people. There will always be those who don't pay anything, but I think they'd be the exception rather than the rule. The power of peer pressure, the weight of expectation and people's sense of doing the right thing would win out, and they'd pay what they could for someone else's service.'

'Seems risky.'

'I know. It's hard to imagine doing, and if it doesn't work or takes too long to work, you go under. And nobody wants to do it first. And the ones that are the trailblazers are usually the ones who fail, but give others a template to improve upon.'

'Hard to convince the music industry to take that approach.'

'True. I don't think you could ever convince a large company like Sony to adopt such an approach, because their economic structure basically forbids it. Hard to imagine the big bands doing it either, since they keep so many people employed.[12] But at the grass roots? It would be a worthy experiment.'

'Which is what you're doing now.'

'That's right.'

'And how is it going?'

'I'm going under.'

She snorted again, and I smiled.

'Well, before you go under for good, perhaps you'd like to introduce the single from your album.'

---

12 As it so happens, a big band *did* try something similar the following year. Radiohead, one of the biggest bands to come out of Britain in the last twenty years, released the album *In Rainbows* online and asked punters to pay whatever they felt it was worth. The actual sales figures were never released, but since they sold three million copies, all reports indicate they made, technically speaking, enough.

* * *

'Mmmm, very smooth; the laid-back grooves of Smokey and his song "Killing Time". For those of you just joining us, Smokey is walking from the Gold Coast to Sydney to promote his album, and after four weeks on the road—or the beach—he's here with me in our Port Macquarie studio. Smokey, why the beach and not inland?'

'Well, the temperature is more constant on the coast because of the ocean, which helps as we get deeper into autumn. Inland I'd either need a tent or I'd be sleeping in town parks or bus shelters …'

'And risk meeting all kinds of unsavoury characters.'

'Exactly. On the beach after the sun sets there's almost nobody about, and if you dig into the dune you can feel the heat of the day stored in the sand.'

'Well I think all of our listeners envy you your liberty, Smokey, if not the lack of showers and decent toilet facilities.'

'I always look like this, Fiona,' I said, and she laughed.

'On that note, I think it's time for a quick news update,' she said.

* * *

'Bit of a downer, huh? Back to the real world?' Fiona asked off mike, indicating the pre-recorded news broadcast telling us of the world's woes.

'Yeah, it's nice being ignorant of the sorrows of humanity,' I said.

'How about your own sorrows? I can't imagine it's all fun in the sun; how bad has it gotten?'

I opened my mouth to answer, but how to tell her that the road shows you who you really are, underneath the civilised layers? The ugliness, the thousand things you are adept at hiding from the world and yourself.

How to tell her that without your life to distract you it's scary, what's under there? There is a reason why the worst punishment tribal people in this country could inflict upon another was exile … we are a social animal, not meant to be left alone with this big brain of ours.

I couldn't even tell her what I was beginning to suspect in the wake of Trial Beach; that after you hit bottom, where everything has been stripped away … once there is no more unknown within to contend with, you can start enjoying the unknown without, and really enjoy the journey.

But I didn't know how to say those things, and it didn't matter, because we were back on the air.

* * *

'Well, sadly we're out of time,' Fiona said, and I was amazed to see by the clock on the wall that I'd been on air for about forty minutes, an unheard of amount of time for an unknown wastrel in obscene flares. Was it really dead in Port Macquarie, or was I exceptionally fascinating? I had no idea and no time to ponder it, because Fiona was saying, 'but before we go, I see you have your trusty guitar with you, Smokey, and are going to be kind enough to play us a song.'

This was the moment of truth, the moment I had been dreading—at least, the part of me that remembered all too clearly my hellish mangling of James Taylor's homesick ode to North Carolina.

'That's right, Fiona,' I began, relieved to hear my voice sounding calm and natural. 'Rather than play something from the album though, I thought I'd play a song I wrote on the beach on the way here.' I hoisted the guitar into my lap, and now I was starting to get the fear, could feel my pulse in my throat, affecting my voice. 'It's called "Ten Seconds", and it's for my girlfriend Di,' I finished lamely, not trusting myself to say any more.

I strummed the first chord, a D Major 7th, and hoped for the best.

* * *

'That was great, Smokey, especially the song you played at the end there,' Kim said as she engaged in some prestidigitation on the computer in front of her. She was the producer, and I assumed she was editing something while the midday news was on.

'Thanks,' I said, wondering if she was just being nice. I hadn't made it through the song unscathed, forgetting the words to the third verse altogether and simply repeating the first again. What I hadn't forgotten was that sudden plunge into silent terror when you realise that bridge is over and you have no idea what comes next. This was a song I had been playing constantly for a month, you understand, as I had done with 'Carolina in my Mind' years before. I doubted whether anyone had noticed the slip, but *I* had, and it bothered me. If I was going to be making a career out of this I had to stop choking when the pressure was on.

Kim handed me the phone receiver, breaking into my reverie. 'It's for you,' she said, her attention never wavering from the screen in front of her.

'Huh?' I said, taking it from her.

'I think you've made an impression,' she said distractedly.

'Hello?' I said.

'Is that Smokey?'

'Yeah.'

'I'm glad I caught you. My name's Paul McCarthy ...'

'Whoa, did you say McCartney?'

'Mc*Carthy*,' he said, and there was a smile in his voice. 'I heard you on with Fiona, mate, and I love it, the music and the whole concept. I'm on the road but I run a business in town and I want you to drop by with a copy of the album. How much does it go for?'

'Ten bucks, or whatever you think is fair, I suppose,' I replied dazedly, and now there was a smile in *my* voice, too.

The ball was rolling.

* * *

McCarthy had been the first of several callers to the station inviting me to visit their workplaces in town, and I was standing in the last of these—a bank—with a dozen or so employees enthusing over my appearance in their midst. From somewhere close by I could hear ABC radio playing softly. I was backed into a corner near the reception desk and surrounded before questions were fired at me like an artillery barrage.

'How long have you—

—what have you been—
—*where* have you been sleeping—
—eating—
—why
why
why?'

I tried to answer everyone at once, but quickly realised it was impossible. So instead I stood there and smiled a lot and carried on seven different conversations, with no idea of what I was saying.

'Chicken. Thank you. Yes. Packstool. Is it? Quicksand. Number Two.'

The novelty of me quickly wore off, however, and people started talking one at a time.

'How did you come up with the idea?' asked a blonde in a tight white blouse and tight black skirt. She looked at me with wide brown eyes that were unnerving in their frank regard.

'It was the weirdest thing. I went to the corner store for milk, got turned around and now here I am …' I expected a laugh but I trailed off as I noticed everyone nodded sagely, as though it had been a nod-worthy—even profound—statement.

'And do you get lonely?' she pressed, still regarding me with those large, fawn-like eyes.

'Ah, sure, yeah, but only occasionally. I talk to myself a lot,' I added, to which everyone did laugh. I chuckled weakly, thinking privately that they only knew the half of it. I also wondered what they'd make of the jawbone stuffed in my pocket.

'Have you had a shower yet?' asked a guy, nudging his neighbour with his elbow. There were more laughs. 'How about deodorant?' he added before I could reply, buoyed by his own wit. There were fewer laughs this time, mostly his own.

'How long until you make it to Sydney, do you reckon?' asked one.

'It took me a month to get here, so my guess is about—'

'How many albums have you sold?' asked an older woman with her hair pulled severely back from her forehead. It was not asked in an unfriendly way, but her voice held none of the admiration or awe the others did, and it threw me.

'Ah, not so many, as it turns out. I'd say maybe five? Six? And some of those were traded for food.'

The blonde girl and the rest smiled in a sympathetic, encouraging way, but the woman who asked the question did not. I didn't blame her. Six albums after four weeks and five hundred kilometres isn't exactly a chart-busting effort.

'So can you say that your idea is working? That it has been a success? Or is it too early to tell?'

A murmur went through the assembled group, one that undoubtedly held a note of disapproval of her line of questioning, but also one of curiosity as to what my answer would be.

The problem was, I had no answer, and had not expected to be asked for one.

'Well, if you measured it in album sales so far, then no, probably not. But since I'll be doing the second half of the walk naked, I'm hoping that will change.'

Everybody laughed again, with somebody adding that my meagre album sales would drop off altogether, which elicited still more laughter.

The woman, however, did not laugh, just looked at me for a moment longer as though she had been expecting more. Then, as though that expectation had gone unrealised, she turned away and walked back to her desk without another word.

I was shamefully grateful her input was over, and welcomed the attentions of the ones who were enthusing over my achievements, originality and wit. For the remainder of the time I spent there, however, I felt a perverse need to seek her out. I wanted to tell her there was more to me … that success could not be measured by album sales alone, and even if it was, thanks to this morning the promotional wagon was rolling at last.

More than those things I wanted to erase that look of hers from my mind; the one that implied I was nothing more than a passing fad, a bit of whimsy for a Thursday morning, a curiosity to be fondled, passed around, then discarded.

I sold and signed a couple of albums, one of whom was for the blonde who also made it clear that should I ever be back in Port

Macquarie to look her up. I posed for photos with some and listened to others tell me of their own adventures—everyone has them, and they're always interesting. I did these things with good grace and a lot of laughter, but haunting me throughout was the question.

Why am I doing this?

DAY 31

Two people approached me cautiously in Bonny Hills' tiny shopping precinct, and I realised they knew who I was. It had only taken twenty-four hours, but already I was getting good at spotting the ones who'd heard me.

'Are you that guy from the radio?' the first one asked. She was a woman in her mid-thirties out to do the shopping. Her friend looked much the same.

'That's me,' I said, smiling.

'I heard you yesterday,' she said, her tone solemn and her demeanour quite serious.

'Right, right. Talking to Fiona. They tried getting me off after five minutes but I had the microphone in a death grip,' I said, hoping to get a smile.

I didn't.

'This is the guy I was telling you about,' she said to her friend, who was staring at me with no expression at all. Then the first woman turned back to me and adopted a similar stare. It was unnerving. What was expected of me? Sing a song? Tell a story? Start krumping?

'So, Bonny Hills ...' I started, not knowing how to finish. The two women did nothing, just stood there, unsmiling and staring. I started to sweat, feeling like I should give them something good.

Something witty.

Something they could tell their friends.

'Bonny Hills, eh …'

I had nothing.

They shifted from foot to foot, but didn't go anywhere or say anything. The breeze fluttered their dresses and stirred my hair, and a car with a dog hanging out the passenger window passed us. A few people went in and out of the newsagency, and the newspaper headlines in their steel frames fluttered like the women's dresses.

There was absolutely nothing to talk about.

I panicked and went for the weather.

'Beautiful day, huh?'

'Oh yeah,' said one.

'Mmmm, beautiful,' said the other.

Okay, not too shabby Allmon, keep it up.

'Thought we might have had a bit of rain last night,' I added.

'Oh yeah,' said one.

'Mmmm, looked like,' said the other.

We stood there, swamped in renewed silence, engulfed in this horrendous, never-ending moment.

'Didn't though,' I said, after a bit.

'No,' said one.

'Mmmm,' said the other.

I couldn't stand it any longer; it had gone beyond all human endurance.

'Well, ladies, have a lovely afternoon, I better get back to it. Sydney, you know …'

'Bye,' said one.

'Bye,' said the other.

I walked on, thinking that fame sure isn't what it's cracked up to be.

* * *

My next fan was a few hundred yards along; this one dressed in board shorts with a small boy holding his hand.

'Hey, aren't you that guy …' he began.

'Yeah!' I said, hoping he meant me.

'Wow,' he said, and sounded genuinely enthused, which was an improvement on the women at least.

He crouched down next to his son and pointed up at me, pitching his voice about an octave higher. 'Hey Kyle, this man is walking to Sydney. You know Sydney? Yes you do! Yes you *do*! You remember the bridge? And the Opera House? Pretty building? Sure you do.'

Kyle looked unconvinced.

Dad pointed at me again. 'This man's walked all the way from Queensland. That's a long way to walk, isn't it? Remember that time we drove to Grandma's house? Well, that's as far as this man has walked. That's amazing, isn't it? Do you want to say something, Kyle? Say something to the man? Go on, say hello to the man.'

'Hey,' I said, smiling in what I hoped was a non-threatening way.

Kyle must have thought his dad had already spoken enough for him, me, and possibly the whole of New South Wales, because he just looked off into the distance and ignored me totally.

'Gee, I don't know why he's so quiet, he never gets like this, even around people he doesn't know,' the man said, eyeing me suspiciously.

'Ah, don't worry about it,' I said, but the guy still looked perturbed. I felt sorry for him and his underwhelmed kid, so I gave him a copy of the album. I signed it and went on my way, wondering if I should have done a kids' album instead.

* * *

The outer suburbs of Laurieton—two houses and a yellow school bus parked on the shoulder—signalled the end of my brief car ride with Tim the teacher.

'Do you realise the only people who seem to offer me lifts are drunks and teachers?' I said to him after he picked me up just outside Bonny Hills. The road had been the only option south, and it had no shoulder to speak of—I'd accepted Tim's offer gratefully.

'I think we're one and the same,' he replied, shifting down gears. 'Gee, I wish I could do something like you're doing,' he added, as we pulled in at the Laurieton Library carpark.

'Why don't you?' I asked.

'Wife. Kids. Mortgage. Job to pay for all three.' He looked at me with an eyebrow cocked. 'Give it ten years, mate, and you'll know.'

'Does it make you sad?' I asked in the sudden silence now that the engine had stopped running.

'A bit, but I'd never trade it, you know? You have kids? No? Wait till you do, Smokey; your life will never be the same. All the adventure you could ever want.'

I started rooting around in the packstool for a copy of the album to give him.

'Are you sticking around the area?' he asked. 'You should come and play for my youth group up at Timbertown. It's this program tailored to disadvantaged kids, and we have all sorts of activities. Having you play would be awesome.'

'Really? That sounds like something I could stick around for,' I replied, thinking again I'd missed a trick not doing an album aimed at the Wiggles demographic.

'Yeah? It wouldn't take too long, and it'd just be all the classics—"Click go the Shears", "True Blue", you know, stuff the kids can sing along with.'

'Oh, I see …'

He saw my pained expression.

'What's wrong? Too small a gig for a big star like you?' he said with a grin.

'No, no, nothing like that. It's just …'

'What?'

'Well, it's terrible and unpatriotic and everything, but …' I trailed off. I took a deep breath and confessed, 'I don't know the words to "Click go the Shears". Or any other "Australiana", for that matter.'

There. My secret shame revealed. Tim looked surprised.

'"I Still Call Australia Home"?'

'No.'

'"Waltzing Matilda"?'

'No.'

'"Kookaburra sits in the Old Gum Tree"?'

'No.'

'"Home among the Gum Trees"?'

'No, nothing with a gum tree in it.'

'Wow.'

'I mean, I'd love to help out, play something, but I'd just be doing my own stuff and a couple of covers I know. The little kids will boo me off.'

'No, no, they wouldn't do that,' Tim said, but I could see the lie in his eyes, those wretched urchins would have me for lunch. 'Well, I guess it'll have to wait for another time, eh?'

'I'm sorry, Tim. Listen, let me give you a copy of the album as thanks for the ride and as an apology for not being a respectable Australian.'

'At least tell me you sing in an Australian accent ...'

'Ah ...'

The truth was, I sang like an American. Which a lot of Australians (and Brits, Germans, French) do, because America is where the action is ultimately at—the size of the Australian industry is a tenth of the American and about three per cent of the international market. Even homegrown artists only accounted for sixteen of the top one hundred selling acts in Australia for the decade. Sounding American was the only sensible way to proceed if you wanted to make it.

Or so I thought.

'Come on, Smokey, be true to your roots, mate. There's no shame in the country you're from.'

'No, no, it's not that,' I demurred, but the truth was that I loathed songs sung in our broad dialect ... and the worst offenders in this regard were the very songs Tim wanted me to play. I said nothing more, feeling like a traitor to my country and kin, and handed him the album. We said our goodbyes, and I set off in the dappled afternoon sunlight, thinking about my cultural cringe.

There was a little more to it than that, if the truth be known. I remembered my own childhood, when the teacher would take us through ghastly rhyming couplets like,

He fired at Trooper Kelly,
And brought him to the ground
And in return from Davis,
He received a mortal wound ...

I'd be in agony, because it either didn't rhyme when every other stanza did, or they *made* it rhyme and destroyed the word's pronunciation. Brought him to the *groond*? Really? Mortal *wound*? I assume that is a reference to the best way of storing the mortal coil, lest it unwind.

'The Wild Colonial Boy' is almost a sacred song in this country, and by merely suggesting such criticism I open myself up to attack from virtually every quarter. So I may as well go the whole hog honesty-wise and say that I was indifferent to the whole canon of Australian folk music. They all sounded the same; always about filthy people doing incomprehensible things in hot and horrible conditions. I couldn't see where they fit into modern life, especially when most of us wouldn't know a 'cove', 'tarboy' or 'bare-bellied yoe' if we fell over one. Bush poetry drove otherwise normal people to adopt broad dialects and slap their knees, calling everyone 'cobber' in fruity tones.

I remember some commemorative event organised by my school for the Bicentenary, where 'Click Go the Shears' was sung with frightening intensity by old folks dressed in flannel and ill-fitting overalls, hats with dangling corks flying chaotically about their flushed and sweating faces ... they'd grab me and try to dance and cajole and scream *'COME ON BENNNN! CLICK CLICK CLICK! WIIIIIDE IS HIS BLOW AND HIS—COME ON! WHY AREN'T YOU SINGING?'*

Why aren't you singing?

Why indeed?

I stopped walking and looked around. I was on the outskirts of Dunbogan, a town that was hit by a small meteorite several years earlier.[13] I knelt and took the guitar out of its case, which I then folded and tucked into the pack—there was a lot more room for it than there had been a month ago.

I started walking again, strumming a new song as I went. I probably

---

13 It went through the roof of the Hancox family home after travelling through space for five billion years. The newspaper report covering the event has this one excerpt that I find remarkable in that it prompted no further lines of enquiry: 'initially he feared a goanna living in the roof had fallen through.' I've had mice that sound terrifyingly loud when scampering above your head, and mice weigh one ounce and grow to about fifteen centimeters. Goannas weigh five hundred times as much and can grow to two metres in length. But no, just that one line, ho hum, clumsy venomous reptile loitering above our heads, 24/7 ...

should have been playing material from the album, but now that I had recorded them I had little desire to linger on them. Something about the recording process had neutered my desire to play these twelve songs anymore. Many of them I'd been playing for years, and I wanted to be creating, not replicating.

If you're not playing the songs from the album you're touring, a voice murmured, *and you're not playing songs people know, then why are you doing this?*

DAY 33

'You have the look of a man who knew the answer before he asked,' the man said, smiling at me over the rim of his cup. He took a sip of his coffee.

'Yes, I suppose I do,' I replied, sipping my own steaming brew.

'Then why ask?' he said, not unkindly.

'Because I like surprises.'

He smiled again and shook his head. 'No surprises in Harrington, I'm afraid. You'll have to go the long way around.'

I took another sip of coffee, not wanting to think about the long way around.

Instead, I enjoyed the early morning dark and the company of the man. He was the owner of the Everything Store. He was in late middle age, tanned, bespectacled and sporting an open, Tom Bosley-ish face.

He sat ensconced behind a counter so cluttered with knick-knacks, bric-a-brac and every conceivable trinket he was barely visible. Newspapers were stacked in front of him, behind him and around him. The walls were covered with old coasters, newspaper clippings, and photos of smiling men holding up fish. There was a rack along one wall stuffed full of cards for every occasion—birthdays, engagements, bereavements, greetings from beautiful Harrington. There were loaves of bread and a fridge full of milk along another wall, and bags of lollies festooned every remaining inch.

The place was a labyrinth of mercantile enthusiasm, the walls a historical record of the area, the man himself an anthropological wonder dressed in flannelette. In the pre-dawn murk, his store shone with a cheery yellow glow, and the hobbit-hole clutter of the place was cosy and welcoming, if a bit daunting in its navigability.

I'd stopped in on my way along the banks of the Manning River, hoping to get a sense of the area, maybe a local map, and most importantly, to see if there was a quick way across the mouth of the river. It was five o'clock, and the guy had just opened the door, yet he looked unsurprised to see me.

'Sun won't be up for another hour. Do you want to come in for a cuppa?'

'I'd love that,' I said, shivering.

'Come on in,' he said, turning and walking back inside. 'What brings you here at this hour?'

'I'm on my way south, and I wanted to get an early start. The cold woke me up, actually.'

'Yeah, autumn's definitely on its way.'

'I didn't think anybody'd be open, to be honest.'

'Five o'clock, every day 'cept Christmas,' he said, disappearing through a door behind the cluttered counter. I stood in the warm glow of the store proper, looking about the chaos and trying to get a sense of where the coffee machine was.

'How do you take it?' he yelled from the next room, and I realised it must have been a kitchenette.

'Black with two!' I yelled back, and heard the kettle boiling not long after.

When he came back out, he was holding two Herculean mugs clearly not of the Styrofoam variety on offer at most cafés these days. I liked him immediately.

He sat on his stool and I leant on the only bare patch of counter I could find. Over the next half-hour I told him about my walk, and he told me about the history of the area.

At this hour the only customers were old men whose sleeping patterns were so utterly scrambled they had been up for hours waiting for him to open so they could get the day's paper.

'Mornin, Clem, you old bastard.'

'Terry,' the old guy would nod, shuffling towards the nearest stack of papers with grim determination. 'See you haven't fixed that bloody light in the fridge. Still flickerin like it's havin a bloody fit or somethin. Useless as an ashtray on a motorbike, you are.'

I looked at the fridge; the light looked fine to me.

'Be nice, Clem, we've got company.'

Clem looked up at me with narrowed eyes that gave no hint at what he was thinking. They flicked back to Terry, and I saw the quick wink the old guy gave him.

'When did you start lettin blokes who look like women in 'ere, Terry?'

'He had no choice,' I said. 'He's a sucker for good looks.'

Clem burst into a wheezing cackle.

'This time of day, I'll take what I can get,' Terry said.

Clem flapped his hand at us both, dumped his dollar on the counter and shuffled back out, saying over his shoulder, 'Get that bloody light fixed.'

'Nice folks around here,' I said, smiling.

'Oh yeah. He's one of the nicer ones.'

After Terry confirmed what I had suspected—that there was no way across the river other than by boat, he went on to tell me the bad news.

'I don't know how long it's going to take you on foot, but to get over to Manning Point by car takes about forty minutes. You'll have to go all the way to the highway, then south to Taree, then cut back east. All told you're looking at about seventy kilometres.'

'*Seventy?*'

Terry just nodded and took my empty mug away to the kitchen, leaving me alone to digest the news.

Seventy kilometres.

I turned and looked out the front window of Terry's store. Between the yellowing newspaper articles depicting local triumphs and tragedies taped to the dusty glass, the day was well and truly begun. The dark, which had seemed so indefatigable, was finally surrendering, revealing a deserted street and a grey glassy river beyond it. I thought I could see the far bank, Manning Point, a scant five hundred yards away.

I swallowed a bitter taste in my mouth and said without turning back, 'It's going to take me two days to get over there, you know.'

'Are you on a timetable?' Terry said as he returned to his stool.

'Well, no …'

'Then what's the rush?'

I thought for a moment. Other than the inconvenience of a sleepless night in Taree, he was right. If anything I should be lingering, cashing in on the Port Macquarie broadcast. And it wasn't as though I was expected anywhere by a certain time. Winter was perhaps my only concern, and that was still a month away.

'The same thing happened here back in the Depression, you know,' Terry was saying. 'Folks would walk from town to town looking for work, coppers always moving them on. They were called the travellers. Or the battlers. My old man spent a couple of years like that.'

'Really? I had no idea that people did that here,' I said, appalled at my lack of knowledge. I knew more about America's history than my own country's.

'You heard of Kylie Tennant?' he said, pointing at a clipping on the window I'd spotted earlier, depicting her Diamond Head writer's hut, which I'd passed the day before. I had never heard of her. 'She wrote about 'em. Walked with them, too.'

'She walked with them?'

'I heard that in '32 she walked from Sydney to Coonabarabran in two weeks to be with her husband … she was only twenty, mind you … thirty kilometres a day, and the roads back in the '30s weren't what they are now.'

I quickly did the calculations and realised we had walked about the same distance, only it had taken me twice as long. Any pride I may have felt in getting all this way was immediately doused.

'Some say she was a feminist, others a communist, but mostly what she did was write about ordinary folks … battlers. Walked everywhere with 'em, she did, to know what their lives were like. That's all that really matters about her; what she did, not what others say.'

'You know a lot about her,' I said, thinking I had the opposite problem—I clearly didn't know enough.

'I'm an old fella, Smokey. Old fellas are like libraries with dodgy filing systems. It's all in there, it's just getting it out that's the hard part.'

He leant towards me, a grin on his face and his voice lowered to a conspiratorial level. 'I know something else about her, too, but it'll probably make you feel a bit inadequate.'

'What?' I groaned.

'She also walked from Coonabarabran to Brisbane.'

'How far is ...'

''Bout seven hundred kilometres, including crossing the Great Dividing Range.'

'Thanks Terry,' I said.

'Don't mention it,' he replied. 'She wrote about how they sung songs to pass the time on the road,' he said, nodding at my guitar. 'You'd know a few of the old tunes, wouldn't you Smokey?'

Oh no, I thought, *not again*.

'I'm a bit rusty, to be honest ...' I began, but he cut me off, for which I was grateful.

'A lot of young folks don't know the old songs, the ones they used to sing on the roads back in those days. Shame, don't you think? Not to know your own history.'

'Yes,' I did, meaning it, hearing again Tim's words from the other day. *You gotta know where you come from* ... was that what he'd said? Something like that. Had I been ashamed of my roots? Maybe, but if Kylie and the families on the road that Terry described were any indication, I had no right to be.

How could I have been so blind, overlooking the Great Migrations of my own people, poor Australians walking the long roads looking for their place in the scheme of things? The folk songs suddenly made sense—it didn't matter if the rhyming scheme was all over the shop, it was what those songs meant, represented—they tied people together, across time and lonely miles. John Williamson's 'True Blue' drawl suddenly seemed right, proper; my own Americanised singing accent a peculiarly insecure affectation. Nano-fame, and seeking anything beyond it, suddenly seemed meaningless, incredibly shallow.

'There's so much I don't know,' I said before realising I was going to, but Terry just smiled.

'That's all right, son. That's what us old buggers are for.'

'Here I am complaining about seventy kilometres ...' I trailed off, hearing again my petulant tone a few minutes earlier. I thought about having to walk seventy kilometres with a wife and a couple of children depending on me to find food, water, shelter, work.

We were both silent, Terry giving me a moment to gather my thoughts, before he reached under the counter and pulled out a loaf of bread. Handing it to me, he said, 'Here you go. It's yesterday's, so it's not the freshest, but it'd just go in the bin otherwise. I figure you'll need all the energy you can get.'

'Thank you, Terry,' I said, touched. For every wretched individual I'd meet, or jerk throwing insults or objects from cars, there would always be a Terry just around the corner.

'No mate, don't thank me for stale bread, for Christ's sake. Just promise to watch out for yourself, especially around Taree. If you have to spend the night there, keep that knife on your belt hidden. It'll cause more problems than it'll prevent.'

'Thanks,' I said, and turned to go.

I had to stop at the door to let another fossil in, this one wearing overalls and a green hat with side flaps. The insides of the flaps were lined with sheepskin. He looked me over briefly, seemed unimpressed by what he saw, and hobbled inside saying, 'Hey Terry, I don't suppose it's too much to ask you to get the damn heater on. Cold enough to freeze the nuts off a tractor in here. Every bloody year it's the same. What are ya, too cheap to buy a bloody radiator ...'

* * *

The van pulled up ahead of me. I was on the highway somewhere outside Cundletown, looking for the exit to Taree. I figured I'd hitch a lift to the next exit; I detested walking along the Pacific Highway, risking the integrity of my body every minute I was on it.

The passenger door swung open, releasing a torrent of loud music.

'Put your stuff in the back!' a voice yelled.

'Okay!' I yelled back, doing so. Climbing into the passenger seat, I barely had time to close the door before we were tearing back onto the highway. I looked at the driver and came to the conclusion that I had made a big mistake.

He could have been anywhere between thirty and fifty, shirtless, his bare arms and chest heavily tattooed. I couldn't be sure, but it looked as though his fly was open.

'I'm Andy!'

'Smokey.'

'*Wooohoooo! Let's roll baby!*' He turned the music up louder still until even I, a veteran of eardrum-bursting volumes, was wincing in pain. Andy was saying something, but all I could see was his mouth moving. He cranked the van up to one hundred and twenty kilometres per hour, and I surreptitiously tugged on my seatbelt to make sure it was sound. I realised he hadn't even asked me where I was going.

The song, which I could not recognise, was mercifully on the fade out, and I took a breath to tell Andy he could let me out at the next exit. I opened my mouth but the opening riff of 'China Grove' came bursting out at bowel-loosening decibels. I closed my mouth and watched the scenery fly past. At this speed I'd be in Sydney in about twenty minutes. That's if we stayed on the road. I should have never gotten in to this hurtling amplifier.

I felt a tapping on my leg, and looked over to see Andy pointing at the glove box, grinning and saying something. I opened it and was immediately inundated by a slithering torrent of crap—napkins, discs, cassettes, and tourist booklets.

He kept tapping impatiently on my knee and pointing into the deeper recesses of the glove box.

I pulled out a battered boiled lolly tin and sniffed it.

This had to be it.

I looked over with an eyebrow lifted in inquiry, and he winked at me.

'*Yeah baby, woop woop!*'

I cracked the lid off the tin, and just as I had expected, saw a healthy stick of marijuana. Before I could do anything, he reached across and took it from me.

I looked over and was alarmed to see him steering with his knees as he fumbled around on the dashboard for his rolling papers. He then proceeded to pull a small pair of nail scissors from his pants and commenced chopping up his weed with leisurely calm. Occasionally he'd sing along, and I assumed he'd already been into his lolly tin at least once today.

'Well you're talking 'bout China Grove ... whoa-oh-OH!'

I fought the urge to lean over and grab the wheel, or offer to chop and roll. Instead, I yelled over the blaring Doobie Brothers to my very own doobie brother.

'Hey, Andy! You can let me out at the next exit!'

'What?'

'The next exit! Let me out at the next exit! The one for Old Bar!'

'Yeah, it's my car!'

'Old Baaaaar!' I bleated. I could feel my head swelling up with music and blood.

'How far to what?'

'What?' I yelled, regretting instantly the fact that I did.

'I've got plenty!'

This couldn't go on. I looked at the sound system in the dashboard, wanting to find the volume control. Before I could, however, he tossed an expertly rolled joint into my lap. I looked up and saw him winking again.

This wasn't a good idea. The memory of Happy Jim's demon weed was fresh in my mind. I had no way of gauging how strong this gear was, and I didn't want to be waking up two hours later still in this van and halfway to Melbourne. However, I also didn't want to offend my driver, so I lit it and surreptitiously bum-puffed it. I had a very mild buzz after a minute or so, but that was all.

Andy flicked some switch on the CD player, and there was blissful, sweet silence at last. 'Just tell me when you want to get out,' he said, his voice hoarse from the smoke and the singing. 'You want a beer?'

'Ah, no. Thanks though. Actually, I was hoping to jump out at that exit back there, the one for Old Bar.'

'You've got to tell me these things, mate. How do I know where you wanted to get out?' He looked out the windscreen long enough to overtake a struggling Volkswagen, cracking a fresh beer. We passed it as though it was standing still. 'I'm not a bloody mind-reader, you know. You like Bowie? I fucking love him. Best musician ever. Fucking genius.'

'Ah ...'

Before I could say anything, he flicked another switch on the CD player, and out came 'Young Americans' at about the same volume as a jet taking off. Ordinarily I love the song, but not when it shakes my fillings loose.

We had bigger problems than Bowie, however, such as the column of signs indicating we were about to enter a roadwork zone. There were warnings of every kind, and it looked as though they were putting in a whole new stretch of the highway.

The speed limit went from one hundred and ten kilometres per hour to eighty, but Andy kept barrelling along, unperturbed.

The limit dropped to sixty.

No change.

We were now roughly doubling the speed limit.

When the forty kilometre per hour sign came and went in a blur, I thought that surely we must slow down, the traffic would simply become too congested. We were now flying along at three times the speed limit. Any moment now one of two things was going to happen: Andy would brake and spare us from ruin, or we would crash and die.

Andy's response to such a choice was, to put it mildly, singular.

He pulled a harmonica out of his seemingly bottomless pocket, took both hands off the wheel, steered with his knees, and played along with Bowie. I sat, mouth agape, watching and listening and thinking that I could be identified by the titanium rod in my back when investigators arrived on the scene.

Up ahead, the two lanes were merging into one, with a line of orange witches hats to prevent idiots from getting confused. Andy—who, it must be said, blew a monster harp—finally showed some acknowledgment of the situation and applied the brake.

Bit too late, as it turns out.

The traffic had bottlenecked, and where Andy's hazy ocular senses had told him people were still moving along, they had in fact stopped completely. A caravan sitting last in line loomed larger and larger until it seemed to fill our windscreen. Andy came to the belated realisation that there was no way he was going to stop in time to avoid turning the caravan into kindling, and us along with it.

'Fuck,' he exclaimed mildly, and swung the wheel to the left, taking us onto a section of highway under construction. I felt the thud of the witches hats getting run over. We fumed with tyres smoking towards a pile of gravel and machinery, the van filled with Bowie wailing,
ain't there one damn song that can make me ...
while I wailed
'FUUUUUUU—'
and there was no way we were not going to crash
'—UUUCCCCKKKKK!'
but then Andy ripped the wheel back to the right, narrowly missing the gravel, the machinery, and one startled guy holding a yellow sign that said 'SLOW'
... break down and cryyyy?
and we slid back into the flow of traffic doing twenty, seamlessly merging as though nothing untoward had happened.

A quick glance in the wing mirror showed a column of overturned witches hats and one angry guy in a torn vest, giving chase. As he seemed to be the foreman, his belly prevented speedy pursuit, and we soon left him behind.

I turned in my seat to face Andy, who was looking for his harmonica. The song was fading out, which gave me the chance to speak at a moderate level and still be heard.

'I think maybe I'll just get out here, mate, if it's all the same to you.'

Andy looked surprised, and said, 'Really? I don't think it's safe to stop in roadworks, mate.'

Safe? We had just escaped becoming a Bowie-blaring suppository for a Jayco Pop-Top, and here he was talking about safety?

'Even so, Andy, I think I should,' I said, keeping my voice neutral.

'Okay, you're the boss,' he said, his tone implying I was being unreasonable and foolhardy in the extreme.

* * *

Andy's Wild Ride had taken us well past the exit to Taree and dumped me near Nabiac, thirty kilometres to the south. It would take a full day to backtrack to Taree.

Consulting the map proved I was now closer to the coastal Great Lakes towns than Taree; given that the latter was an inland town and ill-suited to rough sleeping, I decided to keep moving east.

* * *

It was after eleven when I found myself standing on the top of a Tuncurry dune. I had made it back to the ocean, my beautiful midnight Pacific, despite my interior navigator being a cobwebbed skeleton grinning at some long-forgotten joke.

I had walked fifty-two of the seventy-six kilometres between here and Harrington, my body was wracked with pain to the point of mutiny and I'd seen my life flash before my eyes with David Bowie singing the soundtrack, but it didn't matter; I was here.

Comprehensively exhausted, I felt something of an affinity with the travellers of the Great Depression ... and had the sense to know I didn't know the half of it.

Chapter Eight: Great Lakes, High Stakes

DAY 37

Lexi and Jason had a good thing going. They also made me look like a piker. They were hitching from Melbourne to Cairns[14] with surfboards, surely the most optimistic hitchhikers in the history of Western civilisation; God knows who picked them up with two Malibus and a couple of backpacks the size of Harvey the Newfie of Woopi.

We were sitting at a table in a campground on the banks of the mighty Wallis Lake called The Ruins, the ruins of our dinner spread before us. I had provided the food and music; they had provided the wine.

'There it is, eh,' Lexi said, her accent pegging her as a Canadian. 'Can you hear it?'

'Water-helicopter,' said Jason, sounding subdued. We were all a bit subdued.

'It's been like this for the past two hours,' Jason said to me as we watched the helicopter thundering its way south through the orange-black sky.

---

14 3500 kilometres, or 2200 miles. The same distance between New York City and Salt Lake City, three London to Edinburgh round trips, a journey from Barcelona to Moscow, or India top to bottom. Maniacs.

Trailing behind it, looking improbable at the end of a long cable, was a gigantic bucket silhouetted against the fading sky. The bucket was full of water drawn from Wallis Lake to fight the rapidly burgeoning bushfire consuming the forest south of the Ruins. With the coming of night it was hard to tell where the glow of the setting sun ended and the glow of the fire began.

'Wonder if we'll have to leave,' he remarked, sounding quite relaxed for a man with no means of quick escape, other than the surfboard.

'I guess the ranger will let us know,' I said.

I had spent the day to the north in Forster, finally securing distribution with Somersault—I could legitimately go to radio now. Invigorated by this long-denied victory, I busked about town for the next few hours, but made no sales. After getting hassled by louts near the pub I walked two hours south to arrive here in the wonderfully named Booti Booti National Park. On the morrow I would push on into the more sparsely populated wilderness of the southern Great Lakes region.

If, that was, the bushfire didn't cut me off.

We all sat silently for a while, watching the action play out in the darkening sky.

'Hey, what happened to the ground next to the toilet block?' I asked, remembering a large patch of burned grass I had seen upon arriving. 'And the trees around it are singed, too.'

'Oh, you saw that, eh? You're an observant fella,' Lexi said, blithely unaware of the truth.

'It's pretty funny … and scary, too,' Jason said, and settled back to tell the story. 'Couple of nights ago, there was a whole heap of people camped here, most of them in caravans. Anyway, this one caravan was owned by an elderly couple who didn't want to walk far to the toilet in the middle of the night, so they parked right next to the block.' He stopped talking when Lexi passed him the bottle of wine we were sharing. Groundmist was beginning to gather around our feet, and Lexi took up the story.

'So we were having dinner here near the barbecues with most of the other folks, you know, talking and drinking and just hanging out. Except the old couple. They'd turned in about seven-thirty.' Jason handed me the bottle, and I took a swig. Lexi continued. 'So we're eating, right, and at nine o'clock, the old folks' caravan explodes! I mean *BOOM!*'

'Boom?'

'It goes up in a huge fireball. Little pieces of caravan flying through the air, it was like in a movie. Little personal items too, like half a watch, melted shoes, clothes, cutlery ... you name it. And we're all like, "No way, did you just see that?" And the first thought was like, "Oh fuck, what happened to the old folks? Shit, check that shoe and see if there's a foot inside it," you know? We ran over to see, but no one wants to get too close, right, cos there could still be gas bottles that haven't exploded. The ground's on fire, there's not much left of the caravan, and no sign of anybody.'

'The trees were starting to catch fire, too,' Jason said, eyeing the glow on the southern horizon, 'so we had to put them out. We were throwing water everywhere, using cups, bottles, and buckets. I think one of the dudes was pouring his six pack onto the grass fire.'

'Did you manage to stop it?'

'Yeah, and pretty quickly too, with all of us helping. And all the time everyone's saying "What happened to Betty and Al?"'

'We thought they had to be dead, you know,' Lexi continued, 'cos nothing could have survived the blast. I mean, all that was left of the caravan was a few struts and tyres. The rest was strewn all over the park or had been consumed.'

'And then we hear this woman start crying, and we turn around and it's Betty, she's alive and coming out of the toilets in her pyjamas and carrying her toothbrush. And we're thinking she's crying cos Al's bitten the big one, that all that's left of him is a burnt slipper and half a watch.'

'Oh dear.'

'Yeah, and then we hear the toilet flush, and a few seconds later out comes Al. *He's* in his pyjamas, and—can you dig it Smokey?—*he's* carrying a toothbrush as well. And his mouth is still foamy, looks like he got bit by a rabid woodchuck or something, and he's not crying, but looks fucking dazed all the same, and wouldn't you be if you went to brush your teeth and came out to find a piece of scorched earth where your caravan used to be? And they stand there holding hands like two little kids in their PJs, and we've all stood still for a second, kinda making sure they're really there and not some collective hallucination, and then we ran over to them crying and hugging them, cos they were pretty cool, and even if they weren't, nobody deserves an exploding caravan,' Lexi finished, taking the wine from me.

'No, they don't,' I said.

'So then somebody called the fire guys and the ambulance and this whole place was a circus until four in the morning,' Jason said.

'Did they find out why it blew up?'

'Apparently Betty liked to have a cup of milky tea or something before bed and left the gas on. They think somehow a spark occurred and up she went.'

'You would have thought they'd have smelled something,' I said after a bit.

I could sense Lexi shrug without seeing it.

'They were pretty old,' she said, as though that explained everything.

On the way to bed several hours later my phone rang, an unusual occurrence. It was my old friend and former bandmate, Myles, sounding unusually serious. He'd spent the last couple of days with me; always a fan of madcap adventures, he'd been waiting until I was within range of Sydney—where he lived—before joining me. After weeks spent on marketing, promotion, making contacts and securing distribution, jamming for tourists with my old Valhalla drummer—even if he was simply using two drumsticks on the Coleman lantern—had reminded me what I truly valued in music.

It had been ten years since we played together, and I'd forgotten just how wonderful that moment inside the music could be when shared, how no other relationship is like it. I'd caught his eye at one point in the middle a song, and there was an instant where we were both eighteen again and something inside rolled over in the grave of memory.

Music used to be fun, a voice said. *Somewhere along the way, you've forgotten that …*

I came back to the present when I heard the urgency in Myles's voice cutting through the crackling line.

He told me he had been severely delayed by the fire, and then re-routed around it on his way home.

'It's a big one, Allms. Roads are cut,' he said. The only way south was a long inland detour; fine if you were in a car, not so good if you were on foot. He told me I'd have to get down to Seal Rocks, the next large village, by coast or not at all. There was a real chance I was going to be stuck in the Ruins, possibly until the end of the week.

'And watch your ass, Allms. I mean it; if you're sleeping somewhere in the bush nobody's gonna know you're there. It's a bushfire, man, and bushfires are things you don't want to fuck with.'

Thanking him, I hung up and looked at the reddish glow on the horizon, thinking about tomorrow. If the fire made it to the thick scrub of the coast, I'd be stranded here; having exhausted the economy of Forster-Tuncurry over the last few days, I needed to be moving on to new opportunities. If I was here for days, I'd be spending money and little else, so if there was a chance I could squeeze down the coast ahead of the fire tomorrow, I'd have to take it.

But as I lay in my sleeping bag, trying to sleep and failing, Myles's words came back to me. *Bushfires are things you don't want to fuck with* ...

DAY 38

Serving as a brief and bizarre reprieve from an increasingly hazardous day was Shelly Beach. There were discreet signs along the main road that informed the bushwalker that Shelly was for those lacking in the apparel department. The word 'naturist' was mentioned, arousing my interest. I hurried down the trail to the beach, where I was about to get a lesson in raising one's hopes too high.

I was the youngest person on the beach by at least thirty years.

The women weren't so bad, but the men ... dear God, it was a hideous preview of coming attractions. Penises hung from grey thatches of pubic hair like gnawed-on gristle; deflated buttocks hung like empty cushion covers. Hair sprouted from places I'd not known hair could grow.

Unwilling to let this dampen my spirits, I dumped my stuff onto the sand and started stripping off. The weirdness of this act cannot be overstated. A lifetime of ingrained behaviour had me looking over my shoulder, expecting to hear a scream and someone yelling for the cops to get this pervert off the beach.

Of course, none of these things happened. There were about half a dozen people in the vicinity, and none of them took any notice as I pulled my pants off and stood there naked as the day I was born. Remembering the Brooms Head Affair, I decided to go for a swim, just in case the excitement of genital furlough translated into something inappropriate even to these liberal-minded folk.

I spent about twenty minutes in the water. There was a steep drop off, and the water was quite chilly. Just how chilly I only became aware of once I emerged from the water. I figured playing a bit of guitar in the sun would restore my self-image, and after all, I *was* on tour.

A couple sauntered over and sat down next to me. They were both smiling happily and seemed completely at ease with the whole nudity thing, which in turn put me at ease.

'Hiya,' said the woman in a thick European accent. Europeans. It figures. I knew Australians would be too uptight to be down here strutting their stuff in the altogether. Too much British in us.

'Hi.'

'Guitar. Very. Nice.' She stepped from word to word with the caution of a tightrope walker working without a net.

'Thank you. Yes. Good day to be on beach,' I said. I had to stop myself from talking louder, as though volume could bridge the linguistic gulf.

They both nodded, smiling politely if somewhat warily. I figured I'd let the conversation side of things slide and just keep playing tunes. As I did, another foreign couple came over and sat down. Soon I had an audience, and at the end of each song they clapped and encouraged me to play on (I assume). By now I had forgotten we were all naked. It is amazing how fast you can adjust; I was more interested in picking the next song than checking out geriatric genitalia.

And so I played perhaps the strangest gig of my life in the queer orange light of that bushfire morning, sand entering every nook and cranny, singing songs for a handful of naked septuagenarians that barely spoke English, totally naked myself, while a few miles away the world burned.

* * *

An hour later I was lost.

I checked the map. No trails were marked. I looked around and saw incredibly dense scrub in every direction. I couldn't even tell where I had come from.

Ash was falling, blackened scraps that drifted down slowly because they were so light. Being so light they could have blown from many miles away, I told myself, but I just didn't know. The day still had a weird orange cast to it, like being on acid. My nostrils would flare and catch a stronger, sharper whiff of smoke, and the primitive Id inside me would bang against the bars of my civilised Super-Ego, telling me to run, any direction was good. I mercilessly throttled that urge. I needed to think clearly, otherwise I could really be in trouble.

Unable to continue walking, I began crawling through a seemingly endless tangle of lantana and dead trees with bony fingers poised to scratch, stab and poke. I hadn't been this badly lost before, even on Big Smoky. My only guide was the position of the sun and the faint sound of the ocean off to my left. I checked my phone, but the reception bars were non-existent.

Watch your ass.

This was in the running for being the worst place imaginable when there was a bushfire about. No avenue for quick escape, no idea where the fire was, no means of communication. I became aware there was no birdsong, no sounds of animals scurrying through the undergrowth, no crickets or cicadas singing. Ash was still falling like malignant snow, coating everything.

I decided to get to the highest ground possible, where the vegetation was likely to be thinner as the soil got poorer. I would have the added advantage of being able to see possible routes to the next beach, as well as where the fire may be in relation to me. What I was lacking was information, and elevation would give it to me.

* * *

By two o'clock I'd reached the high ground. Standing on an enormous granite boulder, and I could see a glimpse of white sand far below through the screen of trees. According to the map it was Boomerang Beach, and it looked truly fabulous after the last couple of hours.

Of the bushfire I could see no sign, other than the pall of smoke in every direction. Even so, I wanted to get down to the ocean, where nature's giant water bucket provided a haven if the fire made it to the coast. I set off rapidly down the hill, climbing over rocks and tangled deadfall, plunging several feet at once.

In my haste, however, I abandoned caution.

My foot came down heavily on a thick log that had rotted through. It collapsed under my weight, sending me tumbling forwards and downwards at a considerable speed. The weight of the packstool only added to my acceleration. The vegetation on the slope looked dense because it was in actuality the canopy of trees growing much further down the hill, and the ground disappeared completely beneath me. Suddenly in free fall, I hurled the guitar away from my body, not wanting to have it broken by my body when I landed.

I went through the canopy and had the shirt torn from my waist in an instant. The slope of the ground ameliorated my landing, and I managed to avoid breaking my leg or snapping my ankle upon impact. Still rolling at speed, however, the world was a greenish-brown blur and I couldn't get my breath or bearings.

A tree trunk abruptly halted my wild descent, and I heard something in my back crack. I lay very still for a moment, sending out mental telegrams to all the parts of my body, wanting damage reports.

My upper body was scratched and bleeding from the branches and rocks, and my legs felt bruised from the impact after the fall. My head was fine, as were my hands, as vital a component of this tour as my feet. Badly winded, I could only take in air in tiny sips.

I couldn't feel any pain, but I couldn't forget hearing that crack. My fear of paralysis since the car crash has never really left me. I moved slightly, trying to gauge if I had done some deeper damage. I felt the packstool, still in place on my back, the jury-rigged strap broken. It had probably cushioned the impact, but still …

Pulling the pack around in front of me, I reached in and happened upon the familiar shape of the empty peanut butter jar I'd been carrying since Hat Head … now cracked down the middle, instead of me. My old friend had come out of retirement to take the bullet, or tree, intended for me.

Standing up shakily and taking a few steps as a test run, I realised I'd just plummeted down a headland and escaped serious injury. Unable to believe my luck, I retrieved the guitar and set off, convinced I'd come as close to disaster as was possible on this journey.

**

Bluey's Beach convinced me I'd been wrong and left me suspecting there's only so many headlands upon which one can try to kill oneself on before one succeeds. The quickest inland route to Seal Rocks was a twenty-kilometre trek along the Lakes Way via the unfortunately named village of Bungwahl.[15] This was the road Myles had told me was cut, however. With no way of knowing if it had been reopened, I followed the road into the smoky woods, the skin of a diamond python now flapping from my Akubra.

Night came down hard as it does on the deep forest roads. The constant taste of smoke coating my mouth made me incurably thirsty, and by six o'clock I was out of water. Every so often fire trucks passed me on their way south-west, but I was unsure if this was a good sign or not. The smoke was definitely getting thicker the further I walked into the Wallingat Forest, and I kept second-guessing myself, wondering if I was making a colossal mistake.

It had been a day of mistakes, really, ever since I had happened to look up and see the antediluvian penises and shrivelled buttocks of my counterparts on Shelly Beach. Mistake #2 had been getting lost on the subsequent headland, compounded by tumbling down the other side and losing my shirt in the uppermost branches of a tree. Mistake #3 had been the fiasco south of Bluey's Beach where I had just about succeeded in imitating the cow for which the place was named. Was this the final, supreme mistake that would categorically and forever thrust me into the company of such illustrious catastrophes as Burke and Wills, the Donner party, and Operation Market Garden?

I was about to get my answer.

Out of the haze a pair of sawhorses across the road appeared, accompanied by a flashing light attached to a small generator and a small blocky man in a yellow fire fighter's suit. He looked surreal standing out here in the middle of the woods, his blackened face made demonic by the pulsing orange light.

---

15 Bungwahl's claim to fame is that it is the Choko Capital of Australia. Why this is a source of pride—so much so that there is a sign on the outskirts of town that proclaims it—is an enduring and endearing mystery, the choko being a ghastly, irredeemable vegetable.

I can only guess at what he must have thought of me.

'G'day,' I said, as though we were bumping into each other at the pub.

'Where're you headed, mate?' he said, clearly not in the mood for pleasantries.

'Right. Ah, Seal Rocks?'

'*Seal Rocks*? That's miles away! Where'd you come from?'

'Today? The Ruins. You know, up in Booti–'

'I know where the bloody Ruins are, mate. What the fuck're you doin out here in the middle of the bloody night, is what I'm sayin.'

'Ah, well. On my way to Seal Rocks, you know ...'

'You do realise there's a bit of a bushfire goin on, don't you?' he said.

'Either that or someone fired up a monster doob,' I said before thinking. The guy just shook his head as though he had expected just this sort of inanity from a longhair out for a nighttime stroll to Seal Rocks in the middle of a bushfire. In an attempt to appear somewhat more intelligent, I said, 'Is the road open?'

'Yeah, but only just. Few spot fires still goin, but the main problem's the smoke. Can't see shit, stinks to buggery and I'm coughin up a bloody lung. I'm tellin you, mate, turn around and come back in a day or two when she's cleared a bit.'

'Cheers, but I think I'll keep going all the same. Thanks though.'

He shook his head as though I was mad, but said no more. I assumed he was going to get a lift, since I couldn't see any vehicles. As it turns out, so was I.

* * *

'You should come to the dance, we need some fresh meat on the floor, believe me. Especially with this fire ... everyone's staying in.' The woman changed gears and slowed down, pulling onto the dirt shoulder. She turned in her seat and faced me, and said, 'Are you sure you won't change your mind?'

'I'm sure, but thanks anyway.'

'Well, if you *do* change your mind, you know where to find us,' she said, indicating with her head the tiny town hall across the road. 'Sorry

I can't take you any further, but there's a campground a little bit further up the road ... Neranie, I think. You'll be able to camp there.'

'Thank you so much, Lisa, and all the best for the dance.'

'Meh. Slim pickings for a young looker like me,' she said, laughing.

Lisa was a banker on her way to a B&S Ball being held in Bungwahl's minuscule town hall. She was country-pretty, and entirely un-spinsterish to my mind. That there was a shortage of eligible bachelors in the region had constituted most of the conversation during the three-kilometre lift she had given me.

I'd been thankful she stopped; I was beginning to think I'd have to spend the night on the muddy banks of Smiths Lake. The smallest of the three Great Lakes, it was still, smooth and gorgeous in the smoky night, but completely infested with mosquitoes.

I hoped Neranie was more hospitable, assuming I could find it in the darkness. I set off just as the town hall's jukebox shattered the silence with Chuck Berry's signature riff filling the smoky air, a surreal soundtrack to complete a surreal day.

An hour later I was bedding down on a picnic table on the northern bank of Myall Lake. Completely blanketed in smoke, Neranie was deserted, the campers having no doubt fled when the fire rampaged through the area.

It was bitterly cold, and I had no sand in which to burrow to get warm. Struggling into the sleeping bag, I lay down unhappily on the hard wooden beams of the picnic table and tried to sleep.

As exhausted as I was, it took a long time to doze off; when I did, my sleep was plagued with dreams involving fire, snakes, and disembodied genitals. It was during a dream in which I was being chased by all three that I actually rolled off the table, thumping onto the wooden bench seat, then onto the concrete slab the whole thing was built upon, thus completing my third, and final, fall for the day.

Chapter Nine: Jawbone Night

DAY 39

The Neranie morning was still, the world seemingly holding its breath. My back ached terribly: from the falls, from the cold, from trying to sleep on a dozen thin wooden rails that constituted the table. I'd given up on sleep hours ago and been waiting for dawn.

But when dawn came, it was as I imagine it must be on Venus. There was smoke everywhere. Adding to the fugue was a mist rolling in from the northern reaches of Myall Lake, whose waters were so still they didn't even lap at the bank. There was absolute silence, all the insects and birds having fled before the fire.

Over this alien tableau a thin disk presided, watery and strengthless. It took a few moments for me to realise that it was the sun; every so often thicker membranes of smoke would overwhelm it entirely before allowing it to reappear like a timid observer. The day pulsed with light like an organic thing, enhancing the Venusian feel of the place.

Then, rising out of the grey mausoleum of the morning came the laughter of a kookaburra, and the spell was broken.

* * *

On the outskirts of Seal Rocks I met Greg. His four-wheel-drive, mud-spattered and of indeterminate age, pulled over onto the gravelly shoulder. He waved me over, and I chuckled at the idea of getting a two hundred-metre lift into town. It seemed pointless, but I was always keen to meet new people, so I got in.

Dressed in flannelette, gumboots and a knitted beanie like those worn by the fishermen I had avoided way back in Pottsville, Greg had been working even on a Saturday morning such as this. I had a fleeting moment where I feared we would have nothing in common, coming from such disparate walks of life as we clearly did. I needn't have worried. I discovered that here was a man in dire need of company; once he started, he simply wouldn't stop.

He told me he'd been fishing here for so long he remembered when there had been seals at Seal Rocks. They had pretty much fled back in the '60s and these days the town was a popular holiday destination in a reasonably unpopulated region.

Greg wasn't the attraction, however. In fact, Greg was pretty rank, truth be told. I don't mind the smell of fish, but it was so ingrained in his truck, and him, that it was a physical presence.

Fortunately, the trip into town was brief.

*Un*fortunately, Greg was in no hurry to go anywhere or do anything in particular once we got there, and held me in his rancid truck with the sheer force of his relentless conversation.

'So anyway, where you headed, because there's plenty to do around here, course there is, plenty to do, oh yessir, my word, do you like fishing, course you do, everybody likes fishing, there's a great spot just off Sugarloaf Point, that's the other side of the headland here, see, and last night I picked up a run of trevally, bream, whiting, you name it, but you knew that anyway, didn't you, that's why you're here after all, and are you hungry cos we could grab a bite to eat at the café, they make a fabulous egg and bacon roll, my shout, whaddaya say, and orange juice, gotta have some of the OJ, the old Vitamin C, the old ascorbic acid, my word yes, and ... hey, where are you going—'

'Ah, just thought I'd get out and stretch my legs, Greg, you know, stretch the old hammies ...' I was grinning, but getting out of the pungent cab and backing away, yessir, my word, I was getting out of the truck and eyeing escape routes as I did.

'—oh yeah you gotta keep limber, gotta stay in shape especially on the road as you are and on the cold mornings even more so, my word, but it's lovely autumn weather isn't it, blue sky and crisp with the southerly and a good day for fishing, trevally are on the run, whiting too, can't forget them, my word no, and I've got just the thing to catch them, just the thing, pipis don't you know, pipis are the thing, just the thing to get a tasty snapper on your hook, got bags of em, I do, all the pipis you could ever want and they make a bloody good feed in their own right and, hang on, where are you going?'

'Just thought I'd ...'

Oh God, I've got no adequate excuse, how the fuck am I going to get away?

'... go to the toilets!'

Allmon, you are a genius.

'Oh. Well, there's a couple of toilets, I mean to say, there's two, no, three—'

'Which one is closest?' I interjected, rapidly reaching the end of my tether with Greg's inexhaustible speed rap.

'That'd be the café,' he said, subdued.

I felt like I had kicked a puppy.

'Cheers. Listen, Greg, I'm gonna have to hit the road, and I wanted to thank you for the ride and the ... conversation.'

He looked absurdly touched, and a tender-hearted part of me wanted to stick around, listen to his insane chatter—he was so clearly lonely and in need of a companion. I felt for him in his earnest madness.

Sadly for Greg, that part was ruthlessly overwhelmed by my desire to escape.

'Oh well, sure, I understand, Smokey, I understand, gotta keep on truckin, keep on the move, make hay while the sun shines, never put off till tomorrow what you can do today, as you sow, so shall you reap, give a man some fish and he'll—'

'*Greg!* I've got to go, I'm sorry,' I said, and turned and ran for it.

I crashed through the café door and looked around for a place to hide, resisting the urge to cry out '*SANCTUARY!*'

A few customers looked at me strangely. I didn't care. I'd spend the whole day in here copping strange looks if it meant waiting until Greg had gone, yessir, my word, you better fucking believe it. Crouching behind the magazine racks, I risked a look out the salt-encrusted window to see whether I had been followed.

There he was!

Standing by the truck, hailing another local. The local put his head down and pretended not to hear, quickening his pace until he was in the clear. I sympathised.

Greg seemed not to notice, and smiled and waved at a tourist couple that had just left the café in which I was presently cowering. The tourists just looked blankly at him and got into their sedan without responding to his greeting. He looked crestfallen and started rooting around in the back of his truck.

I felt sorry for him all over again. He was just being friendly after all.

I had to stop looking at him, otherwise I was going to go out there and strike up a one-sided conversation out of pity. To distract myself, I decided to pick up some food for the fifty-kilometre beach trek that lay between here and the next town, Hawk's Nest.

After a cursory glance, it was clear that in Seal Rocks the spirit of mercantile competition is well and truly dead. As the only store in town or for miles around, they were free to charge what they liked. Parting with five dollars—twenty-five per cent of my funds—for a small jar of peanut butter that normally retails for a buck and half was hard, but without it I would have nothing but three muesli bars to eat for two days.

I took the clerk's ill-mannered attitude with as good grace as I could muster, but her rudeness when compared to Greg's annoying but helpful nature was stark, and made me feel even worse about ditching him. When she simply dropped my change onto the counter and left me to scrabble for it, I decided I'd rather risk it outside with Greg than spend a minute longer accepting their protection, and stalked out through the door.

As I did, I turned and saw Greg spring up from the seat that sat against the café wall where he'd been waiting for me.

'Smokey, jeez, I thought I'd lost you, yessir, couldn't let you go, *couldn't* let you go—'

'Hi Greg, listen, I appreciate the ride and all, but I've got to get moving if I'm going to get to Mungo Brush by tonight, so—'

'She's right mate, I know, my word, don't I know, all good things must come to an end, but before I let you go, cos I couldn't let you go, could I, not without giving you something I know you'll need, blow me down, you'll bloody love this, when I saw you I thought "now here's a bloke that'll *really* understand the value in this," and here it is, Smokey, a bag of pipis, all yours, all yours, my word, all yours.'

And he held out a plastic shopping bag that bulged with pipis, dozens of egg-sized molluscs that I could smell even at this distance. I numbly watched as I reached out an arm, looked on in silent amazement as the hand attached to it grasped this dubious offering, listened with disbelieving ears as I thanked Greg for them.

'Nah, she's right mate, she's right, and they'll cook up nicely, they will, cook up a treat, but make sure you rinse them in fresh water first, my word yes, or you could fish with them, and did you know your rod was broken? I can fix that for you, if you like, in fact, have one of mine! Yeah! Come on over to the—'

'*Greg!*' I snapped, feeling mildly ridiculous standing there with a guitar in one hand and a bag of bivalves in the other.

'Yeah?' he said, looking immediately contrite. It was as though some part of his brain knew he was blathering on, was wishing he could shut up but was helpless to stop.

'Thanks mate, I appreciate it,' I continued in a softer tone. He wasn't a bad guy at all, and generous to a fault.

'Oh mate, it's the least I could do, the least, it's nothing, not compared to what you're doing, what you're doing for all of us,' he said, and I wondered just what it was he thought I *was* doing. From what he'd just said, it sounded as though I was walking for world peace or the rights of oppressed peoples everywhere instead of promoting a bizarre album that owed much to black coffee and insomnia.

'Yes, well. When I'm tucking into these babies tonight, Greg, I'll have a few for you.'

He smiled, and we shook hands. He walked back to his truck

without a word, and when he pulled away he waved at me. I raised the bag of fragrant pipis in a salute.

It was a nice, quiet way to part company.

* * *

As I wandered around looking for the way south I copped more suspicious glances than even I am used to. As anybody who has carried a sack of raw pipis around town will tell you, those things get heavy after twenty minutes. I didn't want to throw them into the bin, however, as this would not only be an insult to Greg's generosity, but also fly in the face of my own belief that if you kill something you better be prepared to use it or eat it. And so I carried them around like some grotesque *bonbonniere*, my arm starting to hurt.

The longer I held onto them the more worried I became. The state of New South Wales has some pretty strict laws governing the collection of pipis, and rightfully so. As such good bait—and for the Gregs of the world a delicacy too—they are in danger of being over-harvested. Therefore, one can only have so many upon one at any given time. I wanted to get out of town quickly before someone reported me to the local ranger, figuring it would be even harder to explain why I also had a snake skin on my hat and a jawbone in my pocket.

I was thirsty; the camel had been dry since Bungwahl. Ever since leaving the Ruins, I'd noticed that almost none of the parks or towns had functioning taps, which made refilling quite the dilemma. As I walked out of Seal Rocks I remembered something Greg had mentioned earlier—among a thousand other facts delivered at warp speed—about how most of the East Coast was in a drought and as such they had removed the knobs from the taps.

'I mean, take Mungo Brush, Smokey; middle of nowhere, no taps anymore and my word if you run out of water there there's all kinds of hell to pay …'

I was headed for Mungo Brush now.

There were no taps that I saw on my way around Seal Rocks, and I was damned if I was going back to the café and making another purchase. I pulled out the map and saw that there was a campground called Yagon about five kilometres south. It was huge.

'Surely they must have water,' I said, refolding the map.

Maybe this is one of those things you don't want to assume, old sock, a voice said.

'Believe me, Yagon will have water. Look at the size of it. It's there for the tourists. Tourists need water. We'll be fine.'

* * *

Yagon was bone dry.

The grass was so dry it crackled under my boots. The toilets were of the chemical variety that don't require water at all, and the rusting tank I did find echoed hollowly when I rapped my knuckles against its corrugated side. There was nobody camped here, and no sign of anyone having been here for a long time. It was a ghost campground, drying up and blowing away in the shadow of Treachery Head.

Disheartened, I sat down heavily at a picnic table. I put the pipis—wallowing in their own pestiferous miasma by now—on the table, staring at them bitterly. What good were pipis as bait when my rod was busted, and I had no water to boil them up in if I decided to eat them myself? Their odour, powerful to begin with, was rapidly approaching intolerable. I simply couldn't imagine walking for the next eight hours to Mungo Brush carrying these wretched things.

It was eleven am. I hadn't had a drink for seventeen hours and I was as parched as the grass that lay dying under my boots. The knowledge that the nearest water was an hour and a half away, back at the world's most exorbitant café, only made me thirstier.

The sound of a car approaching filled the empty campground, and I turned to see an old station wagon piloted by an equally old guy pull up right beside me.

He had a fishing hat on.

Great. Another fisherman. What's this one going to offer me, a garbage bag full of seaweed?

'G'day,' I said warily.

'Hi. Nice day, huh?'

'Yeah. Going fishing?' I said, relaxing a little. He seemed normal.

'Uh-huh. Since I retired I find I have so much free time, it helps to fill the hours. You?' he said as he lifted up the back door to his car and started pulling out rods and buckets.

'I'm heading for Mungo Brush.'

'On foot?'

'Yeah.'

'Long walk.'

I watched as he pulled out a two-litre water bottle and unscrewed the cap. My mouth fell open like a rusty drawbridge with a creak and a puff of dust. I could see the heat had caused tiny beads of moisture to gather on its sides like perspiration, and I wanted to lick them off.

He noticed me looking and paused before taking a drink.

'Ah, do you need a drink?'

I licked my lips and nodded. I couldn't speak.

'Here you go,' he said, holding the bottle out to me. I took it from him with thanks. I took a tiny sip, trying to be restrained.

'I've got four of these things, you know.'

I took a bigger sip.

'I always bring a few extra just in case I end up spending the night. My wife died a few years ago. Not much point in going home if the fish are biting, you know.'

'Oh hey, I'm sorry.'

He waved this away. 'Do you want to take the bottle with you?'

Two litres would be ample for me to walk the twenty-five kilometres to Mungo Brush. Five and a half weeks on the road had taught me that much, at least.

'I'd love that. But are you sure?'

He waved this away, too.[16] I sat there, sipping and nibbling at a muesli bar as he got the rest of his stuff unloaded. He had two big surf rods, two buckets, a folding chair, a blanket, and a tackle box.

Something was missing though, and I thought I knew what it was.

'What do you use for bait?' I asked.

---

16 One universal characteristic of the people who helped me along the way was their embarrassment at being thanked.

'Oh, pipis mainly. Bloodworm if I can get it, but pipis are best.' He chuckled. 'Half my day is spent digging in the sand for the buggers.'

Unbelievable, I marvelled.

'Is that so? Well, you'll never believe this, but ah, I've got a whole bag of pipis here, fresh, and I'd like you to have them.'

'Eh?'

'See?' I said, holding up the grocery bag. 'I'm not going to need them, but I don't want them to go to waste. I'd like you to have them. As thanks for the water.'

To his credit he didn't ask why I was out here in the middle of nowhere with no water but a hundred pipis in a bag, simply taking them with thanks.

We both saddled up and made our way to the beach.

'Well, all the best, son. A word of advice, if you don't mind taking advice from an old bugger like me.'

'Not at all.'

'Get to Big Gibber before the tide turns. If you don't, you'll be stuck for the best part of the night on the north side. I'm no expert, but in soft sand and with all that stuff with you, you're going to have to hustle.'

'Cheers. I'll punch it, don't worry.'

We shook hands and went our separate ways. I hadn't gotten far before I heard him whistle. I turned around and saw him standing on the top of the dune.

'Watch out for dingoes …'

I waved my acknowledgment; he waved back and resumed walking toward Treachery Head. I turned south, looking at the golden crescent stretching ahead to the very limit of my vision.

Dingoes? a voice asked, sounding apprehensive.

'Hey, I'm just glad we're shot of those fucking pipis,' I replied, walking on.

DAY 39/40

They came for me after the moon rose.

They had been following me since the sun set, but the darkness this far from any major town was total, and they had remained mostly hidden.

Mostly.

One pair of glowing green eyes, joined by another, then another. There were always at least three, sometimes as many as five or six. In this fashion we walked for about five kilometres.

Then, at around nine o'clock, the moon sailed up from behind the clouds. As the beach was washed white by the moonlight they slunk forward, dark shadows cut from the night. They made no sound as they came.

Their heads bobbed up and down, as though they were all in agreement about something. I knew what they were doing—sniffing the air. Testing my scent.

Perhaps smelling my fear.

There was plenty to smell.

One dingo poses little threat to a human adult. Skittish by nature, they will rarely attack unless provoked. Children are in more danger of an attack, and the smaller the child, the greater the vulnerability. As incidents on Fraser Island and the tragic Chamberlain case of 1980 have shown, dingoes will sometimes go for babies.

But a lone dingo against a fully grown man?

Forget it.

A pack, on the other hand ...

I was tired, having negotiated miserably soft sand since Big Gibber, where I'd beaten the incoming tide only through scrambling over the huge boulders at the base of the headland. After yesterday's antics and having slept poorly the night before, I was exhausted and dehydrated despite the water I'd received in Yagon. I had no idea what a pack of dingoes—all of them fully grown too—might do if they sensed weakness in me. I had the knife on my belt and the guitar to defend myself, but neither seemed adequate when compared to the size of the dogs.

I kept walking long after I would normally bed down. Three of them were herding me against the ocean—one in front, one on my right, and one behind me. With the ocean on my left I was surrounded.

We kept moving in this fashion for half an hour before I stopped, curious to see what happened. They stopped too, each about twenty feet away. The one in front of me was grinning, and I could see the white flash of its lower canines in the moonlight. My heart started beating faster, and in my over-tired state I fancied they could hear it pumping hot salty blood through my soft body.

I sensed movement out of the corner of my eye and spun around to catch the rearward dingo creeping in closer. It slunk down and backed away ... but not too far. I got the impression they were growing less afraid of me, and wondered what would happen when curiosity outweighed caution, appetite overcame apprehension.

I reached into the pocket of the packstool and pulled out the torch. I shone it on the nearest one. Its eyes flashed green as it straightened up, and its fur went from a silvery no-colour to the familiar dusty tan shade. The light didn't seem to scare them at all, only made their eyes do that creepy reflective thing that conjured up memories of old Hammer films or vile fiends from early *X Files* episodes. I switched it off and stowed it back in the pack.

Feeling that the packstool might be a hindrance should I need to fight or flee, I unshouldered it and knelt down to put it on the sand. As soon as I knelt they came forward with more confidence, and I hurriedly stood up again. They didn't back off this time, however, and I raised the guitar up like an executioner's axe.

'*Har!*' I yelled, and they scurried backwards, lingering just outside swinging distance, grinning and bobbing. I held the guitar by the neck in one hand and drew the knife with the other. Feeling only marginally better, I pivoted slowly, trying to keep all of them in view.

Looking beyond them, I couldn't see a single light in any direction. Mungo Brush was just a campsite in the middle of nothing. As with the predicament on the headland at Bluey's Beach the previous afternoon, I was a long way from help if things went wrong. To make things worse, I could see more shapes coming over the dunes, dingoes from the forested swamp country that lay to the west.

The fear was on me now.

One darted in and I turned and swung the guitar.

'*HAR!*' I yelled, the sound of panic just under the surface. I was getting closer to the edge now, and every minute the pressure and fear built within me.

I stomped my feet in the sand and made as if to charge them. Each time I did this I would growl and shout at them. At first they retreated a bit further, unsure of what I was capable of. But they quickly realised I was all bark and no bite and resumed their advance, always keeping me pinned against the sea.

I knew I could retreat into the surf if it came down to it, but how far out would I have to go, and how long would I be forced to stay there? There had been a strong rip running this afternoon, and there were deep trenches out there, too. I could easily be exchanging one life-threatening situation for another. I didn't want to retreat into the sea unless there was no alternative.

Emboldened, they advanced in unison, and I had to do something—the guitar was hollow and the knife short and rusty. Without thinking I put them down and reached into my back pocket, pulling out the jawbone I had found all those weeks ago in the Sandon Golgotha, and a peculiar thing happened.

The hot, panicked congestion in my mind disappeared; it felt right in my hand.

I stood still and held it out so the dingoes could see it. One by one they stopped moving about and stood as still as I. It was in this tableau that we stood, frozen in the light of the rising moon, black shapes on the white sand. The dingoes grinned at me, but I no longer feared that grin. The jawbone grinned too, its time come round at last, the reason I had carried it over all the miles and weeks now revealed, and I grinned as well, for it was meet. The teeth bit into my palm, but the pain was good. I no longer felt afraid.

I sat down in their midst, and more came forward to see, to smell, and to know I was not afraid. I was in some other place, beyond Di, beyond everything I'd known. Somewhere old, ancient, somewhere that intellect and rational thought had no place, where all that remained was instinct and intuition.

One by one the dingoes bobbed heads in acknowledgment and disappeared, off to scavenge the refuse left by the day's fishermen that had drawn them out of their forest haunts in the first place. The original three dingoes sat down on the sand, as though waiting for me to get up and moving again.

'Forget it, fellas. I'm done for the day.'

They sat and looked at me expectantly.

'I don't know where Mungo Brush is, I should have hit it ages ago. I'm gonna rest here for awhile.'

One of them cocked his head.

'Go on. Join your buddies—we've got no issue with each other.'

The largest one shifted and scratched the back of its ear, the action of an animal with no particular place to be.

'All right, all right, I'm getting up. See?' I saddled up, and my new companions stood and backed away. One yawned, and I could see the big canines quite clearly in the moonlight. I tightened my grip on the jawbone; these were still wild animals. Accustomed to humans, maybe, but by no means domesticated or tame. And with the biggest the size of an Alsatian, I could not afford to forget that.

We set off at a slow pace. I was now coping with spent adrenalin on top of a long day's walking. The sand was as soft as meringue and churned up by the four-wheel-drive tyre tracks of the same fishermen who had drawn the dingoes with their refuse.

We passed other members of the pack feeding on dead fish and with their snouts in plastic bags, but my three did not join in or stop to feed. If one fell too far behind me, it would trot to catch up.

After twenty minutes, I realised I was being herded away from the water and towards the dunes. I went with it, although I felt uneasy at the idea of not having the sea as an option of retreat in case my buddies descended on me.

Suddenly they stopped, and I stopped too.

I reached around and, without releasing my grip on the bone, pulled the torch out again. Flicking it on, I swung the beam around to see where we were going. It seemed there was nothing but sand, until at the very end of my sweep the light from the torch reflected off something shiny. Something metal.

It was a signpost.

Hurrying forward, my companions keeping pace, I got close enough to read what it said.

Mungo Brush Campground.

I looked around at the dingoes, but now they were melting away, retreating back into the shadows of the dunes, reintegrating with the night just as I would have to somehow reintegrate with society when this was over.

Had they led me here, three dingoes?

I stood there for a moment, rubbing the jawbone with my thumb, feeling the smooth grain, the ridges of teeth, seeing in my mind's eye its perpetual grin, stark against the black night sky as I'd pointed it at the ring of teeth and green glowing eyes that had surrounded me.

My old life seemed very far away.

What was happening to me?

Who cares? Let's just get to the campground and get some water and sleep, a voice said, ragged with some emotion … fear, perhaps?

'I care,' I said. 'I … I don't feel normal anymore. How did I know that would work? The bone, I mean. Why am I even carrying a bone?'

I could hear the voice sigh, like a parent who can no longer deflect their child's questions and is forced to deal with them honestly.

Maybe there are no answers. Maybe, in the end, there's no coincidence, no fate, no reason. Maybe it's all just a bunch of stuff that happens.

'Just a bunch of stuff that happens,' I echoed numbly.

I started up the sandy trail away from this strange beach, stowing the jawbone in my back pocket as I went.

BOOK THREE
THE ROAD HOME

'The makar's wierd[17] is to be a wanderer:
The poets of mankind go through many countries,
Speak their needs, say their thanks,
Always they meet with someone, in the south lands
Or the north,
Who understands their art …'

—*Widsith*, from *The Exeter Book*, a collection of Old
English poetry compiled late 10th century.
Widsith—*far traveller*—is the name of the poet
and the poem, and is thought to be from the 7th century.

---

17 The poet/musician's fate.

Chapter Ten: Out of the Wilderness

DAY 41

I sat at a picnic table opposite the Tea Gardens pub with a tube of super glue bought at the supermarket, and was applying it liberally to every surface in the vicinity, including on occasion my boot and packstool strap, which needed it. It was a misty eight am world I inhabited, an hour before the first ferry of the day departed for Nelson Bay.

I had enough money for a ferry ticket or a cheap pair of shoes, but not both. If the super glue worked in conjunction with the rudimentary sewing job I'd done with fishing line to hold the boot together, then I would use the money on the ferry. If not, then I would buy the shoes and walk around Port Stephens, adding three days to my trip. I hated the idea of the boots not making the whole journey, but I couldn't continue barefoot or with them as they were, and I wasn't going to call off the walk this close to Sydney because of a sentimental attachment to a piece of cowhide.

I took a test walk around the little grassy park. The boot held. It wasn't as good as it had been before, but I thought it would do.

Just as I was sitting down I was hailed from behind.

'You wouldn't be Smokey, would you?'

I turned and saw a man in his forties wearing gloves and leaning on a garbage bin. The truck idling behind him was clearly the Tea Gardens garbage truck, and I assumed he was the Tea Gardens garbologist. I was surprised to be recognised this far south of Port Macquarie.

'Yeah, that's me,' I said, not sure what else to say.

'I thought it might be. Heard you on the radio a few weeks back, when you were on with Fiona. When I saw you sitting here, I did the maths in my head and figured it must be you. You're going bloody slowly though,' he added with a smile.

'Yeah, I'm pretty out of shape. I didn't know the interview had been broadcast this far south.'

'I dunno if it does, mate. I live up in Krambach, north of here. I heard you play, mate, loved the song. A little bit country, you know. I love me country. Can't wait to tell the missus I met you.'

'Oh, well, I'm glad you liked it …'

'Pete. Name's Pete,' he said, and stuck his hand out, glove and all. We both looked at it for a second, then laughed. He shook his head, embarrassed, and took it off. I shook his bare hand.

'Nice to meet you, Pete.'

'Cheers. Hey, don't go anywhere, all right? I'll be back in twenty minutes. Just got the rest of the street to do, then I'll come back and have a yarn.'

I nodded, smiling. I still hadn't gotten enough of being recognised, hadn't grown inured to the little thrill it sent through me. As I was to discover, there were other perks to being a nano-celebrity.

* * *

'Come on, Smokey, get stuck in mate, don't be shy,' Pete said, pouring me another cup of coffee from his thermos. The warmth was fabulous after the chill of the morning, and I watched as steam billowed up from the cup between my hands.

'Oh man, this is good, Pete. Just the thing.'

'No worries. Hey, are you hungry?'

'Oh, well, you know, I wouldn't say no to a …'

I trailed off, watching as Pete produced a lunch box the size of a footlocker. Out came two apples, a banana, a couple of fun-size chocolate bars, sandwiches, rolls, biscuits, more sandwiches and some cheese.

'What takes your fancy, mate? Reckon you'd go for the roll, eh? I've got a curried egg one and a ham and cheese. If you don't mind, take the curried egg. The missus always makes it for me, and I haven't got the heart to tell 'er they make me fart all day long.' We both started laughing. Then he added, 'It's pretty rough mate, when you smell worse than the garbage you're collecting.'

I unwrapped the roll. I didn't care if I farted all the way into Nelson Bay; this was food made by loving hands and smelled divine.

'Cheers, Pete,' I said, and he waved it away as if it were nothing. We ate in silence for a few minutes, and I looked at him from the corner of my eye, intrigued. It shouldn't surprise me but it constantly does. The ones with the least to give always give, and with good grace and a willing spirit.

'This is the life, eh Pete?'

'Sure is, Smokey. Tell us about your walk, mate, I'd love to hear it.'

I found I was getting sick of talking about the tour … and myself. After all that had happened, it—and I—seemed less important now, somehow. What seemed more important was getting to know this man who had just provided me with breakfast.

'Actually Pete, I'm more interested in you. Have you always lived around here?'

He looked a bit surprised at this, but shrugged and said, 'Yeah, pretty much. You know, I travelled a bit when I was younger, before getting married and all that. Have a biscuit, Smokey, they're Kingston's.'

I obliged with great and terrible reluctance.

'How long have you been married?' I said between a mouthful of chocolate and crumbs.

'Shit, I dunno,' he scratched his stubbly chin, 'must be nearly twenty years. Nicole's seventeen this year, so yeah, I'd say it's twenty. Time flies when you're having fun.'

'Where's Krambach?'

'Up in the hills north of here, past Nabiac. I love it up there, nice and mellow, you know? Not like down here. You better have that banana, mate, she's just gonna go to waste otherwise.'

I looked around the streets of Tea Gardens, skinning the banana as I did, and saw one older gent with a newspaper in his hand shuffling towards the park. Not exactly the teeming masses and clamour of industry that Pete seemed to think it was. I've been in funeral parlours with more ruckus going on.

'I remember when I saw the house, Smokey. I can remember it as though it was yesterday, although it'd have to be fifteen years ago now. I drove up past the front gate, saw the place, and the land, and I knew. I called up Sharon as soon as I got back into town and said "C'mon darl, we're moving."' He smiled at the memory of it, and I smiled too, because there are good stories out there, stories of good times that never grow old in the telling, if you're willing to listen. 'She flipped out, cos we had the mortgage and Nikki was a baby, but when she saw it she knew, too. I sold the car and worked me ass off. Took a second job, this one, and we settled on the house two weeks later.'

'What's your other job?'

'Groundskeeper over at the school. This job isn't so bad, you know. You're out and about, your own boss, no one standing over you, telling you what to do. And it meant we could have the place up in Krambach. Never going to move, Smokey, they'll have to bury me up there. Have that apple, mate, don't be shy.'

I took the apple and bit into it. It was tremendously sweet, better than the biscuit had been. Pete took the other apple and munched on it thoughtfully, drawn into talking about himself as though for the first time in a very long time.

'You know, Smokey, it may not be a glamorous life, or one you'd write a song about,' he gestured at my guitar, 'but it's a good life. Shaz and me are solid, you know. Never been interested in cheating. Nikki's a good girl, going to send her to uni next year so she can become a vet. I don't mind me job and me health's good. What more could you ask for, eh?' He turned and looked at me, wanting an answer.

'Nothing more, I'd say.'

'Too right. Have that chocky bar, Smokey, I don't want it. Too sweet for me.'

'Sweet enough already?'

'Don't I know it,' he said.

'Pete, I've eaten almost all of your food.'

'Yeah mate, don't worry abut it. You need all the help you can get.

Anyway, I'm just carrying on and I don't even know anything about you.'

'Trust me, Pete, I prefer to listen,' I said, barely able to contain my excitement at the chocolate bar. Unwrapping it, I crammed the whole thing into my mouth in one go. Pete laughed.

'So mate, how long till you get into Sydney?'

I swallowed and said, 'I don't know. A week, maybe, probably two. I've got a lot of work to do in Newcastle and the Central Coast, promotion-wise. Radio, maybe, some gigs too, if I can get 'em.'

'What about the telly?'

'Nah, I think that's a bit too much to hope for, you know.'

'I dunno mate, it'll be a pretty big achievement, walking all that way. Don't sell yourself short. A lot of people I know heard you on the wireless. Thought what you were doing sounded amazing. I can't wait to tell 'em I had brekkie with you.'

I laughed nervously, unsure as always how to take this sort of stuff. The thing was, Pete's own story sounded like the real achievement, the real deal.

'Who knows,' he was saying, 'one day you might be famous, and I'll say, "Yeah, I know 'im, bugger ate all me food in Tea Gardens one morning".'

We stood up and watched each other as we went about the routine of saddling up. There was a funny look in his eyes, until finally I smiled and said, 'What?'

'Oh, nothin mate, nothin. Just seeing you all kitted out and picturing where you've been and how far you've come, you know.' It startled me, because I'd had the same thought looking at him.

He stuck out his hand. I was very happy he'd spotted me. 'Thanks Pete,' I said as we shook hands for the second time.

'I should be thanking you, mate, for listening to me babble on.'

I wanted to say that's exactly what I was thanking him for, but I didn't, because I couldn't. Men can only talk around the edges of things. Maybe he knew, anyway. I hope so.

'Best way to start a new week,' I said instead.

He looked pleased and bid me good luck. He turned and walked back to his truck, and I turned and set off for the ferry.

***

The town of Anna Bay sat at the northernmost tip of what some call the Golden Bight and the map called Stockton Beach. Thirty-two kilometres away was Stockton itself, the northernmost suburb of Newcastle, the largest city I'd encounter other than Sydney. I had no money and very little food. It was imperative that I got there quickly, not just to replenish my dwindling resources, but also to take advantage of the Easter holiday crowds.

It was humbling to think I would make it all this way with only one radio interview and no coverage besides that. My great fear seemed to be coming true; that the whole expedition had been a bust, a waste of time. Essentially, nobody knew who I was, where I was, or why I was. But I consoled myself that the greatest chances still lay ahead: Newcastle, Erina and Sydney. I had sent my newspaper submissions. I had the names of the ABC radio producers, courtesy of Kim Honan back in Port Macquarie. All was not lost.

I passed the Anna Bay Hotel, the last bastion of civilisation before the unknown quantity of the beach. As stated, Stockton Beach goes by a few names, but the one the locals have for it is, to my mind, the most apt.

The Sahara.

It is not only long, this beach, but *wide*. It makes the peculiar little desert near Hat Head look like a child's sandbox. This is hectares upon hectares of dunes. They dwarf the observer, hurt the mind, and confound the eye. Stark angles and brutal geometry combine with the setting sun to transmogrify each pyramid of sand into two-tone temples, black and gold, sun and shadow. It is a panorama that lingers in the memory, not for its beauty, but for its strangeness. It is no surprise this is the place they used to film *Mad Max*—it is truly an apocalyptic setting.

Taking the inland route to Newcastle would take me two days. By crossing Australia's second longest beach I could be there by the following night—in time to get set up, maybe get on the radio and announce my presence before the Easter long weekend. The payoff for expedience was, of course, there would be nowhere to restock my water supply during the day.

I looked down at my road-worn camel and thought about the litre and a half of water sloshing about inside. Thought about the reserve bottle in the bottom of the pack from my friend in Yagon. Then I looked back at the blasted wasteland ahead. There was no escaping the fact that my meagre water supplies would not last the distance, especially considering the temperature was expected to be a toasty thirty degrees tomorrow.

After all this time, all I had experienced, I thought I could handle a little dehydration if it meant improving my chances of gaining an audience.

I knew what it was to suffer.

Or so I thought.

DAY 42

Midday. The sand was murderously soft. Every step I sank down past the ankle, my legs burning with lactic acid. It was hot, hotter than it had been in weeks. I tried to ration my water, but it was hard. I hadn't reckoned on sand like this—at this glacial pace the Sahara was going to be a two-day journey no matter what. I looked behind me at the headland rising above Anna Bay, still depressingly close, wondering if I should admit defeat and backtrack. Again, something inside rose up against this reasoning, and I turned back south, taking another sip of water.

I scanned the horizon, looking for the wreck of the *Sygna*, a Norwegian tanker that ran aground in 1974. I knew that the *Sygna* lay close to Stockton. Once I saw it, I would know I was within shouting distance of the end of this desert.

But there was nothing before me but sand, sea and sky.

I drained the last few drops of water and tried not to think how far I may be from the next drink.

* * *

Deeper into the wastes, and there were camels loping through baked white valleys, people riding them and pointing at me. My own camel banged against my hip, an empty husk.

Deeper still and there were ghastly tin dwellings half buried in the drifting dunes like the last pockets of post-Armageddon humanity. What manner of man lived in these forgotten husks behind the skyscraper dunes?

Deeper, always deeper, my eyes bugging in their sockets and my lips cracked, my tongue a dusty sponge left in an old cupboard, too horrid for words. My blisters burst; precious liquid seeped out of me, but the blisters wept on regardless.

Long hours passed in a grey fugue, punctuated by coughing fits, longing looks at the seawater

ah, but that truly is the fast route to madness, Allmon

and on one startling occasion the appearance of two Hornets—fighter jets out of Williamstown on a strategic bombing run that took them down to a few metres above the crashing surf like monstrous seabirds cruising for prey. I had to resist the urge to duck as they passed by with a sound like the sky being rent open.

I staggered on, pride keeping me from backtracking, keeping me from surrendering. Pride, the curse that got me into this sort of trouble and then saw me through it. I hoped.

* * *

Finally the *Sygna* appeared, glowing like scarlet fever in the twilight. It was startlingly close to shore. It had been six hours since I ran out of water. The sun set, turning the *Sygna's* rusted corpse into a blackened skeleton, something unspeakable washed ashore and already picked clean by the scavengers.

I lay down on the sand and discovered it was rock hard and wind-scoured after a day of soft, syrupy dunes. I found no comfort in the irony. I dozed off and dreamt I was wringing out clouds, drinking the cold clean water they carried.

I woke up again and again throughout the night to dry misery.

The soundtrack to the long broken night was the ocean moving through the dismembered carcass of the *Sygna*, the ghost ship, the haunted house, and it was a lonely sound; it said that nothing comes to good, that all endeavours must end this way, in hopelessness by the light of the moon.

Chapter Eleven: The Sleeping Giant

DAY 43

It was half past ten when I stopped walking and just drank in the sight of a maintained building.

I looked back at the Sahara. I had been a fool to take it on; I knew that now. It had nearly done for me, but now here I was, with a day up my sleeve to prepare for the Easter long weekend and the hordes of holidaymakers in need of entertainment.

Turning around and shielding my eyes against the morning sun, I spotted a tap sticking out of the building and found enough strength to break into a shambling run; I was going to drink until I puked.

I didn't bother with the camel pack or the little plastic water bottle that acted as my reserve. Instead, I lay down and stuck my head directly underneath the tap, and turned it on. Water sprayed out in a large bell shape, cold water hitting my face like a slap. I sucked in a shocked breath and felt the pores on my skin open up like a thousand tiny mouths, all trying to take a drink. I drank until I did, indeed, puke.

* * *

Although I managed to keep enough water down to begin the rejuvenation process, I was still weak, and wondering whether I'd done some permanent damage to my body over the last thirty-six hours. The walk into Newcastle served to distract me from this unsettling thought.

Unquestionably it was the largest city I'd seen so far, bigger even than my home on the Gold Coast. People hurried along footpaths like blood cells in a congested artery; a line of buses nose to tail disgorged still more cells, unnecessary transfusions for an already replete organism. The clamour of car horns, truck engines, and a church bell proclaiming midday with ecclesiastic abandon seemed to rush in on my wilderness mind, overwhelming me. I remembered some old Tarzan movie where they took him to London and he freaked out, his simple jungle brain obliterated by the horrors of the Victorian era.

In that instant I wanted to be back on the sand. At least there the dangers were ones I understood—thirst, hunger, survival. Here, in a city whose population was six times that of Coffs Harbour, there was a myriad of new threats I could fall prey to. I had been in the silence too long, was now a creature of open spaces and far reaches. Who was I kidding? I had no business here. A street sign proclaimed I was on Hunter Street, but I didn't feel much like a hunter ... I felt hunted, like I had with the dingoes, and the jawbone wasn't going to do me any good this time.

This is where you're going to make a name for yourself. This is what you've been working towards, isn't it? A decent sized city with enough clout to break your album nationally?

'I guess,' I said, standing by the side of the road, my pack and guitar at my feet, feeling small, insignificant. Whether I liked it or not, the truth was clear.

My time in the wilderness was over.

* * *

While I was in an Internet café getting directions to the ABC station, lunchtime had come to downtown Newcastle, and all the office workers had descended onto the street mall to compete with the bums, the buskers, the schoolkids, and the shuffling elderly for space.

Emerging from the café, a wave of intense agoraphobia threatened to drown me. I found myself holding my breath, back pressed against the door, looking for avenues of escape. There were none, just the ever-shifting, impenetrable flesh of Crowd, the great monster of the twenty-first century, and its body was a Hand, and an Eye, and a Mouth through which issued all the miserable dissonance of our age. My mind, already weakened from the trials of Stockton Beach, began to totter.

I was bumped and jostled. People were yelling, children screaming.

Buskers competed with each other in cacophonous chaos, actively pursuing passers-by that ducked and wove until they eluded them.

I shut my eyes and took a deep breath, and the rancid stink of all that humanity pressed in on me, coating my tongue, filling my nostrils. I opened my eyes and saw that no one looked at anyone else; eyes were blank, glazed, their owners caught in the headlong rush to the next thing, never happy, never still.

I should never have come here. I had been lulled by the smaller towns along the way, been lured by the bright lights of the Coal City and the jumpstart to my career that they promised.

'I've got to get out of here,' I muttered, close to panic. I pushed off into the press of bodies, no plan other than to escape. It was in this state that I stumbled—purely by accident—across the ABC station on Parry Street.

They'd been anticipating my arrival, thanks to my promotional package sent from Evans Head and a phone call from Kim in Port Macquarie. With shocking haste the Newcastle producer told me I was to be interviewed then and there.

'You mean now?'

'That's right, Smokey, just take a seat over there, someone'll be out shortly.'

I sat down, dazed, obedient.

That I had been in a solitary, desiccated fugue on Stockton Beach mere hours ago and was now about to address an audience of a hundred thousand[18] pushed new limits for the bizarre in a tour that had been overburdened with bizarre from the very beginning.

---

18 ABC1233 has approximately ten per cent market share in the million-strong Newcastle broadcast area, according to Nielsen ratings.

* * *

'All right, you ready?' the man said, hustling out through a door that I assumed led to the control booth and various recording suites. He was wearing some sort of high collared purple velveteen shirt and had a microphone in one hand, from which ran a cord to a funny-looking contraption on his back. It seemed that this was my interviewer, so I nodded, wondering where we were going to do the interview.

'Name's Maynard. You must be Smokey. Relax, Smokey, you look a bit puzzled, but trust me, this is gonna be great. I figure we'll record you in your element, that is to say, outside, where we can glory in the glorious *alfresco* world you have gloried in for the past few weeks. Come on, right this way, out the front door, that's the ticket, and we've only got about ten minutes so we've gotta get it right the first time,' he gibbered, guiding me to stand by the road outside the station.

It was a quiet time of day and the traffic was light, and I was quite taken with this unconventional concept for an interview and the obvious eccentricity of my interlocutor.

'Not that right is necessarily what we want and sometimes wrong is so much better but regardless we should get going right now and—' his voice changed ever so slightly, '—I'm here with Smokey, a lunatic troubadour who is loitering down the coast as he tours his debut album. Have you been molested in any way on your journey from Queensland, Smokey?'

'Huh? Ah, no, although there's still time, Maynard,' I said. His face brightened.

'Aha! A fellow of wit and indiscretion, I see,' he remarked joyously.

The rest of the interview was a frenetic blur. I haven't the faintest idea what he, or I, said. Then it was over and he gave me his card and bid me good luck before disappearing back into the station, leaving me standing flat-footed by the side of the road. Someone honked at me good-naturedly and yelled my name, and I snapped out of my stupor.

The only thing I was sure I'd mentioned was that I would be in town for the Easter weekend, playing in the Hunter Street Mall and on Merewether Beach. The stage was set, the audience informed—now all that remained was to put on a show.

* * *

I busked for an hour or two in the mall, gradually acclimatising myself to the crowds and the concrete environment. I had the hat upended for generous passers-by, and alternated between originals and covers. I made a few dollars and decided to spend the rest of the afternoon asking the restaurateurs and café owners if they needed any in-house entertainment over the Easter weekend.

None did. I should have recognised this as an ominous sign, but I was basking in the joy of getting recognised by those of their patrons who had heard the broadcast.

'Hey look, it's that guy walking to Sydney. *Hey Smokey*! Good luck, mate!'

'Play us a tune!'

'Welcome to Newcastle, Smokey!'

'Tell Maynard he owes me twenty bucks …'

I'd shaved and tidied myself up in the public toilets, so I don't think it was my appearance that was deterring the café owners. Furthermore, I had the copies of my album with me; it always helps to convince a potential establishment owner of your credibility if you have a semi-professional disc to hand when they ask what you can play.

Bemused, I decided to call it quits and come back tomorrow.

DAY 45

Good Friday.

Newcastle was a ghost town.

I wandered through the mall, but instead of Crowd I encountered Forsaken. Closed doors, stacks of chairs, dead neon signs and alleys innocent of cars or people. Sparrows hopped about, free to fossick without fear of feet. Pigeons bustled around self-importantly. The piercing chatter of a mynah echoed off the naked stone. A page of newspaper whispered over the pavement, sounding like the sea rushing over hot dry sand.

On the fringes, at the edge of perception, people hurried around this mercantile sepulchre like phantoms, their collars up as if to ward off a chill, even though it was a warm day. Nobody other than me ventured into the centre of the square, as if somehow sensing that if they did, the emptiness would be overwhelming, impossible to reconcile.

It has to be said, this was my most favourable impression of Newcastle to date.

This was a Newcastle I could get down with.

This was a Newcastle I could get used to.

This was a Newcastle that now held no opportunities for me.

Shit.

'Shit!' I said, looking around and really understanding what I was seeing for the first time. With a four-day weekend ahead, everyone had packed up and headed for the hills. Or—in a hideous and far more likely irony—the small beach villages I'd just left.

My biggest audience had all left before I could come onstage.

* * *

The little village of Redhead marks the extreme southern edge of Newcastle, the City That Never Woke (at least for me), and I got there just as the sun went down. I'd decided to push on to the coastal towns of Belmont, Blacksmiths and Swansea; I figured that was where most of Newcastle had gone anyway and, with the massive ABC broadcast area, were home to a large local audience.

Redhead also marked the end of the day's walk, and indeed the isolation of the tour; beyond this, it was unbroken humanity all the way to the finish line.

Nowhere was this more apparent than in the southern sky as night fell. A whitish-yellow glow suffused the sky, as though a fire of unimaginable proportion burned just over the horizon, negating the stars with its luminescence. I knew what that glow was, and what it meant.

That glow was Sydney, and it meant the end was at hand.

Chapter Twelve:
Richard and the Rising Tide

DAY 47

It had been a couple of good days. So far this tour had netted me next to no sales, but Belmont South, Blacksmiths, Swansea and Caves Beach were different, and it was in these towns that I finally cashed in on my radio appearance.

I played in parks and on the beach, met people who had either heard of me or were just keen to hang out, and quickly sold six albums for the unthinkable sum of one hundred dollars. I was flabbergasted. It had taken me forty-six days, but I was finally promoting this wretched album with a modicum of success. For the first time since Port Macquarie, I thought about the possibility of the snowball effect of national attention.

I set off from Caves Beach in high spirits, following the rocky coastline around the base of towering cliffs, about to discover that not all kinds of attention are good.

* * *

I awoke in the early hours of Monday to the sound of rustling, and my head being moved around by something other than me. I was lying on wet rock, and judging by the stars it must have been about two o'clock.

I'd reached an impassable sea canyon around sunset and, unwilling to risk backtracking to the beach in the foaming darkness, I had reluctantly spread out my sleeping bag at the rocky base of Wybung Head and lain down, using a loaf of bread in the packstool as a pillow. Figuring I would never fall asleep on this freezing rock, I had dozed off.

But now this rustling, this furtive sound was coming from near my head.

I sat up and saw a long tail poking out of the side of the packstool.

'Holy shit!' I exclaimed, and woke up properly. I realised the furtive sound was squeaking, the rustling caused by whatever was attached to the long tail protruding from my pack.

A water rat.

It sensed it had been discovered and backed out of the hole it had made for itself in the wall of my pack. The size of it was astonishing. There were breadcrumbs on its whiskers and in its greasy hair. It had been a few centimetres from my cheek as it gnawed a hole in the bag to get at the bread inside. How long had it been there? Had it touched me, pawed my face? I pawed my face now, wondering as I did what sort of diseases rats carry.

Typhus? Y. pestis? Lumbago?

I didn't know what lumbago was, but it sounded bad.

Alarmed by my movements, it bolted for the safety of the cliff face, leaving me with a ruined pack, a ruined loaf of bread, and zero chance of returning to sleep for the rest of the night.

I sat for the next few hours shivering as I watched the east, waiting for dawn and jumping any time I heard movement in the dark. Despite my certainty that sleep was out for good, I dozed off at some point, and in my dream I was lying on a giant loaf of bread, trying to get comfortable. Every time I moved the loaf squeaked.

Loaves shouldn't squeak.

I woke suddenly and to my horror the rat was back, but with a buddy this time. Scrambling to my feet, I watched in atavistic loathing as two tails wriggled and writhed out the side of my pack, looking like beheaded snakes.

I kicked the pack and first one, then the other emerged, both totally covered in breadcrumbs. It had been an orgy of bread eating in there, a midnight feast in the ever-fucking dormitory. They waddled away into the night—slowly, because they were full of Tip-Top Extra Fluffy—and I made a mental note to find a shop first thing and restock my supplies.

DAY 48

As I saddled up in the pre-dawn light, I noticed something sticking out of the cliff face that shouldn't have been there. It was an iron peg, jutting about nine inches out of the red rock at eye level. I bent in closer to inspect it, gripped it and pulled, but it was stuck fast, like Excalibur.

I craned my neck back and looked up the cliff face. It was easily fifty feet to the top. I looked around and saw nothing but boulders, and about twenty feet below, the receding tide. There was nobody around, no sign that anyone ever came here, and yet here was an iron peg, clearly driven with great force into the rock. People don't do such a thing without a good reason. Looking up again, I got my answer.

About three feet above the first peg and maybe two feet to the left, another peg poked out. Once I knew what to look for, it quickly became apparent that they went all the way up the cliff. I assumed they provided a quick way for fishermen or rescue crews to get in and out of this region rather than by taking the seaward route. If that were true, then that had to mean there was a road at the top of this cliff, and a less perilous route southwards than the way I'd come the previous afternoon—not to mention saving me hours of my least favourite pastime, backtracking.

I slung the guitar across my back, figuring it was a better bet to take up first as it was lighter and if I got into trouble wouldn't hinder movement as much as the pack. Pushing off from the ground, I swung up and grabbed the next peg, putting my right boot where my hand had been.

In this fashion I made swift progress up the cliff, making sure I didn't look down. I don't have a fear of heights as such, but the jagged rocks and pounding surf below reminded me forcibly of the fiasco at Blueys Beach.

I hoisted myself over the rocky lip and sure enough, found I was in a dirt carpark. There were no cars here at this early hour, so I felt little fear in leaving the guitar propped against the railing before climbing back down for the pack, happy to leave this region to the bread-engorged rats.

* * *

'What did you say your name was?' the man said, forking scrambled eggs into his mouth as the morning traffic cruised past. The steam from his coffee rose from the polystyrene cup, switching in the conflicting breezes that swirled around the café. We were sitting at a wooden table underneath a sun umbrella and were the only patrons at this late breakfast hour.

The town was called Lake Munmorah.

The man was called Richard.

He must have been a regular, because when he arrived the owner brought out his meal without him having to place an order. I'd already replenished my diminished bread stocks and bought one last jar of peanut butter to go with it, having thrown out the last of the muesli bars on general principles; although they looked unmolested, there was no telling what those two rats had been up to. Even though I'd already eaten, the smell of crispy bacon coming from Richard's plate was almost unbearable.

He caught me looking and invited me over. The guitar sparked the usual questions about who I was and what I was doing. He gave me some of his bacon, and I gave him a copy of the album in return.

He now turned it over, inspecting it as I swallowed the morsel of bacon.

'Ben.'

'It says here on the back that "Smokey" wrote most of the songs.'

'That's me. I'm also Smokey.'

'Any reason why you chose a pseudonym?'

'I don't know,' I said, surprised by the question. 'I thought it would be cool, you know? Give me some sort of added freedom. And I thought it was more memorable than just Ben.'

'Just Ben.'

'Yeah. But after almost two months of being Smokey, I'm pretty sick of it,' I said, astonishing myself with this unsuspected revelation. 'It's hard work being Smokey.'

'My advice is to abandon it. Go back to being "just Ben".' He waved the album around and said, 'You'll need to reprint this, as well, with your actual name on it. Pseudonyms rarely work, you know. Too often they indicate the possessor's reluctance to really own their work. It's different if you're famous, of course, but I assume you're not?'

'No.'

'No. For somebody famous it may be a desire to see whether their work is appreciated on merit rather than brand recognition, but for those just starting out, it is usually better to be yourself. Not just in music, but life in general, wouldn't you say, Ben?'

'Uh, yeah. Definitely.' Nobody had spoken to me about such a concept, or in such depth as it related to the album, as this. Most folks just asked me questions about what artists I liked and how long it took to write a song. I began to suspect that Richard might not just be some old guy with a penchant for crispy bacon.

'So what made you decide to adopt such a peculiar method of promotion?'

I thought about it for a moment. Asked so many times why I had chosen this unorthodox approach, I'd formulated several stock answers that, through repetition, were now thoughtlessly trotted out. But with Richard I felt the need to go beyond the standard answer ... maybe because I'd never really answered it to my own satisfaction.

'The initial catalyst was reading about the Great Migration, and the gleemen of the Dark Ages and the troubadours and minstrels of the Middle Ages. Also, I looked at the usual ways you'd push an album, or go on tour, and I just couldn't do it. I've played a lot of gigs in pubs and clubs and coffeehouses and outdoor venues where no one gives a toss, and you wonder why you bother. Competing with televisions blaring sport, poker machines blaring tuneless songs of false hope and drunks blaring obscenities just seems inimical to storytelling, connecting with someone in a way that seems worthwhile. I've been at it since '94, and touring that way just seemed depressing. When you play originals you get very used to seeing four people grooving along amidst a sea of backs.'

'You played no cover material?'

'In the early days. But the more originals I came up with, the more I lost the willingness to do other people's stuff.'

'It's still a handy talent to have. Part of entertaining people is to give them what they want. And what they want is something they know, something that is familiar, something they can sing along with or dance to.' He finished the last of his toast and pushed the plate away with an air of accomplishment. 'When I was younger, I could eat a plate like that and ask for seconds without breaking a sweat. These days it seems like I'm full on the smell of breakfast. That's the thing about getting older—you eat less, you sleep less, you remember less. The only thing you do more of is go to the toilet. Hell of a thing, getting old.'

'Not for the faint of heart,' I said, smiling.

'No. Now, going back to what you said about playing originals. Those are what people need. Not what they want, necessarily, but what they most definitely need.' He gestured to the empty plate. 'Sort of like eating—I don't particularly want to eat, but I know I need to. Otherwise I'd starve.'

'And eventually die,' I offered, to which he nodded.

'Precisely.'

'But what about the musician?' I said. 'Surely there must be more in it for them than simply regurgitating musical hot dog and occasionally slipping in a tasty morsel of originality?'

'Why?' he said. 'The food asks nothing more than to be consumed, to provide nourishment. Its value is inherent, and when consumed fulfils its purpose. Whether it is a hot dog or caviar, in the end it all comes to the same thing.' He frowned and took a sip of his coffee. 'But going back to what people want and need. Say that what you really want is cover songs; hot dogs, as you put it. What would happen if all you ever ate were hot dogs? Day after day, year after year, hot dogs.'

'I'd get pretty sick of hot dogs,' I said, smiling, but Richard didn't return it.

'What else?'

'I don't follow.'

'Think about what would happen to you, physically.'

'Oh. Well, I guess after a few days, maybe a week, I'd start to get sick because I wouldn't be getting all the things I need. Vitamins, you know, that kind of stuff ...'

Understanding dawned.

'Eventually, receiving nothing else, you'd die,' Richard finished for me. 'Just as surely as if you ate only caviar. Or nothing at all.'

'So what you're saying is that you need both; caviar and hot dogs, originals and covers. That by touring the way that I have—avoiding playing regular gigs and covers—I've starved myself of an audience, thereby never getting the chance to give them something they need?'

'Maybe. Or maybe the audiences you *have* had were the ones who were starved, fed a diet of your choosing. By only doing what *you* want, you're flouting the basic rule of the wandering musician, from the buskers of ancient Rome to the bluesmen who inspired you; give the people what they want.'

I didn't reply, *couldn't* reply. I'd been looking at this whole thing backwards, from the perspective of what *I* wanted, not the audience. The revelation was not an easy one to accept, but undeniable.

I remembered reading an interview with Johnny Shines, the bluesman who had been Robert Johnson's travelling partner for so long, discussing Johnson's ability to play polkas or Polish folk songs on guitar. '*Well, you had to do it ... lots of times you wake up in the morning and you didn't have no money at all. Somebody ask you to play a song, maybe they'd give you a dollar ... that meant about four meals ... and if you couldn't play that song, you miss that money. So you had to learn to play some of everything you heard.*'

What had I been doing?

We sat in silence for a while, and Richard finished his coffee.

'I think what you're doing is admirable, however. I didn't mean to diminish what you're trying to achieve.'

'No no, it's fine,' I said, suddenly depressed. 'It's just hard to accept that by not deigning to play songs people might actually want ...' I suddenly felt miserable and confused.

'Don't forget you're on tour though,' Richard said, no doubt trying to cheer me up. 'It'd be a bit strange if Sting went on tour for his latest album and played mostly Beatles songs ... how have the songs from your album been received?'

I felt my cheeks redden. I'd spent most of the time playing new songs that weren't on *The Dark Carnival*. Because that was what *I* had wanted to play. Covers? Please. Songs from the album I'm actually touring? Well, if you insist but I'd really rather just ignore that too and do what I want to do.

'Well ...' I began.

'Don't tell me. You haven't been playing them either.'

'Not exactly.'

'You do realise you're selling a product, and part of that is performing songs people can expect to hear if they buy the album. Which I presume is something you desire?'

'Well, yes.'

'I understand the desire to not confine oneself to playing the same few songs ...' he began, before I leapt to my own defence.

'Surely if a painter only ever painted ten scenes over and over again, they'd be dismissed as a hack. Or a writer, for that matter. Whoever heard of a writer writing the same book over and over again?'

'You're thinking of it the wrong way. Think of what you're doing as more like acting—an album is like a movie, performed one way and frozen forever, infinitely repeatable and always the same. Your tour is to your album what the stage is to movies. People go to the theatre to experience a unique, once-only performance, where everything is live and real and variable. But the variables exist within a framework of expectation. And the expectation is they are going to see the show advertised. Imagine going to see *King Lear* but the actors deciding they were bored with it and shifting to some unknown play one of the cast wrote that morning. Would you feel ripped off?'

I sat there silently.

Jesus, it's a wonder I'd made it this far and sold anything, I thought. Richard sat quietly, seemingly in no hurry to get to wherever he was going to spend the rest of the day.

'It's little wonder I haven't met with much success,' I said after the silence got uncomfortable. 'Hardly anyone knows I've done this. I've sold about twenty albums.' I paused, fiddling with a napkin. 'Maybe it's been a waste of time.'

'It depends on how you define success,' said Richard, and I was suddenly struck by the strangeness of it all, sitting here at a café having a deep philosophical chat with a stranger after spending the night on a wave-washed, rat-infested slab of rock and climbing a cliff face this morning to get here.

'You mentioned the Great Migration,' he was saying. 'The mistake a lot of people make is to assume the country bluesman's goal was simply to get to Chicago and make it big themselves. But the truth is, once they had recorded their works, most simply wanted to return to the Delta and the life they knew. Charley Patton, Son House … I think it was Mississippi John Hurt who said he never wanted to get away from home.'

'I didn't know that,' I said, genuinely surprised. I thought the goal of all musicians was to make it big, as it were. But then, that is what celebrity culture has conditioned me to think, and I have swallowed it with nary a hint of indigestion.

That wasn't all that surprised me. Richard's knowledge of the bluesmen was coincidental … but perhaps the voice at Mungo Brush had been right, that there *was* no such thing as coincidence.

'It was only Muddy Waters and Howlin Wolf and their ilk who possessed the ability and determination to "make it", as it were, and because of this they are the ones we know about, therefore they become the representative of the whole. The truth is, most of the bluesmen knew what they wanted, and it wasn't in the big city.'

I thought of Newcastle, of the feeling that I didn't belong, couldn't belong. There were too many people in too small an area—who in their right mind would willingly throw oneself into such a threshing maelstrom? Had it been the same for those sharecroppers and levee-workers-turned-musicians? Had they taken one look at Chicago or

New York and turned back for the Delta as fast as their legs could carry them?

And here I was, about to walk into the largest city on the continent, ten times the size of Newcastle. How on earth was I going to get heard in that seething morass? I felt a traitorous urge to avoid Sydney and its teeming millions. But that would be a terrible betrayal of everyone who had helped me get this far, as well as myself. What had I sacrificed everything for if not for that?

'I don't know what the hell I'm doing,' I said, before realising it was going to be said.

'It all depends on what you wanted to get out of it. If you wanted to be famous by the time you got to Sydney, or change the course of music and how it is performed then that's asking an awful lot. If, however, you simply wanted an adventure then surely you must be satisfied. Just by looking at you I can tell you must have had a hell of a trip.' He chuckled and shook his head and said, 'Anyone who takes such a bizarre backpack is guaranteed an interesting journey.'

'You shitting on my packstool, Richard?' I said, smiling.

'No no! Far be it for me to impugn another's …'

'Packstool.'

'Packstool. I'm fairly certain that in the Middle Ages they called such a contraption the Iron Maiden.'

We both laughed for a bit, and then my curiosity got the better of me.

'You seem to know an awful lot about music, Richard.'

He smiled enigmatically, but said nothing.

'Do you mind if I ask what you did before you retired?'

He looked down at his hands as they folded, unfolded and refolded themselves again. 'I used to be a producer,' he said at length.

'I knew it had to be something like that. Who did you produce?'

He waved his hand, unwilling to be drawn. 'A lot of people, over the years,' was all he would say. 'I'm more interested in you. You haven't answered my earlier question,' he said, shifting to look at me more directly. 'What did you want out of this?'

Why you are doing this?

'You sound like someone I know,' I said.

'Really? And what did you tell them?'

'I didn't tell them anything.'

'Don't you know?' he asked, leaning forward on his seat, intrigued.

I sat for a moment. The owner of the café came out and collected Richard's plate and cup, asked if either of us wanted anything else. Neither of us did. A couple of cars did a *pas de deux* at the nearby crossroads, and a little butcherbird hopped around in the dirt, looking for morsels. Richard sat patiently, realising perhaps that he had hit the main nerve, hooked the big one.

'I thought I did … it seemed pretty clear when I started in Pottsville: walk, play, and eventually arrive in Sydney to acclaim. I wanted to start a revolution of how we listen to live music, how musicians perform. I figured it was only a matter of time before I changed the world, but now … everything's gotten all mixed up.'

Richard sat silently, and eventually I went on.

'As the weeks passed, I realised I wasn't cut out to be a revolutionary, or famous. Maybe not even a performer.' I sighed, knowing what needed to be said, but dreading it nonetheless. 'Today I realised I was actually going to make it to Sydney, and I also realised that maybe, after twelve years, a music career isn't my thing. I've spent over a decade devoting myself to something that maybe I'm not meant to do. I've forsaken education, shunned lovers and sacrificed friendships for a dream that never came. I've spent my adult life in debt because of it. I've risked my life and my sanity out here because of it.'

I stopped; suddenly embarrassed I'd said so much. I consoled myself that I would probably never see Richard again. 'Does that answer the question?'

'Yes,' said Richard, looking at me calmly.

No, came a small voice, but I ignored it. Again.

'I'm sorry, I didn't know all that was waiting to come out,' I said, unwilling to look at him.

'That's all right,' he said, and he didn't seem embarrassed or shocked. He just went on sitting there looking at me.

'What do I do now?'

We sat silently for a few minutes, watching the cars pause at the crossroads, on their way to wherever. At length, he spoke.

'My wife died two months ago. And I asked myself the same question you just did. "What do I do now?"'

I could see that he too was deeply conflicted about whether to continue. I said nothing.

'We were married for forty-one years when the cancer got her. And ever since, I've been asking myself the same question. "What now?" "What next?" It's nice coming here every morning to read the paper over the same breakfast, because I don't have to think about what comes next.' He paused and gave me a sidelong glance. 'But I'm a little bit older than you, and I know something you may not. There's *always* something else. Even if it's death, there's always something else. So I don't worry too much, you see.'

'I'll have to take your word for it,' I said, subdued. I didn't want to contemplate a life where I no longer considered myself a musician—it was so much a part of my identity I was afraid of what I might see when it was gone. We both got up to leave.

'I have my doubts that you have spent twelve years at your craft and achieved nothing of value. Just as I doubt that you have walked all this way and not been changed by what you have seen and done. But even if that *were* the case, it does not diminish or change the fact that you have done these things. And by so doing you are one step closer to finding what it is that you are truly meant for. There will be other roads than the one you're on, Ben, ones that are better suited to the shape of your feet and measure of your gait.'

'With lines like that you should be a songwriter, Richard,' I said, to which he smiled a sunny smile, and I saw what he would have looked like when he was my age.

'Well, you pick up a phrase or two here and there when you hang around enough of them.'

'You're not going to tell me who you worked with, are you?' I said, smiling myself. He looked at me for a moment before deciding to cut me a break.

'Tell me someone you know in the industry and I'll tell you if I know them.'

I said the first name that came to mind. 'I worked with Heather Field in Nashville …' which was as far as I got before he cut me off.

'She worked with Rick Price, didn't she? And Tina Arena? Won an ARIA, I believe,' he said, looking as if he was consulting some inner library index. 'Yes, I know of Heather,' he concluded simply.

I nodded, strangely unsurprised by the coincidence—after all the coincidences along the way, what was one more? Still, I had to chuckle at the idea of sitting here with a man who knew someone I had worked with on the other side of the world six years ago. Of all the roadside bacon-and-egg joints in all the east coast I could have walked into ...

We shook hands and parted at the crossroads, Richard leaving me to wonder whether the road to Sydney was the one I wanted to take after all, now that I doubted myself.

In the end I chose Sydney, of course; I had put too much in to quit now. As I set off, however, I wondered whether Robert Plant had been right when he said there's still time to change the road you're on.

DAY 49

I checked the time; I was on air in ten minutes. I was standing outside an enormous shopping centre called Erina Fair, having a cigarette. Situated in the middle of the mall was the ABC station where Scott Levi would interview me. Called the Fishbowl, the studio walls were glass and afforded passers-by the chance to ogle the deejay and whomever they were interviewing.

About an hour ago I'd walked into a room jammed full of computers, electrical cables, and paperwork-smothered desks. A woman sat in the middle of this chaos and smiled and waved me over.

'So you're the guy who walked from Brisbane,' she said, clearing a space in the debris for me to sit.

'Pottsville,' I said, which garnered me a nonplussed look. It occurred to me that it was easier just to agree—nobody outside of Pottsville knew where Pottsville was.

'So what have you got for us today?'

'I'm happy with anything, to be honest. In Port Macquarie I did a long interview and played a live song as well as one from the album. In Newcastle it was a five-minute quickie with Maynard, then they spun a track. So anything is fine by me.'

'Okay, good. Scott got your album and read the article you sent. He's been looking forward to meeting you. We could slot you in before the news, how does that sound?'

'Suits me. I can get listeners in the mood to hear the latest disasters and government spin.'

'That's the spirit.'

I walked out with a spring in my step. For the third time I was going to be on the radio. That I now had doubts as to my *raison d'être* mattered not one whit—I was going to be on the radio playing something I created. You can't do better than that for feeling good, unless it's checking your phone messages to discover a journalist from *The Manly Daily* has tried to reach you and says she'll be calling back to interview you for a feature piece in the Sydney newspaper. Perhaps Robert Plant had been onto something after all; the road I was on was changing, and, finally, for the better.

The phone rang.

'Hi, this is Lisa from the *Manly Daily*. Do I have the pleasure of speaking with Smokey?'

'You do, but please call me Ben,' I replied, feeling a mixture of pleasure and panic. Pleasure at the idea I was going to have another iron in the promotional fire after this conversation, panic because I was due on the air in five minutes. When this woman had said she was going to call back and do an interview, I hadn't anticipated it to be immediately. I was now in the uncomfortable position of doing a very important interview at exactly the same time as I was due for another very important interview.

I thought of the last forty-eight days where I would have done anything to get the phone ringing, the endless hours where it had sat mute in my pocket, all the time I'd spent talking to myself when I could have been talking to others.

And now it was happening all at once.

'I assume you were expecting my call,' Lisa said, perhaps detecting an odd note in my voice.

'Yes,' I said, looking at the time. Four minutes, forty-nine seconds.

'Excellent. Okay, let's get started. What was it that drove an ordinary young musician to such extraordinary lengths to promote his album …'

* * *

'... and the crack I heard wasn't my back at all, but the peanut butter jar,' I said, checking the time yet again—I only had a couple of minutes at most, but I forced myself to concentrate on Lisa and make sure I gave her intelligible answers.

'Wait a minute. You broke your back? When? Were you paralysed?'

'Yes, back in '95, I was few millimetres from being a paraplegic—' I began, but she cut me off in an excited voice.

'Do you think that's the reason you've toured in this way? To prove to yourself that you can do it ... or a celebration of the fact that you *can* still do it?'

The thought had never occurred to me, and although it sounded nice and psychologically satisfying, it wasn't true.

'No ...'

'Do you know anyone else who has done something like this?'

'Well, a lot of musicians went for long walks besides the American bluesmen—Syd Barrett of Pink Floyd literally walked away from the London music scene in 1978—eighty kilometres, all the way to Cambridge and a quiet life of art and gardening.'

'How do you feel now that you've almost made it?'

I'd been thinking about this a lot since Richard, and despite the dwindling sand left in the hourglass before going on air, I decided to try to put it into words.

'Goals are funny things—they only work when you're far away from them. As you get close to realising them, they become strangely unsatisfying, relics of a more naïve you—they are one-dimensional in a three-dimensional life. I want to be thin, I want to be Prime Minister, I want to quit smoking. The day you quit smoking is a good day for sure—but it is the first in a long line of cigarette-less days. And you have to populate those days with things and events and ongoing maintenance routines like not smoking. The point is, until you die there is never a moment like in the movies where your life pauses when it's in great shape, riding a tandem bike with the love of your life outside your dream home as something suitably triumphant plays from some unseen source. It would be nice, but it isn't life.'

I paused, before deciding to be totally honest. 'I feel a great apathy about getting to Sydney. I simply want to either keep walking, or turn around and walk back, see who I meet *this* time, see what crazy things happen. A life in motion. All of our songs and movies and books and myths are about freezing that motion at the best possible frame. And the mistake is to chase *that* moment, forgetting that the chase is the *whole* story.'

'But of course, without the promise of that moment, many of us would never chase to begin with,' Lisa replied. 'Interesting, Ben, but a wee bit philosophical for a daily paper, I think,' she said, and I could hear the smile in her voice. 'So, last question: what day do you expect to make it to Sydney?'

'I hadn't really pinpointed it to a day. Does it matter?'

'Well, yes. I mean, not just for you and your fans, but also for us. We want to make sure we're running the story on the right day.'

'Oh, I see, that *is* important. Um, okay …' I hurriedly tried to compose my thoughts, conscious of the fact that in about twenty seconds I was going to have to sprint to get to the Fishbowl in time to go on air.[19]

'Today's Tuesday,' Lisa said helpfully.

'Yes, thank you. Okay, why don't we say Friday?'

'Thursday's better.'

'Thursday it is, then,' I said, picturing Levi sitting there in silence, fashioning a voodoo doll that sported a tiny black hat. 'Thanks Lisa, this was great, you were great, we'll have to meet up when I get there okayseeyoubye …'

* * *

'Scott's introducing you now!' Kelly practically shrieked. Scott was looking around with that look you get when your ass is out in the wind and you're waiting for a tailor. 'Go! Quick, get in there. Quick!' she yelled, opening the door and shoving me—packstool and all—inside.

Too late I realised I'd left the guitar in the other room.

---

19 The trick to being a successful independent amateur is being professional, funnily enough, and missing a slot reserved for you is not the way to spread the good word amongst station producers.

***

'I have with me a young man who has been walking for the last seven weeks from Queensland to promote his album. Hi Smokey.'

'Hi Scott. And please, call me Ben.'

'Well Ben, I can believe you've been on the road for seven weeks just by looking at you. For those of you not pressed up against the Fishbowl, you'll have to use your imagination, but believe me, he certainly looks every inch the wandering minstrel. Is that a snakeskin on your hat? And a bone poking out of your back pocket?'

'Well, it's a long story …'

***

'… and led me up the path to the Mungo Brush campground. I spent the night sleeping on the barbecue hotplates. Dingoes patrolled the picnic area all night, so I didn't feel safe sleeping on the ground. By two am it was getting cold, so I'd turn the hotplates on for a bit and then … well, sit on them to warm up.'

'Not really the approved use of campground barbecues, Ben.'

I smiled and fondled the jawbone and remembered that strange night, the aura of otherworldliness that had dominated the midnight sands of Mungo Brush.

When Scott had seen I'd not brought the guitar, he'd quickly thought to ask me to go through my bag, telling the story of the items therein. People outside pressed up against the glass to see such treasures as my one remaining sock, an empty jar of peanut butter—and damn if I hadn't gotten teary just looking at it—and the snakeskin from the cliff face at Blueys Beach.

'It seems we have a caller. Go ahead, please.'

'Yeah, g'day Scott,' came a roughened voice of a man in late middle age. 'Well, I've fished up around Mungo Brush, and I think I can dispel some of the more supernatural elements to your experience, Smokey. The dingoes are very accustomed to people, getting fed and even harassing fishermen. You said you had a bag of pipis on you that morning … they probably smelled it on you and thought you were packing.'

'Yes, I've fished up that way myself, and that makes sense,' Scott said. I sat there, beginning to feel mildly ridiculous I'd ascribed such paranormal overtones to the event.

'Yeah, and the other thing is, they respond to dominance. Smokey said when they were circling him he got panicky and whatnot, but when he grabbed his bone—'

'Not what it sounds like, folks,' Scott interjected.

'—yeah, so when he grabbed it he felt calm, and that woulda calmed the dogs down too. Nothing much more to it than that, I'm afraid. Sorry for ruining the mystique, Smokey.'

'No, that's okay, it all makes sense,' I mumbled, and thanked the caller.

'Still, an encounter with a pack of dingoes has got to be a bit unnerving,' Scott said, perhaps noting my chagrin. I was struck by how easy it is to slip into mythologising our lives, how we construct elaborate explanations for the smell of rotting fish.

Scott was talking to me again, and I snapped back to the moment.

'Ben, we've covered the survival aspect of your tour, but what about the music? How has it been received? Are you making any money?'

'If anything I'm going backwards, financially speaking. As for the reception, I don't think people expect a vagrant to start introducing songs from his latest album,' I said, remembering Coffs Harbour and the marked lack of success I'd had there. 'Actually, I think most passers-by think I'm a bit crazy.'

'Let's have a listen to one of the less crazy songs. Folks, this is "Sinner", by Ben "Smokey" Allmon, the Walking Man.' He hit a button and my song started.

He switched off our mikes and leant across the desk to address me in a more relaxed voice. 'So tell me, what's it really like?' he asked, his eyes bright and curious.

'Well, every day I wake up somewhere new,' I began, unsure which 'really' he wanted. 'Every day I can be a whole new person for a whole new set of strangers. Every day contains tiny, simple joys—the feel of the sun on your wind-cooled cheek, the sound of that same wind through the casuarinas as you doze after lunch … it's the sound of nowhere to be and no one to meet. When it's good, this life is better than anything I've found in civilisation.'

'But?'

'Being somewhere and someone new every day can be exhausting after a while. I think everybody needs to stop, even nomadic peoples. And at least they're together. With nobody to share it with, those good days I mentioned can never be truly great. Other people can be a pain, but the payoff of having them around is greater than the outlay. A thousand things I've seen and had nobody to turn to and say, "how amazing was that?"'

'Every musician needs a band?' Scott said succinctly.

I thought of Myles and how I'd forgotten just how much I missed that musical bond. I'd spent years in voluntary musical exile, from bands and labels, determined to be different, to reinvent genres with *The Dark Carnival*, to reinvent touring with a long strange walk. But all I'd managed to achieve was a weird uneven album and a deep tan. I was tired, lonely. Maybe it was time to come in from the cold.

The song ended, and he switched our mikes back on before I could answer.

'So when you get to Sydney, how are you going to define success? Certainly not in monetary terms. Survival-wise you've done okay … and you are truly the definition of the independent musician—you've recorded the album, produced it, marketed it and toured it with no—'

'—with a *lot* of help from people at home, and people along the way,' I interjected, thinking of Bill, of Crescent Head, of my family, and of Di. 'I don't think there is such a thing as a truly independent musician.'

'So how will you know if it was worth it when the usual methods of determining success are gone?'

'Maybe it really is just the act of doing it, and if you do it for the love, you've succeeded already.' I paused. 'Sounds like loser talk, doesn't it?'

Scott smiled. 'Oh, totally. But maybe you're onto something. We define things like success in such narrow terms in this era of celebrity and fame. If you don't sell a million or get into the media, you're deemed a failure. What about simply getting a record deal?'

'*Tres* disingenuous when I'm flying the DIY indie flag. Smokey Sell-Out, they'll call me.'

'Catchy name though. What about deeper personal change? That can be a form of success.'

'Maybe, but most of the time when I have a profound experience I change briefly and then change back.'

'So what do you want out of it, in the end?'

I thought for a second, trying to think of an answer.

'There's a song by Harry Connick Jr called "Booker". In it he says *"some people play for fortune or fame, some just play a part"*. I think at the start I wanted the former, and now I want the latter.'

'Thank you for sharing yourself with us, Ben, and good luck in your travels.'

* * *

'You've got to be the guy I just heard on the radio,' a lanky guy in a clean white shirt said, holding out his hand for me to shake. I was standing outside the Fishbowl, having a cigarette. 'My name is Craig. I'm a cameraman for NBN, and I just heard you being broadcast over the speakers in the food court.'

'Really? In the food court? You mean they actually broadcast the station in the mall?'

'Yeah. Why did you think all those people lined up outside? They wanted to catch a glimpse of the idiot who walked from Queensland.'

I grinned and said, 'I thought that was a bit odd, but then I am in New South Wales.'

'Get stuffed,' he shot back. 'I want to do a piece on you. I've been in touch with the office, and they seem interested but it'll be awhile before I know whether I've got the green light or not. I don't want to get your hopes up, you know, but I think a story like yours makes bloody good telly.'

'Cheers,' I said, happily stunned.

'Anyway, here's my card. What's your number so I can get in touch with you when I get an answer from the office?'

I gave it to him.

'I'd love to stay and chat, but it's my day off and I'm supposed to be looking after the kids. I left them in the food court, which means the whole place should be dismantled by the time I get back. It was great meeting you, Ben, really great, even if you are a Queenslander.'

'Thanks, Craig, likewise,' I said.

I looked down at the card in my hand, and realised I had just been given a real chance at getting on the nightly news, something I had dismissed as pie in the sky back in Port Macquarie.

Newspaper, radio and television.

Perhaps there was hope for a rambler after all.

* * *

'Hop in,' she said through the passenger window of her old Mitsubishi, and I did.

She said her name was Karen, but really, it was Temptation.

Chapter Thirteen: Temptation

DAY 49/50

She wasn't immediately striking. In her late thirties, with close-cropped brown hair framing a narrow, elfin face, she had large eyes and a slight body under a shirt and trousers. She drove well. Beyond that I didn't take in too much, only that the car sounded like it needed a service and that she was probably a teacher.

'Where are you going?' she asked as we pulled back into traffic. It was late afternoon, and I'd given up busking in the mall to give myself time to get to the coast to spend the night.

'The coast. Terrigal, I guess. But anywhere in that direction is fine. Thanks again for this,' I added.

'Normally I don't pick people up, especially men, but I saw the guitar and thought, "there's got to be a good story to that guy".' She looked across at me for the first time, and I saw she was smiling. 'Well, is there?'

I laughed shortly, embarrassed. 'Ah, I don't think there's a way to answer that without sounding conceited.'

'I won't think you're conceited,' she replied, and I realised she had an accent.

'Where are you from, if you don't mind me asking?'

'Terrigal,' she answered, not looking at me and smiling.

'No, I mean—'

'Oh, you mean originally?' she interrupted, a wide-eyed, too innocent look on her face.

'Yeah. Scotland?'

'Bite your tongue. Ireland, you silly man.' She looked at me again and rolled her eyes. 'Scotland. How dare you?'

'I'm terribly sorry, I don't know what came over me. I guess this means you're kicking me out at the next set of lights.'

'We'll see,' she said, a cryptic expression on her face. I found myself warming to her, to her sense of humour and her accent. 'You didn't answer my question. What story lies behind the man with the guitar by the side of the road? And what are you doing outside Erina Fair, for God's sake?'

'I was doing a radio interview at the ABC. I'm on tour, believe it or not.'

'Really? I never listen to the ABC, it's usually so boring. Now I wish I had.' She turned to face me while we waited for the light to change, looking at me with renewed interest. 'Are you famous? What's your name?'

'Ben,' I replied with a nonchalant air.

'Ben! Oh my God, I can't believe it! *Ben!* In my very own car.'

'I know, what are the odds?'

'Seriously, would I have heard any of your songs?'

'No.'

'None of them?'

'No.'

'Are you really bad? I mean, do people boo you when you start playing?'

'Only when I play my own stuff.'

'How terrible. Is that why you went to the ABC? They play anything, you know.'

'That's why you don't listen.'

'Exactly.'

'Would you like a copy of my album?'

'No, I really don't think so. If you were on the ABC, I don't think it's going to be my cup of tea.'

'Fair enough.'

'Are you staying in a hotel while you're on tour?'

'No, I'm sleeping on the beach.'

'Why?'

'It's cheap. No, seriously, it's actually one of the core tenets of this tour. I've walked here from Pottsville.'

'Just north of Brunswick Heads?'

'*Yes!* You know, you're the first person who's known where that is.'

'So you've been sleeping on the beach all this time? How long have you been on the road? Or should I say beach?'

'Seven weeks as of today.'

'Seven weeks?' she breathed, the quick-witted banter gone for a moment. She regarded me again, this time with something else in her eyes. 'You *do* have a good story behind you.'

I stayed silent, feeling embarrassed again.

'I live in Terrigal, you know. I can take you right up to the beach. That's where you want to go, right?'

'That would be fantastic. Is it a nice beach?'

'Beautiful,' she said, smiling.

'Good. I think this may be one of my last nights, so that's good.'

'I live two streets back from it, so I walk on it nearly every morning. You'll love it.'

'Have you always lived there?'

'No. But my daughter and I would never live anywhere else,' she said, and I automatically looked at her ring finger on her left hand when she omitted any mention of a husband.

It was bare.

'Sounds good.'

'Do you have somewhere nice to go back to after this is over?'

I thought about it for a second. No job, no home, no car, and no Di for five months (and possibly a lot longer if her career in the Bahamas took off).

'Not really. This has been the best home I've known so far.'

'The beach?'

'Yeah. I know it sounds funny, but there's no rent or mortgage, no annoying neighbours and I wake up to a different view every day. Beats living in the city.'

'I guess so. But surely you need a roof over your head from time to time.'

'True. I do miss hot showers and fluffy pillows. But after a while I feel the need to get going again. Call of the beach, or something.'

'Well, part of me envies you and part of me is glad it's you sleeping on the beach and not me. I'm glad I picked you up though.'

We drove on in silence for the next ten minutes, but it was a comfortable silence. My feet were happy to be getting a five-kilometre ride out to the coast, but my head was in trouble. My mind kept returning to what Karen said as we drove towards the beach; that she was glad she had picked me up. I didn't want to admit it, but part of me was glad she had, too.

Di seemed very far away.

* * *

'Well, here we are,' she said as we pulled into her driveway. 'Beach is thattaway,' she added, jerking her thumb over her shoulder.

'Thanks again. I know it's worth nothing to you, but I insist you take a copy of the album. I haven't got any money. I'm a musician, you know. Here, take it.'

'All the same, you musos. Take, take, take. What's a girl to do?'

'Well, at least let me carry your shopping in. It looks as though you've got enough here to keep you going through a nuclear holocaust.'

'That's what happens when you've got a teenage daughter who brings her friends around every weekend. Gotta have enough to feed the troops.'

We got out, and I opened the back door, pulling out all six shopping bags. God knows what she had in there but they weighed a ton. The plastic cut into my fingers, turning them rapidly purple. I said nothing. Part of being a man is never admitting you've started something that you probably shouldn't have—the tour was the supreme example of this—so you just grit your teeth and soldier on, even when you start to lose feeling in your extremities.

'Are you sure you're right with all of those?' Karen said over her shoulder as she opened the front door to her house.

'Fine,' I said, secretly wondering if I would ever play the guitar again.

'It's very kind of you,' she said, flicking on the porch light and the one in the living room. Evening was coming on fast, and Karen's little cottage was thick with shadows. I sidled in through the front door, careful not to bump anything in the bags that might be breakable. Following her into the kitchen, I gratefully put the shopping on the counter.

'I'm sorry the place is such a mess, I keep meaning to do a proper clean but, well, you know. Life goes on,' she said.

'No need to apologise. I used to live in a place called the Dungeon.'

'Right,' she said, not returning my smile for the first time. She looked at me strangely, and I wondered briefly if I had said something rude. The bright, witty woman of the car ride had vanished, replaced by wariness.

'I guess what I mean to say is don't worry. It looks lovely, actually, very comfy,' I said, hoping to regain the lighter mood, before it occurred to me that her abrupt change might be explained by her being suddenly aware there was a strange man in her house, physically bigger and looking pretty rough into the bargain. Not only that, but a weirdo who claimed to have walked over eight hundred kilometres to promote an album.

Unnerving was possibly an understatement.

'Well, I'd better be—' I began.

'Would you like a glass of wine?'

This was unexpected.

'Uh, yeah, I guess …' I began.

'It's not very good.'

'That's okay.'

'As thanks for bringing in a lady's shopping.'

'Right.' It was my turn to feel awkward. Maybe I should just leave, end things on a good note, before things got too intense. A few yuks, a good exchange of life stories, then a smooth exit with no lingering weirdness.

The longer you stay, I've found, the harder it gets.

I didn't leave though, instead accepting the wine and further enmeshing myself in her life through the evening that followed.

* * *

She had a teenage daughter who was staying with the father for a few days. Unlike many women in her position, she gave no voice to any bitterness or malice towards him, only to say that she preferred it when her daughter was here and that his new wife was very uptight and straight-laced.

'How can someone be so square in this day and age, Ben?' she said. We were sitting on her couch, feet on the coffee table.

'I blame the decline in psychedelic drug use.'

'Maybe you're onto something. She could use a dose of mushrooms, that's for sure … do her good to run naked around the garden singing "Kung Fu Fighting".'

'Those kicks were fast as lightning,' I said solemnly, taking another sip of red. It tasted better now we were onto our second glass. 'Does your daughter like her?'

'Katie's too sweet to not like anyone. She looks for the good in everybody, that girl. I just hope that old maid doesn't rub off on her.'

'I doubt it. Old maids just aren't cool to a fifteen-year-old.' I spotted a three-quarter-size guitar leaning against the wall and got up and went over to it. 'Is this yours?' I asked, giving it an exploratory strum.

'Katie's,' she said from the couch, taking another sip of wine. She was looking at me over the rim of the glass with that peculiar expression again, the inscrutable one that could have been fear, desire or just gas.

'It needs tuning. Do you mind?' I was glad to have something to do.

'Knock yourself out. I'll be in the kitchen. Does spaghetti bolognaise sound good for dinner?' she said in an offhand manner as she strode out of sight.

'Dinner?' I called.

'If you want it. It's nice to have some company while Katie's away, but if you'd prefer to get going I understand.'

I stood there flat-footed, wondering what I should say. I had to say something before my silence could be misconstrued.

'Ah, yeah, that'd be great, as long as you don't mind.'

'My pleasure,' she called from the kitchen, and the sound of pots banging and cupboards being opened started up. 'I figure it's been a long time since you had a home-cooked meal.'

'You bet,' I said as I walked around the corner into the kitchen doorway. I started tuning the guitar while she went about the creation of dinner. 'It seems all I've eaten for the last two months has been peanut butter.'

'Do you like garlic?'

'Yeah, love it. Can I do anything?'

'No, you'd only get in the way. Play me something instead. Something you wrote. I promise not to yawn.'

'That's a pretty bold statement. I've been told my singing is a soporific second only to Valium.'

'Come on, let's hear it. I've always wanted to be serenaded while I cooked.'

I smiled and started playing 'Under the Sun', remembering too late the lyrical content, especially given the current circumstances. I forged on, thinking she must be reading all kinds of things into my song choice.

Lay down lady the night is young
Speak your sin with velvet tongue ...

Karen didn't yawn or start booing as my song filled her kitchen, just went about her preparations and occasionally smiling to herself, and after a few minutes I finished and put the guitar down. She was silent for a moment, which always makes me feel awkward after I play something, like I've revealed some deep part of myself and am being judged on it.

'Take a seat,' was all she said, however. 'Dinner's almost ready. It's not much, I warn you, but it's better than the wine.'

The food was much better than the wine, and we said little while we ate. A cat appeared and wound its way between my legs beneath the table, butting its head into my calf and purring ingratiatingly. It was all in vain—there was no way I was parting with a morsel of home-cooked food.

'She loves you,' Karen remarked in a surprised tone. 'Hermione hardly ever likes strangers, especially men. Comes from being in an all-girl household.'

'Hermione?'

'Harry Potter's big in our house,' she said, smiling.

I finished eating, pushing the bowl away and leaning back in the chair. I was full and sleepy.

'That was amazing,' I said. 'How can I ever repay you?'

'You can't. You'll be forever in my debt,' she said, standing up and taking the bowls back to kitchen.

'I'll do the dishes,' I said, struggling into a standing position and shuffling after her.

'No you won't.'

'Yes I will. You cooked; I clean. It's the way of things.'

'Not tonight it isn't. Go sit on the couch or something, these can wait,' she said, putting the two bowls into the sink and filling them with water.

I ambled back into the living room. I thought of sitting at the dinner table we had just vacated, then decided I wanted something soft and comfy after my meal and went to the couch.

'Do you want any more wine?' Karen called out.

'No, I'm fine, thanks.'

'How about something else? Ice cream? Coffee? Pot?'

Coffee pot?

'Did you say coffee pot?'

'No,' she said, smiling, coming back into the room drying her hands on a tea towel. 'Coffee *or* pot. Do you smoke? You must, you're a musician. I have a little plant growing in the bathroom. It gives me all I need.'

'Yeah, that'd be great.'

'Back in jiffy,' she said, heading in the direction of the bathroom, presumably.

I looked around the living room and spotted a bookcase jammed with books and topped with knick-knacks and photo frames. I walked over to it and read some of the titles, noting that Karen was a fan of some pretty eclectic genres. Gardening guides, romance novels, a few archaeological books on ancient cultures, and a smattering of Stephen King.

'I like your collection of books,' I called out, but got no answer. I looked at the pictures on top of the shelf, drawn in particular to one of Karen and Katie taken several years ago judging from how small the latter was. They looked happy and relaxed, caught in a candid moment that elevated the photo above the usual staged professional shots you pay a fortune for and where everyone looks slightly constipated.

Seeing this picture reminded me that this was all real, put my own time here into perspective, a brief visitor into the long-running Karen & Katie Show. Or the Spider Show. Or the Tea Gardens' Pete Show. There are eight million stories in the naked city.

'I'm warning you, this stuff is pretty strong,' Karen said as she came back into the room. I turned around hurriedly, feeling as though I had been eavesdropping. She didn't notice. 'I've built up a tolerance to it over the last few months, but you might want to go easy, at first anyway.'

'Thanks for the heads up.'

'You don't mind rolling a joint, do you? Mine always fall apart,' she said, sitting down on the couch and patting the cushion beside her. I sat down and took the bowl from her, looking in. A finely chopped pile of green herb sat at the bottom of the bowl, and the smell was strong. I started constructing the joint while Karen got up and put the radio on. The Stranglers were telling us there was never a frown with golden brown, as that weird harpsichord pulsed beneath.

Golden brown, finer temptress

When I got to adding the weed, I found it to be sticky, always a sure sign the stuff is going to be potent. I reminded myself to take only a little puff—it would not do to green out and fall asleep on Karen's couch. I had to maintain for a number of reasons, Karen sitting a few feet from me being the main one, the finer temptress.

'Good job,' she said, looking at me with admiration. 'I always make such a mess of it.'

'Practice makes perfect,' I said, handing it to her, our fingers brushing briefly as I did. She lit it and inhaled gently, and I watched the cherry flare against the darkness pressing against the window behind her. I looked at the clock and was startled to find it was only seven-thirty. My body clock was telling me it was dark and to go to sleep, and the hearty meal weighing me down wasn't helping. I realised I would be leaving this lovely warm nest shortly for a cold windy beach, and the thought had little appeal.

'Here you go,' she said in a husky new voice, handing me the joint.

I took a tentative drag. It was smooth. I felt my fingertips start to tingle, and my head start to get itchy, both sure signs that this was gear of the first water, the mad note.

'Thank you,' I rasped, passing it back.

'Thank *you*,' she said with a slow, sultry smile. 'I made it myself.'

This struck us both as quite amusing, and we chuckled. The chuckling felt good, so we did it some more.

'I'm hogging it, sorry,' she said, passing it back. I took a few quick drags, realising on the third one that maybe I had gotten a little bit too much of the stuff.

'Whoa. I think I just cast off from the wharf, Karen. You were right, this stuff is …' I trailed off, unable to complete the thought. Karen didn't look as though she minded, just smiled that feline smile and took the tiny stub from my numb fingers.

'I told you to be careful,' she said, sounding as if she was a long way away. I watched as her hand moved from mine and raised the joint to her lips. It seemed as though this action took far longer than it should have. My eyes were swiftly narrowing down to slits, and my eyebrows felt like they were creeping up my forehead, trying to escape.

'My eyebrows …' I began, then thought better of it. Karen didn't need to know about my fugitive brows.

She giggled, and it was a deep liquid sound that tickled my nerve endings and set my hairs standing on end. The cat appeared for no reason, rubbing herself on my legs, before darting off into some other part of the house.

'Would you like a drink? Coffee? Tea? More wine?' Karen asked, unmoving except for her hand weaving sinuous patterns in the air as 'So Far Away' by Carole King came on the radio.

'Coke, if you've got it, thanks,' I said, feeling the need for something cold and sweet. 'What radio station is this?' I asked.

'ABC, in your honour,' Karen said, gliding towards the kitchen on socked feet. 'I haven't got any Coke. Will water do?'

'Perfect.'

I slumped back into the soft cushions. Never could I have anticipated when I got into Karen's car at Erina Fair that I would finish the night thus. I smiled and folded my hands over my stomach, letting my thoughts scatter like dandelion seeds on the wind, while King's song wafted through the autumnal night air.

I didn't notice that Karen had come back into the room until I felt a hand on mine. I started and saw her sitting next to me on the couch. Before I could say anything, she slipped a glass of water into the hand she was holding.

'Oh. Thanks. I was miles away.'

So far away ...

'I have to tell you something,' Karen said, not retreating back to her end of the couch yet, but perched on the edge of the seat, knees bent towards me and a serious look on her face. I opened my mouth to say something—I have no idea what, probably something about Di and how we shouldn't do anything we might regret—but she beat me to it.

She leant in closer to me, lips moist and parted, and said, 'My neighbours think I'm a witch.'

I hadn't been expecting this.

'Huh?'

'My neighbours think I'm a witch. I know how it sounds, but it's true.'

I sat there, my mind struggling to go in this unexpected direction. I could only think of one appropriate thing to say.

'Are you?'

She scooted back on the couch and leant back on the cushions, smoothing her trousers and tucking her socked feet underneath her, eyes never leaving mine.

'Maybe.'

I sat there absorbing this new information, and now the radio was playing The Sunnyboys' 'Alone with You'. I had no idea what to say, so I looked around the room for inspiration. My eyes returned to the fabulously packed bookcase, and I spotted some tomes I had missed earlier.

Witchcraft, Demons and the Occult.

The Succubus.

The Golden Bough.

'Do you mind if I turn this off?' Karen said, indicating the radio.

'Go for it,' I said, feeling completely adrift now. 'So, hang on. Are you saying you *are* a witch? Cos that's cool if you are ...'

'My neighbours think I am,' she said, switching the radio off and plunging us into silence. I struggled to straighten up and get some sort of handle on the situation. Unfortunately for me, the weed was too strong. Stoned and adrift, all I could do was watch as this possible witch returned to her seat, looking at me with that mysterious expression.

'Do you mind singing me a song?' she asked. 'I loved the one you played me in the kitchen.'

'Not at all, although I think I've forgotten everything I've ever written, so just bear with me a minute,' I said, looking around for my guitar.

'That's all right, don't worry about it. What if I sing you a song? Would you mind?'

'No.'

'It's been a few years since I sang it, you understand.'

'That's okay.'

And she closed her eyes and started to sing. She had a soft voice, coloured with that gorgeous accent that evokes images of medieval fairs and deep woods and ancient castles brooding over windswept moors.

'*Ta na paipeir da saighneail is ta na saighdiuir ag dul anonn*

Ta drumadoir aoibhinn aerach le Clanna Gael ag gabhail go Tir na Long ...'

The labyrinthine melody spun out from her, wrapping itself around me and sending me into a trance-like state. I was being hypnotised and was helpless to stop her.

Maybe she is a witch after all, was my last coherent thought.

* * *

'*... da mbeadh agamsa nach duit a bhearfainn cead is dha mhile bo*

Ar a chuntar thu bheith I d'fheirin liom go Contae Mhaigh Eo ...'

The song finished, and silence descended.

I sat, feeling the spell woven around me gradually loosen its hold. I realised I was straightening up at last. The room seemed a little clearer, sounds a little sharper, the cat a little less startling.

'My mother used to sing that song to me, when I was little,' Karen said at last, sounding a little more like her old self. Whatever strange aura had engulfed us seemed to be dissipating, and in a way I was relieved. For a while it had seemed like anything could happen, anything at all.

'It's beautiful, but sounds so sad. You've got a lovely voice, Karen. You should be a singer.'

'Thank you. I used to be in bands back in high school, but then I stopped one day. I can't remember why. Now I just sing along with the radio or in the shower, you know. Do you want any more water?' She got up, banishing the last of the spell.

'No, I'm cool.' I yawned and sat up a bit on the couch, trying to wake up.

'It's getting late, and you must be exhausted.'

'No, it's—' I derailed into another yawn. And she smiled at me in that "you were saying?" way. I smiled sheepishly. 'Well, I guess I *am* used to going to bed when the sun does.'

'I'm sorry I've disrupted your routine,' she said, with a hint of the old cheekiness.

'You should be. I'm on a strict regime here, you know. Even the tiniest alteration could have grave ramifications.'

I followed her into the kitchen. She stood next to me while I rinsed the glasses, and I became aware of her proximity again, was reminded of her womanhood. I found myself scrubbing with a meticulous attention to detail that made Lady Macbeth look like a slacker. I thought of Di, and of Trial Beach, where the memory of her had pulled me through the long wet night.

Thought of the necklace buried far to the north.

'I'd ask you to stay the night—' Karen began.

'Karen, there's something I need to—' I interjected.

'—but I just picked you up by the side of the road, and I don't know anything about you, other than you're on a crazy adventure … I'm sorry, what were you saying?'

'Nothing. I mean, I understand totally. I wouldn't feel right anyway, you know, sleeping indoors. And besides, you've done so much for me already.'

'I'm sorry. I mean, you seem lovely and normal, but I—'

'It's fine. I actually can't sleep anywhere now that doesn't have crabs ... no wait, that sounds bad.'

We both laughed, and it felt good. With the unspoken sexual thing between us resolved, I found myself relaxing. We chatted for another twenty minutes, and I told her tales of Spider and his 'never make it' catchphrase, of Happy Jim constantly mispronouncing my name, of the Shelly Beach Crew.

Karen laughed in all the right places as she went about putting the leftover spaghetti into microwave containers. Caught up in the storytelling, I didn't notice the other things she was collecting until she handed me a paper bag.

'... so I'm trying to remember the chorus and there's this penis in my face and ... hey, what's this?' I said, taking the proffered bag.

'Provisions. Something to keep you going to Sydney. I hope you like apples,' she added shyly.

'Wow, you didn't need to do this.' I opened the bag and saw a container of spaghetti, two apples, a hunk of cheese and two bread rolls. There was also something wrapped in foil that I assumed was some kind of perishable food. 'This is so wonderful, thank you.'

'Thank *you*, for making this place a little less empty while Katie's gone. And I couldn't send you out into the night without supplies.'

We walked back to the front door where my packstool and the guitar waited patiently. I saddled up, feeling both happy and a little sad that the night was over. Karen looked the same, and I was suddenly very grateful to have met her, not because she represented a victory over Temptation, but simply because she was a lovely person. A little odd, but then, so am I.

'Thanks,' I said, and we shook hands. She pulled me into a hug, made awkward with the packstool on my back, but genuinely affectionate all the same. I think if I weren't already in love with Di, I probably would have stuck around for a few days; gotten to know her better, maybe see what might have been. As it was, I left it at a hug, and a promise that if I ever returned to Terrigal I'd look her up.

We both knew it would never happen, but we said the words anyway.

***

I couldn't sleep.

I was tired, yet I couldn't drift off.

There was something bothering me.

Di.

I wondered whether she was asleep or working or partying. She wasn't much of a party animal, but then, people change, especially when they are far from home and in a strange place. I knew that better than anyone.

I lay there, listening to the waves hurl themselves at the earth. Those waves had travelled a long way, perhaps all the way across the Pacific, only to end it all here on the Australian coast by the light of the silvery moon. I couldn't decide whether such a journey was impressive or pointless. On Ben's Head Radio, the only song playing was that old one by Max Merritt and the Meteors.

Oh, you're slippin' away from me ...

She wasn't—our conversation in Port Macquarie had proven that—but I still worried about the

appreciation of a woman over here

distance that was bound to grow between us, fill up with new people and new experiences and

it's breaking me in two

new guys. Was she having nights with other men similar to my night with Karen? And if so, was she resisting temptation as I had?

'Come on man, snap out of it. You gotta get some sleep, tomorrow's a big day, people're going to be ...'

watching you

'... watching you, judging you on how well you finish this.'

It seemed like a long time since we'd spoken, longer still since we'd held each other, and no matter how I worked it around in my head, I couldn't escape the fact that I felt she was

slipping away.

'Slipping away. Right on, Max.'

As I lay there my phone beeped. I pulled it out, figuring it would be Bill telling me how sales were going up north. I was wrong.

It was Di, of course.

There *are* no coincidences. I know that now.

Can't believe I've got reception so I'll be quick. I'm so proud of you and wish I were there to see you finish. PLEASE stay safe and remember that I love you. Your Di.

I sat there and re-read it. Then read it again. I savoured every word, the feeling of warmth that flooded through me. I could have read it a thousand times and never had my fill.

Your Di.

She loved me.

Chapter Fourteen: Bring it on Home

DAY 50

Wednesday morning passed slowly. I cut inland, running south-west towards the port village of Ettalong. From Ettalong I could catch a ferry across Broken Bay to Palm Beach, Sydney's northernmost suburb and near where I'd lived the first ten years of my life.

Palm Beach was forty kilometres north of the Sydney CBD; a full day's walk, so I'd have to go across tonight. Lisa had emphasised how important it was to get there on Thursday in order to capitalise on publicity and readership circulation. NBN hadn't called yet, however, and if I crossed the Hawkesbury River I'd be leaving their jurisdiction.

I desperately didn't want to pass up the opportunity to get my shaggy bonce onto the television, but I didn't want to make Lisa look a fool either, especially after she had so kindly promised me half a page with photo. Torn by indecision on this, the penultimate day of the tour, I trudged on.

* * *

Just after I left the town of Kincumber I got a call from someone at NBN. The reception was terribly patchy. They wanted to confirm I was still walking to Sydney, as though I had suddenly lost interest after nine hundred kilometres and fifty days and had decided to open a haberdashery instead. I told them I was definitely still walking to Sydney.

'But I wont be for much longer,' I warned the person on the phone. 'I'm leaving Kincumber now.'

'I'm sorry, do you just say you're kneading your cucumber? Hello? Ben?'

'*Nooo*! I said I'm almost finished, I'm leaving *Kincumber*, north of Ettalong, right now. I'm due in Sydney tomorrow and—'

I realised I was speaking to the dial tone. Whoever had called had decided to give up on the maniac on his way to Sydney, clearly in an advanced state of decline and raving about vegetables.

My chances of being televised seemed to be getting slimmer.

Probably for the best. As my so-called friends have told me, I have a good face for radio.

* * *

Besides having a name that wants you to add 'little doggies' every time you say it, Ettalong has a pretty, tree-filled park where families and the homeless alike can feel a little closer to the sylvan life. Which was where I sat now, caught on the horns of my dilemma. Was a newspaper in the hand worth a television in the bush?

I decided to wait until the last ferry left at five. That way I could give NBN the maximum amount of time to get in touch.

It was four pm.

'Come on, Craig, come on …'

* * *

'You wouldn't be that young man in the paper, would you?' a grey-haired woman asked as we stood about waiting for the ferry.

'Ah … paper?'

'The *Manly Daily*, dear. Are you the fellow who has walked all the way from Queensland?'

'Pottsville,' I said distractedly, wondering where she had gotten such information. Perhaps she was crazed. 'Did you say the *Manly Daily*?'

'Yes, today's paper. There's quite a big article with a photo of you in your regalia. You look just like your picture.' She regarded me for a moment. 'Even wearing the same clothes,' she added with the faintest note of disapproval that is the province of older women.

'*Today's* paper?' I said, trying to get up to speed.

'HEY, WALKING MAN! SMOKEY! FUCK YEAH!'

I looked over at the car park and saw two big guys getting out of a Camaro. They were both grinning, yellow hard hats tucked under their arms as they strode down the wharf, clearly just finished work.

'Huh?' was all I had time to mumble, before more people started arriving, the peak hour rush, all of them recognising me and asking me questions.

'How do you feel …'

'… Is that the guitar in there …'

'… You looked taller in the paper …'

'… How long has it taken …'

'… play us a song, Smokey.'

Overwhelmed, I gave up trying to answer any questions and just stood there, smiling and shaking hands and nodding a lot. I saw from the corner of my eye the ferry coming in fast over the water and was almost grateful for its approach. It was a little bit unnerving to be the centre of such attention, especially when it was so unexpected. I had been mentally preparing myself for it tomorrow; why had Lisa run it a day early?[20]

The disappointment of not getting a call from NBN was ameliorated somewhat by this small but enthusiastic reception. I desperately wanted to see the article, but nobody had a copy of the paper with them. I turned to see one of the deckhands jump off the ferry onto the wharf, tying a large rope around a post.

'This is the guy from the paper!' someone yelled, pushing me up to the front of the line. Too late I realised that with the article printed I was

---

20 I never found out, but I suspect it was a case of the editor saying 'okay folks, slow news day, whaddaya got ready to go?'

under no obligation to leave NBN's jurisdiction … but I couldn't think of a feasible way to stop this circus now that it was in motion. Looking behind me, there was a large clot of people blocking any chance of retreat, and the deckhand was pulling me into a half embrace.

'Hi,' I said, feeling a bit embarrassed by it all.

'Looks like we've got a special guest,' said the deckhand in a loud voice, clapping me on the back. As I boarded I could see passengers looking at me, nudging their companions and pointing.

One of the benefits of being a nano-celebrity is that, for a day or so, you don't have to pay for certain things. Not a trip to Vegas, mind you, or a Rolls Royce.

Nano-things, if you will.

'How much, man?' I asked the deckhand.

'Nothing, mate,' he replied, pulling me past him with a nod and a wink. 'Reckon the boss won't mind this time.'

'Cheers,' was all I could think of to say, unprepared for such largesse.

'You'll be wanting to see this,' said the captain, emerging from his cabin with a copy of the paper in one hand and a beer in the other. 'And you better have a cold one while you read,' he added, also with a wink.

'Oh, hey, thanks,' I said. 'I thought this was a dry vessel,' I said as I raised the bottle to my lips.

'Well, I reckon you've earned this one, Smokey. Pleasure to have you aboard, mate. Enjoy.' He disappeared back into the cabin with a wave, and I stood there for a moment, overwhelmed.

I took a seat on the lower deck and opened the paper. From a speaker above me a voice suddenly crackled.

'Welcome aboard everyone. I'd like to say a special hello to a passenger who has travelled a long way to be with us this afternoon. Welcome aboard, Smokey, and congratulations on making it to Sydney.'

I sat there feeling embarrassed again, especially as the couple nearest me clearly had no idea who I was. I turned my attention to the article.

They had used a photo taken in Port Macquarie before I went on air with Kylie. It seemed like a long time ago, now. Looking around to see whether anyone was watching me read about myself—a gross *faux pas* for the nano-celebrity—I noticed the couple nearest me quickly make a show of looking out the window. Clearly they were trying to place me. I heard the man mutter to his wife, 'Probably one of those nitwits from *Big Brother*.'

Smiling, I went up onto the top deck for some fresh air.

Watching Barrenjoey Head grow larger filled me a strange mix of emotions. Memories of childhood washed over me … an eight-year-old clutching his new *Slippery When Wet* album in one hand and a guitar made from a shoebox and a ruler in the other; a gulf of nearly twenty years stretched between that little boy and the man who now stood on the roof of this ferry. Tempus had been fugiting along, as it tends to do.

Feeling pleasantly melancholy, I wandered towards the back deck, where the bulk of the passengers sat. One man in his thirties caught my eye, for the simple fact that he was giving me a large grin. He waved, and I couldn't help but smile at the child-like way his hand moved back and forth enthusiastically.

'Hello,' I said, smiling and sitting down next to him. An older woman sat on his other side, a maternal hand on his knee. He regarded me with a joyous face that was quite beautiful in its way. He wore a T-shirt that had a smiling Garfield on it and tracksuit pants an alarming shade of green.

'Hi,' he said, shaking my hand vigorously. 'You w-w-were in the paper.'

'Yes, I was,' I replied.

His mother smiled and said, 'I told Henry about you this morning when we got the paper, and told him if we were lucky we might see you today. We couldn't believe it when we saw you getting on, could we, Henry?'

'You w-were in the paper,' Henry said again, patting me solicitously on the shoulder. 'You play guitar.'

'I do,' I said.

'W-why did you w-walk all that w-w-way?' he said, squinting at a point above my head.

And there it was again, the big question.

Why are you doing this? the voice had asked a month and a half ago, but our society is always examining motives, questioning itself, gazing inward, and I get sick of it. It's better to just do it and not overthink it. Sometimes the mystery is better; pulling apart the device to see how it works often ends up breaking it.

Still, I felt I owed that voice an answer, after everything that had happened.

Furthermore, I owed it to Henry, who was waiting patiently beside me.

'Well, you see, Henry, I wanted to promote my album in a way that …' I trailed off, seeing Henry's face contort in confusion. I tried a different tack.

'The music industry has ruined music, Henry, and I wanted to get back to the essence of …'

Blank look.

'You know when someone tells you a thing can't be done? Well, a lot of people told me that I would never make it, and …'

I gave up on this avenue of explanation as well, seeing Henry yawn and not bother trying to cover it. I thought for a little bit longer, searching for the essence of what it had all been about. Fame? Fortune? Neither of those things had occurred, and if anything, this tour had cost me money.

The sun sent out its final farewell across the water and the colours of evening exploded above us. The wind carried the smell of the Pacific, that perfume of far places and endless adventure, and suddenly I had it.

'You know why I did this, Henry?'

'W-why?'

'For fun.'

'Fun,' Henry repeated.

'Yeah. Fun.'

Henry smiled and nodded as though that was the answer he had been waiting for, and turned his head to let the sunlight wash over his upturned face. He patted my shoulder again, comfortingly.

We sat that way for the rest of the trip.

Epilogue, Part I

DAY 51

The *Manly Daily* has a readership of about one hundred and fifty thousand. On the morning of 20 April 2006, a good deal of them acknowledged me as I limped like Esu towards Mona Vale Hospital, where I'd been born and where I decided I'd stop walking. The article had made a point of me being a hometown boy, even though I hadn't lived here for nearly twenty years. Nobody cared; in the eyes of all, I was theirs to claim as their own, which suited me fine.

NBN rang and said they were all set to go for the interview, cucumbers notwithstanding. They declined my helpful offer to backtrack into their jurisdiction and called the whole thing off.

In the days that followed I would never get past the front desk at Sydney ABC's monstrous Ultimo headquarters—the goal that had seemed so important back in Pottsville. The sleek young receptionists there had never heard of me, had not received any of my missives from the road, and were singularly unimpressed with my tale of a journey now over. Security gave me the bum's rush, and that was that.

Scott Levi rang, however, and did a live follow-up interview as I walked the final miles that morning, having to yell as around me cars slowed down, horns were honked good-naturedly, people approached with hands ready to be shaken and smiles waiting to be answered. I shook and smiled and waved an awful lot, and told Scott that however success is determined, I was a lucky man.

* * *

I stood on Mona Vale beach, alone again for the moment. The sun beat down without mercy or hint of reprieve. That's the thing about Australia—longer than anywhere else on earth, the sun has beat down upon it. For millennia it has seared the continent, stripping it of all but the essential ingredients for life.

Gone too were all *my* non-essential ingredients. From the packstool, which was practically empty, to me; I weighed fifty-eight kilograms, all trappings of citified luxury stripped from my body. As for that curious grey onion floating in its cranial soup …

I looked back the way I'd come. My footprints blended into a thousand others until it was all footprints, a convoluted story written in the protean sand, of which mine was but one. It seemed right, now, that it should be so.

And then a wave came and washed away all trace of my passage, ready for the next traveller to leave their mark.

And that seemed right, too.

Epilogue, Part II

DAY 1261

'How much further?' she asked from behind me, only a little out of breath by the sound. It was quite a hike up Middle Head. Neither of us had had a lot of sleep, either, what with being on our honeymoon and all.

'Not far,' I said, trying not to let my voice betray how out of shape I had become since quitting smoking nine months earlier and putting on fifteen kilograms. It was a good thing our car was parked nearby in Scotts Head.

It was almost three and a half years since I'd been here.

'Do you think you'll remember where you put it?' my new wife asked, a note of doubt in her voice as she surveyed the vast massif of the head.

'Yes,' I answered simply, for I did. A moment such as the one I'd had up here, a young man on a grand adventure, was burned into my memory as few things are. Moments like saying 'I do' to the girl who, without knowing it, had pulled me out of the darkness on Trial Beach. Moments like that are treasures, buried in the earth, sometimes waiting years for us to return and claim them.

'Is this it?' Di asked as I stopped walking, and I could hear the excitement in her voice, and beneath that, wonder.

'Yes.'

The rock was half buried in the mud of the narrow trail, and I toed it over with my boot. Lying there, clogged with dirt, was the necklace she had given me the day I left, and that I had buried here in the autumn of 2006.

We looked at each other in amazement.

'Still here …' she breathed, and I bent to pick it up.

Feeling it in my hand, I felt a stirring in my bones, an ache that only adventure can sate. But I have someone beside me now, a travelling buddy, and that makes all the difference.

ACKNOWLEDGEMENTS

Neither the adventure, nor the writing of it, was done alone. Thanks to Liz, Don, Sarah-Jane, and my family; to the Clan (they know who they are); to Bill, Myles, and Sue, who each saved the day in their own way; to Ma, that voice of unconditional support; and to my wife and son, the best travelling companions you could ask for.

ABOUT THE AUTHOR

Benjamin Allmon is a journalist by trade. He has a column in *Punchnel's*, and his work has appeared in RACT's *Journeys Magazine*, *Jetstar Magazine*, *The Writer* and *Aurealis*, to name a few. A songwriter with twenty years experience, he's a member of APRA, the Australian Songwriters Association, and is an accredited audio engineer, as well as being an active member of the Gold Coast writing community.

www.ingramcontent.com/pod-product-compliance
Lightning Source LLC
Chambersburg PA
CBHW031100080526
44587CB00011B/756